THE HIDDEN FREUD

THE HIDDEN FREUD
His Hassidic Roots

Joseph H. Berke

Routledge
Taylor & Francis Group

LONDON AND NEW YORK

First published 2015 by
Karnac Books Ltd

Published 2018 by Routledge
2 Park Square, Milton Park, Abingdon, Oxon OX14 4RN
711 Third Avenue, New York, NY 10017, USA

Routledge is an imprint of the Taylor & Francis Group, an informa business

British Library Cataloguing in Publication Data

A C.I.P. for this book is available from the British Library

ISBN-13: 9781780490311 (pbk)

Typeset by V Publishing Solutions Pvt Ltd., Chennai, India

CONTENTS

ACKNOWLEDGEMENTS

I am very grateful for all the help I have received in the writing of this book.

In particular I wish to acknowledge the contribution of my friend and colleague, Prof. Stanley Schneider, of the Hebrew University. Much of the work I present is based on the papers and book which we have jointly researched and written.

I also wish to give special thanks to my wife, Shree, for her patient support, wise comments, and helpful editing.

Many friends and colleagues have enabled this work to come to fruition. Thank you so much for your contributions.

Rabbi Shimon Cowen
Dr. Sanford Drob
Dr. Michael Eigen
Rabbi Mendel Gordon
Professor Robert Hinshelwood
Ms. Ilany Kogan
Rabbi Shmuel Lew
Professor Naftali Loewenthal
Professor Kate Loewenthal

Mr. Alistair Mann
Mr. David Morgan
Mr. Matthew Rosen-Marsh
Mr. Ephraim Rosenstein
Mr. Henry Rotstein
Dr. Morton Schatzman
Ms. Ann Shearer
Rabbi Yossi Simon
Swami Sadasivananda
Mr. Rod Tweedy

My appreciation to Oliver Rathbone, managing director of Karnac Books for commissioning this book and to his staff for preparing the manuscript, and especially to Kate Pearce and Cecily Blench, project managers, and James Darley, copy editor, who have all done so much in seeing the book through to publication.

My appreciation to Rabbi Nathan Lopes Cardozo for sharing with me the correspondence between Dr. Samuel Eisenstein and Rabbi Alexandre Safran, and for permission to reproduce it.

My appreciation to the Freud Museum for permission to reproduce in Hebrew Jacob Freud's message to his son Sigmund on the occasion of his thirty-fifth birthday.

My appreciation to the staff of the Royal Society of Medicine, London for assisting my research.

ABOUT THE AUTHOR

Joseph Berke is a psychoanalytic psychotherapist working with individuals and families. He is a lecturer, writer, and teacher and has lived in London since 1965. Beforehand he attended Columbia College of Columbia University and graduated from the Albert Einstein College of Medicine of Yeshiva University in New York.

Dr. Berke moved to London to study with Dr. R. D. Laing and assisted in establishing the Kingsley Hall Community. There he helped Mary Barnes, a middle-aged nurse who had been diagnosed with schizophrenia, to pass through a severe regression. Barnes later became a noted artist, writer, and mystic. The book which Barnes and Berke co-authored (*Mary Barnes: Two Accounts of a Journey through Madness*, 1972) was adapted as a stage play and has been performed in many countries. It has now been optioned as a feature film.

In 1970 Berke and colleagues founded the Arbours Housing Association in London in order to provide personal, psychotherapeutic care and shelter for people in emotional distress. Later he founded and was the director of the Arbours Crisis Centre.

Berke is the author of many papers and books on psychotherapy, social psychiatry, psychosis, therapeutic communities, and transpersonal psychology as well as Kabbalah and Hassidism. For further information, please visit his website: www.jhberke.co.uk

INTRODUCTION

This book began in the 1980s after I was asked to give a talk about psychoanalysis and Kabbalah at the Leo Baeck College in London. The subject aroused my interest because I am a psychoanalytic psychotherapist and I had been attending seminars on Kabbalah, the Jewish mystical tradition. This led me to explore the relationship between the two disciplines in depth. My question was, "Is there a connection between psychoanalysis and Kabbalah." The answer I found was, "Yes, a very profound one". So much so, that I concluded that psychoanalysis is a secular extension of Kabbalah. Subsequently I wrote a paper on the subject entitled, "Psychoanalysis and Kabbalah" (1996, pp. 849–863).

A few years later, while meeting with my friend, Rabbi Shmuel Lew, a Lubavitch emissary in London, he told me that the fifth Lubavitcher Rebbe, Rabbi Shalom Dov Ber Schneersohn, known as the Rashab, had been to see Sigmund Freud. My reaction was utter disbelief, for Freud was known for his antireligious views and I hardly thought that the leader of the Lubavitch movement would need to consult a therapist, especially a secular one. I told Rabbi Lew that I did not think this was likely. He replied that he had attended a *farbrengen* (hassidic gathering) at 770 (the name of the Lubavitch headquarters in Brooklyn) in May 1962 when the Rebbe (Menachem Mendel Schneerson) gave a long discourse. In it he referred to the diaries of his predecessor, Yosef Yitzhak Schneersohn (the sixth Rebbe, known as the Rayatz), who said his father (the Rashab) had consulted "a famous professor" in order to overcome "lowness of spirit." The Rebbe revealed that "the famous professor" to whom the Rashab had turned to for help was Sigmund Freud.[1]

I further discovered that a number of accounts had been published in Yiddish and Hebrew about the encounter between the Rashab (fifth Lubavitcher Rebbe) and Freud. Friends translated these for me. Reading them led to the publication of two papers. The first concerns the encounters between the Rashab and Freud in the period January–April 1903. The second has to do with the mysterious trip that the Rashab and his son made to Pressburg (now Bratislava in Slovakia) just before the Rashab met Freud.

I have included these papers in the initial chapters of this book. The rest of the book has to do with the relationship between Freud, his work, the Jewish transcendent tradition, and Hassidism. This is a mystical and religious renewal movement rooted in the Kabbalah, and applied to everyday life.

There were many Freuds: the scholar, the academic, the researcher, the neurologist, the founder of the new discipline, psychoanalysis, and the Viennese professional. All were noted for their rejection of religion and their identification with the prevalent German culture. This was the picture painted by Freud's principal biographers: Ernest Jones, Peter Gay, and Ronald Clark. They agreed that Freud came from an assimilated Jewish background and he was a completely secular intellectual.

However, more recent studies, especially those of David Bakan, Yosef Yerushalmi, Marianne Krüll, and Emanuel Rice show a very different and more complicated Freud. This Freud emerged from a deeply religious Hassidic background, with generations of distinguished rabbis and scholars on both his maternal, paternal, and marital sides. They show that Freud was very knowledgeable about Jewish ideas and practices and that he was conversant with both Hebrew and Yiddish.

It is clear that Freud was a master of dissimulation. This Freud was extremely ambitious. He denied what he knew in order to be seen and treated as an eminent German doctor. He was also determined to deflect the pervasive anti-Semitism in Vienna away from himself and his creation. We can say that there was a revealed or overt Freud and a concealed or covert Freud. The former has been well documented. This book will consider the hidden or covert dimension of Freud's persona and explore how it reflected his struggle with his Jewish, indeed Hassidic antecedents. Concomitantly, the title, *The Hidden Freud: His Hassidic Roots*, does not just refer to his encounters with different rabbis, but also to disputations with his rabbinic *alter ego*.

This is not to say that Freud was or wanted to be a believing Jew, far from it. The overt Freud was closer to the genus *Judaeus Psychologicus* (psychological Jew), a term the renowned historian, Yosef Yerushalmi, coined to denote a man who was charmingly ignorant of Jewish culture and customs (1991, p. 10). Yet, as Yerushalmi also emphasized, Freud maintained some "strikingly mutant traits" (pp. 10–11). The covert Freud was proud of and strongly asserted his ancestral lineage. He willingly joined the board of governors of the Hebrew University (p. 12). And, he vehemently objected when a friend did not refer to his beloved chow dog by her correct Hebrew name, *Jofie*. Indeed, his writings are littered with Hebrew and Yiddish words and phrases (pp. 69–70).

Why did Freud choose to denude his work of religious content? Certainly, as an adult, he needed to establish his own identity, in the face of strong familial pressures to follow in the footsteps of his father's father after whom he was named. Hence we see Freud the rebel, who tried to reject his Hassidic heritage. But, his rejection of religion was more closely connected to a deeply felt sense of maternal deprivation.[2]

Sigmund was born to Amalie Nathansohn, a new bride and his father's third wife just past her teens. At the time the Freud household was still mourning the death of his grandfather, Shlomo. Amalie became pregnant again with her second son, Julius. This baby also carried the same name as Amalie's brother and beloved companion.

Baby Julius died when Sigmund was two years old from an infection and Amalie's brother passed on at around the same time from tuberculosis. Both losses left his mother heartbroken and emotionally unavailable to Sigmund. He was then passed on to a Czech Catholic nursemaid, Resi Wittek, to whom he became very attached, emotionally and physically. Suddenly, at the age of three, while his mother was confined with his sister, Anna, Resi disappeared, never to return. Sigmund's older stepbrother, Phillip, found that she had stolen some household money and had her sent to prison (Krüll, 1986, pp. 116, 119–122).[3]

Both his mother and nursemaid were very religious. I think Freud transferred the sense of rejection and rage he felt for being abandoned into disdain and contempt for Jewish religious observance and ritual, and subsequently, all religious practice. These views reflect the overt Freud. They seem to have surfaced in his grandchildren and their descendants, none of whom have maintained an attachment to Judaism. The covert Freud was more dutiful. He visited his aged mother every Sunday, even though he suffered from headaches or gastric upset beforehand. And he did try to grapple with his Jewish inheritance through the questions he posed in his last book, *Moses and Monotheism* (1939a).

Freud's lasting legacy is manifold. His creation, psychoanalysis, is a method, a way of thinking, a discipline through which we can find meaning in the experiences which make us human. It is a science of subjectivity.

Psychoanalysis carries the added cachet of opening a door to the discoveries and mysteries of Kabbalah. It is a way by which the Jewish mystical tradition has entered and enriched the mainstream of Western culture. Kabbalistic ideas include the concept of bisexuality, methods of dream interpretation, the dialectic between good and evil, and the significance of reparation, perhaps the most important imprint of them all (see: Bakan, 1965, pp. 62–63, 253–257).

CHAPTER ONE

Sigmund Freud and the Rebbe Rashab

B y 1903 Sigmund Freud was evolving from a neurologist to a psychoanalyst. This term had been proposed by Freud several years beforehand. He first used the term in 1896, in French and then in German (Gay, 1988, p. 103). It denotes an expert in matters of the mind who aims to alleviate emotional and physical distress through psychological means. But Freud's transformation was by no means straightforward. For years he explored physical treatments for the relief of physical and emotional illness. One of these was the use of cocaine as a stimulant and cure for morphine addiction. In fact, Freud narrowly escaped becoming famous for discovering the analgesic and anesthetic properties of coca. He was very upset that he had missed a chance for professional recognition and advancement (Clark, 1980, pp. 58–62). However, such a success could have undermined his emerging focus on psychological processes.

Freud wavered between his identity as a rational scientist and his explorations of subjective worlds: Dreams, free associations, and kindred eruptions of the unconscious. He was not the first to note the power of unconscious impulses. Toward the late nineteenth century writers like Carl Gustav Carus declaimed: "The key to the knowledge of the nature of conscious life of the soul lies in the realm of the unconscious"

1

(ibid., p. 115) and the prominent psychiatrist, Henry Maudsley, insisted that the most important part of mental action was unconscious mental activity (according to Clark, ibid., p. 116). Freud was the first to systematically investigate the hidden basements and subbasements of the mind. He showed how they are built, what they contain, and how they affect ordinary thoughts and behavior.

Initially Freud turned to hypnosis as a means of delving into these psychic recesses. He had some success with helping people to part with their disturbing symptoms through the power of suggestion. He would put a person into a trance and direct him to relinquish whatever was bothering him when he woke up. He quickly realized, however, that there were many people who were not amenable to hypnosis. Even in those who were, he found he could achieve the same results by ferreting out the onset of their troubles and by allowing them to talk freely about their experiences.

"Anna O" was "the germ cell for the whole of psychoanalysis," according to Joseph Breuer, Freud's older colleague, collaborator, and co-author of his first major book, *Studies on Hysteria*, published in 1895. Anna, whose actual name was Bertha Pappenheim, came from a wealthy, Jewish, bourgeois family (ibid., pp. 101–106, 132–133; Gay, op. cit., pp. 63–69). Freud remarked that she was a young woman of exceptional cultivation and talents, charitable and clever. She had consulted Breuer some years beforehand after the death of her father, a man whom she dearly loved and to whom she was devoted during his final illness. Subsequently Anna became increasingly weak, anorexic, and paralytic. Among the many alarming symptoms, she alternated lethargy and excitement, "saw" skeletons and black snakes, and manifested two different personalities, one charming, the other unruly. Breuer visited her every evening. He encouraged her to talk freely about anything and everything. When she did, he found that her terrors diminished. She described this process as "the talking cure" or "chimney sweeping." We might say this that was her way of slaying demons and getting rid of emotional debris.

Then, during the particularly hot spring of 1882, Anna found that she could not drink water, even though she was very thirsty. Breuer helped her enter a hypnotic state during which she recalled an incident when her English companion allowed her dog to drink out of a glass. Along with the memory, Anna reexperienced the tremendous disgust she had felt at the time. The result of this emotional catharsis, as Breuer put it, was that her hydrophobia disappeared. He repeated this again and again with her other symptoms. They too dissolved. Breuer thought he had found an antidote for mental disturbance—the release of hidden emotions. He pronounced Anna cured. Unfortunately this was not to be. She suffered many relapses, some no doubt brought about by his sudden rejection of her once he realized that she was sexually attracted to him and wanted to have his baby. Breuer could not tolerate his attraction, indeed love, for her. In any case his wife had become increasingly irritated at the time he spent with her and clearly conveyed this to him (Krüll, op. cit., p. 7).

Freud saw the sexual interplay between them. Breuer was uncertain. Sometimes he agreed that sexual conflicts lay behind mental disturbance, and other times he dismissed the notion. Perhaps a further reason for backing away from Anna was that her real name, Bertha, was the same as his mother's. These differences resulted in a bitter conflict between Freud and Breuer and a rupture in their relations. As for Bertha Pappenheim, aka "Anna O," she became a distinguished social worker and feminist. The German government has even issued a postage stamp in her honor.[1]

It is said that behind every famous therapist there lies a famous patient. For Freud this was certainly true. Although it might be better to use the word "subject" or "person," because many of the people who contributed to his clinical practice and ideas were friends, colleagues, or even close relatives. These included his daughter, Anna; his son, Martin; Irma (Emma Eckstein?, more likely Anna Hammerschlag, the daughter of his Hebrew teacher); Emmy von N. (Fanny Moser, at the time the richest widow in Europe); Frau Cäcilie M. (Anna von Lieben); Dora (Ida Bauer); Elisabeth von R. (Ilona Weis); Katharina (Aurelia Kronich, a peasant girl); Miss Lucy R. (an English governess); Little Hans (Herbert Graf); the Rat Man (Ernst Lanzer); Enos Fingy (Joshua Wild), and the Wolf Man (Sergei Prankejeff). Other notables included the conductor Bruno Walter; the composer, Gustav Mahler; the poet, H. D., and Princess Marie Bonaparte (Fichtner, 2010, pp. 149–151).[2]

But the most notable man Freud "treated" was himself. And the work which most reflected his self analysis (Clark, op. cit., p. 177) was *The Interpretation of Dreams*, first published in November 1899. Really it was Freud's autobiography, for so many of the dreams and dream processes he discussed were his own. Freud said the book had a powerful "subjective meaning" and saw it as "a piece of my self-analysis, my reaction to my father's death, that is, the most significant event, the most decisive loss, of a man's life" (Gay, op. cit., p. 89). Essentially Freud applied what he learned from "Anna O" and his other patients to himself, a method of systematic introspection and acute observation of the resistances that arose when he looked into himself. He then extended this procedure from his waking life to his dream worlds and back. In this way he saw how the unconscious mind acts, for example, through condensation (combining several thoughts and symbols into one), displacement (redirecting thoughts and feelings away from their intended recipient), repression (of forbidden desires), and dramatization (mental theater). He also observed other operations all of which served to conceal overwhelming conflicts about sex and death.

Like a master novelist, Freud compared the elucidation of dreams to a "guided tour" of the self. In a letter he wrote in August 1899 to his close friend and confidant, Wilhelm Fliess, he observed, "The whole is laid out like the fantasy of a promenade. At the beginning, [there are] the dark forest of authors (who do not see the trees), hopeless, rich in wrong tracks. Then a concealed narrow pass through which I lead the reader—my model dream with its peculiarities, details, indiscretions, bad jokes—and then suddenly the summit and the view and the question: Please, where do you want me to go now?" (ibid., p. 106).

Freud saw *The Interpretation of Dreams* as his "own dung-heap, [his] own seedling and a nova species mihi (sic!)" (Clark, op. cit., p. 177). Not surprisingly he was full of conflict about what to include, or leave out. "… if I were to report my own dreams, it inevitably followed that I should have to reveal to the public gaze more of the intimacies of mental life than I liked, or than is normally necessary for any writer who is a man of science, and not a poet" (p. 178). But he also acknowledged that the temptation to conceal certain embarrassing bits was very strong and that he "took the edge off some indiscretions by omission and substitutes" (p. 178). No doubt a lot of what he secreted away were his own sexual fantasies and death wishes (Gay, op. cit., p. 124). Nevertheless, he was skillfully able to uncover them in others, so much so, that he became world famous, many would say notorious, for describing a particular constellation of murderous and erotic feelings known as the "Oedipus complex." This referred to the wish of a maturing boy to kill his father and marry his mother. The counterpart in maturing girls is the "Electra complex," the wish of a girl to kill off her mother and marry her father. Both terms come from Greek mythology, a subject with which Freud was very familiar. He asserted that these highly emotive constellations not only occupied much of dream life, but also a large portion of people's unspoken thoughts and feelings.

Freud elucidated what happens inside a person's black box, that is, his or her private, subjective space. This is something that his adversaries claimed was impossible. They insisted that all one can know about other people is how they speak and act, because only these events can be verified by external observation. Freud demonstrated that this was not the case, that people contain an intense, dynamic, complicated inner domain which they are constantly trying to share with others. In so doing he wrote with the flourish of a novelist and poet, but also systematically with the discipline of a scientist.

Initially Freud gained renown as an anatomist, being the first person to dissect the testicles of an eel (ibid., p. 32). Subsequently, he devised a new method for staining sections of the brain, elucidated the structure of the medula oblongata (the back part of the brain to do with breathing and circulation), and made major contributions in neurology, particularly to do with aphasia, the inability to use or understand words (Clark, op. cit., pp. 56, 75, 109). His book, *On Aphasia* (1891b) remains a seminal study of the condition.

These undertakings arose within the context of nineteenth-century science which emphasized measurement and verification. Not surprisingly, Freud, the natural scientist, looked for palpable facts to support his developing theories. By the spring of 1895 he was consumed by a new undertaking, to elaborate a "Psychology for Neurologists," which he eventually called "The Project" ("A Project for a Scientific Psychology", 1950a). In it Freud tried to describe mental functioning in the language of classical physics and cerebral physiology. He foresaw the time when psychological functions could be described by "the amounts of energy and their distribution (or 'discharge') in the mental apparatus" (Gay, op. cit., p. 79). In other words he aimed "to represent psychical processes as quantitatively determinate states of specifiable material particles, thus making those processes perspicuous [i.e., lucid] and free from contradiction" (Clark, op. cit., pp. 153–154).

To begin with, Freud was elated with the manuscript, but he quickly decided it was a nonstarter. It did not explain what he hoped to know in objective terms. Even so, this thinking permeated his formulations (such as the buildup and release of sexual energies). He never gave up the idea that psychological functions might have a material basis (ibid., p. 155).

Above all Freud was ambitious. He lobbied prominent colleagues and journalists to have his books reviewed. He continually pressed influential friends and patients to intervene with the Austrian Ministry of Education to have his status upgraded, first to *Privatdozent* (lecturer), then *Professor extraordinarius* (associate professor), and finally, twenty years later, *Professor ordinarius* (full professor). Apparently the price of his first professorship was a valuable painting given by the family of Frau Marie Ferstel, a patient and wife of a diplomat, to the Minister of Education (ibid., pp. 208–210).

These efforts were consistent with Freud's relentless determination to "spread the gospel" about his work and theories. He once confessed to Fliess, at that time a confidant, "I am actually not at all a man of science, not an observer, not an experimenter, not a thinker. I am by temperament nothing but a conquistador, an adventurer … with all the inquisitiveness, daring and tenacity characteristic of such a man" (ibid., p. 212). The resistances he encountered had to do with his theories of sexuality, which the Viennese found shocking, and anti-Semitism.

At the turn of the twentieth century Vienna was a world center for Jew hatred led by its populist mayor, Karl Lueger. He proposed, for example, that all Jews should be crammed into ships and sunk without a trace. Almost certainly Freud was passed over for academic appointments due to his Jewish background. In the circumstances one might have expected Freud to convert to Christianity in order to further his ambitions, as many of his associates had done. Yet Freud strongly retained his Jewish identity. He insisted, "My parents were Jews and I too have remained a Jew myself" (Gay, op. cit., p. 6). Among his heroes were Joseph, the dream interpreter, the son of Jacob, and Moses, who led his people into the Promised Land. As if to emphasize these attachments, he refused to accept royalties from any of his works that were translated into Yiddish or Hebrew (ibid., p. 12). Yet, at other times, he went to great lengths to hide his Jewish knowledge and to avoid religious observance.

Freud's mother, Amalie [Nathanson], came from Galicia, the northwestern part of the Ukraine, and a center of Jewish mysticism. Among her ancestors there were rabbis and rabbinical scholars (ibid., p. 8). Amalie was a beauty when, at the age of nineteen, she married

Freud's father, Jacob, who also had come from Galicia. By then he was a middle-aged man with two grown boys by his first wife, Sally.

Freud was their first son and was born on 6 May 1856. At the same time he was named Shlomo (in German, Sigismund, later shortened to Sigmund) after his father's father who had died six weeks previously. Thus, Freud was born into a house in mourning. This was a major factor in his life, and especially, in his relationship with his father which varied from affection to hostility. Surely, this ambivalence reflected Jacob's uncertainty toward his own father, Shlomo, and the clash with the Hassidic culture of his childhood.

Hassidism, a mystical and religious renewal movement, began in the eighteenth century in the Ukraine and southern Poland and, within a few generations, it spread to other parts of Eastern Europe (Poland, Rumania, Hungary). Hassidic teachings are rooted in the esoteric or concealed dimension of Judaism, specifically the Kabbalah, the Jewish mystical tradition, as expounded by Rabbi Isaac Luria (the Ashkenazi Rabbi Isaac, or ARI) about 500 years ago. The Hassidic movement itself was founded by Rabbi Israel ben Eliezer, known as the Baal Shem Tov (Master of the Good Name) 200 years later. He revolutionized Judaism by reintroducing the powerful imagery of Lurianic Kabbalah in conjunction with an everyday language that could reach the most uneducated person. The Baal Shem Tov emphasized a direct, heartfelt relationship with God that touched every aspect of life through prayer, study of the Torah (the first five books of the Bible), and inner contemplation. His followers were known as *hassidim*, Hebrew for the "pious ones." The opposing group of religious Jews who did not accept this direction were known as *mitnagdim*, which is Hebrew for "opponents." The *mitnagdim* practiced a dry, scholastic, "establishment" Judaism and looked upon their Hassidic brethren as heretics. They often instigated pitched battles which resulted in many injuries and fatalities. At the least the *mitnagdim* (opponents) would denounce their fellow Jews to the police as traitors, whereupon they could be jailed and tortured.

By the 1800s a third force, the Haskalah or "enlightenment" arose in Germany, Austria, and other areas with large Jewish populations like Galicia. Its followers called themselves *maskilim* ("enlightened ones") and encouraged their compatriots to give up the yoke of religious practice and immerse themselves in the secular world. Many Jews saw this as a small price to pay for overcoming the hatred of the gentile world and gaining professional advancement. These three groups feared and vehemently opposed each other.

Even before Sigmund was born, the Freud family was caught up in this struggle. His father, Jacob, his grandfather, Shlomo, and his great grandfather, Ephraim, were all *hassidim*. But around the age of thirteen, at the time of his bar mitzvah, Jacob began to break away from religious strictures by traveling widely and learning the ways of the non-Jewish world. Unusually for a man with his background, Jacob had three marriages. His first wife Sally died in 1852. Presumably his second wife, Rebecca, also died, although almost nothing is known about her (ibid., pp. 6–7). By 1855 he had married Amalie, a striking young woman who was half his age. A year later Sigmund was born. This was not an altogether happy occasion, for the baby entered an ambience of death and depression. In these circumstances, it would not be surprising if the love and rejection that Jacob harbored toward his father was subsequently redirected to his son, who carried the same name. He was clearly "a replacement child," that is, a template for a future pattern of relationships based on his namesake.

In 1860, around the same time that Sigmund entered the world, a son was born to Rabbi Shmuel of Lubavitch. The child was named Shalom Dov Ber, after his great-grandfather, and was destined to become one of the most distinguished leaders of Lubavitch Hassidim. Lubavitch refers to the town in White Russia (Belarus) where the followers of their founder, Rabbi Schneur Zalman (The "Alter Rebbe") settled. Through his writings, and, in particular, *The Tanya* (Teachings) which was first published in 1796 in Slavuta, the "Alter Rebbe" expounded a form of Hassidic thought and action which is both highly intellectual and deeply heartfelt. It focuses on the inner spiritual life of a person and attempts to serve as a guide by which the reader can overcome the divisions in himself between righteous thoughts and wicked temptations. The book also seeks to present the essential insights of Jewish mysticism to a general audience.[3]

Lubavitch Hassidim are also known by the term *ChaBaD*. This refers to the first letters of the Hebrew words, *Chochmah*, *Binah*, and *Daas*, or, Wisdom, Understanding, and Knowledge. According to the Kabbalah these attributes represent the higher or most profound emanations of God. Many hassidim dwell on these characteristics as a means of spiritual contemplation.

The leaders of Chabad, and other Hassidic communities, were disciples of the Baal Shem Tov and then disciples of disciples. They were respected as *tzaddikim* ("the righteous ones"), and also by the title, "Rebbe." A Rebbe is far more than a rabbi. The latter is a person who is knowledgeable about Jewish laws and practices. The Rebbe, on the other hand, not only possesses such revealed knowledge, but is also an expert on the inner essence of life, the concealed knowledge. This is exemplified in the basic text of Kabbalah, *The Zohar* (The Book of Illumination) as well as in other mystical texts. The Rebbe is often described as a person touched by God, someone who possesses immense powers to sustain the lives of his followers, his hassidim, on earthly and spiritual planes. The hassidim, in turn, feel dependent on their Rebbe for guidance and help in accessing divine grace about all matters—spiritual and mundane.

A Rebbe may share some qualities with a psychoanalyst. Both are experts about human nature as well as esoteric matters. For the Rebbe this includes spiritual or supraconscious realms, while for the psychoanalyst this includes inner reality, or the unconscious. And both encourage intense real and transference relationships among their adherents.

The father of Shalom Dov Ber, Rav Shmuel, was the fourth leader of a large community of Chabad Hassidim and was known as the Rebbe Maharash (our teacher Rabbi Shmuel). He was very much a "political Rebbe," traveling extensively to combat the anti-Jewish pogroms that occurred throughout Russia and other parts of Europe too. At one point, and at great danger to himself, he personally reprimanded the Russian Minister of the Interior for reneging on his promise to suppress anti-Semitic outbreaks. In all this he was aided by a great intellect and capacity to speak several languages. Unusually, he urged his followers to study the Kabbalah as a basic prerequisite for understanding their own humanity. He also had a good sense of humor. Among his memorable sayings, he exclaimed, "You cannot fool God; you cannot fool others either. The only one you can fool is yourself. And to fool a fool is no great achievement".[4]

Rav Shmuel died at the early age of forty-eight and was eventually succeeded in 1883 by his second son, Shalom Dov Ber Schneersohn (known by the acronym Rashab). Even before he became Rebbe, it was clear that the Rashab possessed profound spiritual powers including the capacity to access paranormal states in himself and others.

Moreover, he was a prodigious scholar and a great organizer. Known informally as the "Rambam (Maimonides) of Chabad Hassidism," he wrote and delivered over 2,000 Hassidic discourses (*ma'amarim*) over his thirty-eight years as Rebbe. Some of these discourses literally took years to deliver, during which time he comprehensively covered the most abstruse Kabbalistic concepts. They were subsequently published as an encyclopedic set of twenty-nine books, *Sefer HaMa'amorim*.[5] And these are only a few of his many works on Hassidic thought.

A second major aspect of his activities had to do with outreach to forgotten or hidden Jews. The first group he focused on was the Mountain Jews or *Berg Yidden* in the Caucasus between the Black and Caspian seas. He sent emissaries to reintroduce them to Jewish life and learning. This undertaking catalyzed outreach activities which have grown to be one of the most successful Lubavitch projects. As of January 2012 there are over 3,300 Chabad—Lubavitch facilities in more than seventy-five countries, a figure which continues to grow each month.[6] In so doing, the Rashab compared the Hassid to a lamplighter, who walked the streets to kindle the sparks of Jewish consciousness in even the most remote person or place.

Thirdly, the Rashab was instrumental in establishing a new kind of yeshiva or school of Jewish learning where the students did not only learn the Talmud (Jewish civil and religious laws), but also the mystical teachings of Chabad Hassidism. This yeshiva was called *Tomchei Temimim*. Literally it means, "Those who support the complete ones." This phrase refers to students whose training emphasizes prayer and contemplation, itself another Chabad innovation.[7]

And as if all these activities were not enough, the Rashab followed in the tradition of his father in fighting for Jews who continued to be oppressed by the czarist and other governments. One might expect such a man to be large, robust, and with the strength of a lumberjack. In fact, his followers have described the Rashab as physically weak and frail. This was a condition exacerbated, no doubt, because he took on the burden of communal leadership at a very early age. Indeed, the Rashab was renowned for his devotion to self-sacrifice and striving for the truth, for working long hours in study, for teaching, and for service to his hassidim.

But by the year 1902 his wife and others recognized that the Rashab was suffering from a severe malaise. He continually compared himself to his distinguished grandfather (the third Lubavitcher Rebbe)

Menachem Mendel Schneersohn, also known as the Tzemach Tzedek (meaning "Righteous Offspring") and his father, the Maharash. In spite of his erudition and accomplishments as a Rebbe, he felt that he was nothing and had accomplished nothing in relation to his father and grandfather. He would often remark, "Where am I? Where do I turn? [i.e., What have I accomplished?] What should I say? Here I have to go in the path of our Rebbe" (Y. Y. Schneersohn, 1992, p. 42).

At that time the Rashab was under great pressure both internally and externally. The outside pressures were related to a slew of social and political events that were impinging on his activities. By the turn of the century the Lubavitch movement had been under threat from other Jews as well as from the Russian government and the Czarist police. In addition to the vehement enmity of the *mitnagdim*, religious Jews opposed to Hassidism, Lubavitch was also threatened by the *maskilim*, militantly secular Jews who tried to spread modern European culture and secular knowledge. Both groups regularly informed on the Lubavitcher Hassidim to the Czarist police. The Rashab and his son had been arrested and jailed on several occasions. In addition, the secularists brought about temporary closures of the yeshiva in Lubavitch and were proponents of the emerging Zionist movement which attempted to replace religion with nationalism.

As to the internal pressures: 1902 was the twentieth anniversary of his father's death and his ascension to the mantle of leadership. His son, Yosef Yitzhak, referred to his father as being very upset and low in spirits (M. M. Schneerson, 1997a). Around this period, the Rashab repeatedly complained to his family that he was unable to study, that he was unworthy, and that he was deficient in his emotional attributes. By this the Rebbe meant that his love for his fellow man, and that his love and fear of God, were not as they should be. He was overheard to cry out, "How can I apply myself to my Hassidim, if [my] Hassidim don't recognize me?" He added, "I have other ways. But I don't want to use them" (ibid., p. 23). Here the Rebbe was referring to his possession of miraculous powers and his reluctance to deploy them.

It was at this point that the Rashab proposed to travel to Vienna to seek help for himself with the renowned specialist, Professor Sigmund Freud. This was a journey which he considered to be the equivalent of going into exile for the purpose of self-refinement or self-purification (Y. Y. Schneersohn, op. cit., p. 23) He asked his son, Yosef Yitzhak (who was destined to become the sixth Lubavitcher Rebbe, the Rayatz), to accompany him. At first his son hesitated to agree. He himself was immersed in learning and did not want to interrupt his studies. But the Rashab promised that if Yosef Yitzhak accompanied him to Vienna, he would reveal to him mysteries that he might never otherwise encounter, nor understand.

The Rashab had a number of meetings with Freud during the months of January through April 1903. As far as I was able to ascertain, Yosef Yitzhak accompanied his father to the first and possibly several of these occasions. The information about what took place is based on the diaries, R'Shimos), of the last Rebbe, Menachem Mendel Schneerson (1997a, op. cit.) and the writings of the Rashab and his son, the Rayatz (see Schneider & Berke, 2000, pp. 42–45).

I have also tried to confirm this encounter from Freud's perspective. According to Michael Molnar, the Freud Museum, London and Marvin Krantz, the Sigmund Freud Archives, Library of Congress, Washington, DC, there exists patient documentation for the period 1899 and before; and for 1910 and after; but there does not exist any patient documentation for the entire period, 1900–1909. Considering Freud's overt disdain for organized religion, it is possible that he or some of his followers decided to suppress his discussions with the Rashab in order to conceal his interest in and knowledge of Judaism.

When they first met, Freud asked the Rashab to give an exact account of his daily activities, including the number of hours he worked and how his day was arranged. He was also curious about the nature of Hassidus, what kind of discipline it involved. After detailing his daily routine the Rashab replied:

> "The discipline of Hassidus requires that the head explains to the heart what the person should want, and that the heart [should] implement in the person's life that which the head understands." (Schneider & Berke, op. cit., p. 43)[8]

Freud had further questions. He asked:

> "How do you accomplish this? Are not the head and the heart two continents that are completely separated? Does not a great sea divide them?" (ibid., p. 43)

In their exchange, the Rashab focused on this issue:

"The task is to build a bridge that will span these two continents, or at least to connect them with telephone lines and electric wires so that the light of the mind, the light of the brain, should reach the heart as well. [Moreover] I must point out that for Hassidim from birth, the matter of the mind, and the matter of the heart, is fit for study and for *avodah*." (ibid., p. 43)

In Hassidic thought the word *avodah* usually means religious practice or service. But in this instance, the Rashab means the process of self-refinement, both in terms of intellect and emotions. I am not referring to a mundane sense of intellect, rational thought, or scientific discipline, rather to thoughts that exist on the highest levels of spirituality. Similarly, with feelings, they should not be in conflict with a divinely inspired intellect, but complement it (Cowan, op. cit., pp. 4–5).

It is possible, given the maelstrom of conflicting political and religious currents that flowed in and around the Rashab, that he felt "pulled down" from the inner unity he had previously achieved. If so, his despondency could be considered to be an "occupational hazard" of his position. In other words, it was not a symptom of illness, rather of greatness.

After more discussions between Freud and the Rashab, his son recalls that Freud came to the following conclusion.

"The head grasps what the heart is unable to contain, and the heart cannot tolerate." (Schneider & Berke, op. cit., p. 44)

The word Freud used, in German/Yiddish, was *fartrought*, which means to carry or to bear (German: *fertragen*, to endure), or to hold or contain. So the diagnosis can also be translated as, "The head grasps what the heart cannot carry/bear," or "The head grasps that which the heart cannot contain/endure" (ibid., p. 44).

The Rashab's son, Yosef Yitzhak, has himself offered another perspective on Freud's analysis:

"The head comprehends what the heart cannot bear to hear, and the heart cannot assimilate what your mind comprehends." (ibid., p. 44)

The implication here is that the Rashab was upset to hear certain things and needed to find a way to obtain relief from an overwhelming despondency. These feelings moved him to seek relief from Freud.

Freud recommended that the Rebbe should try to avoid sources of tension and to change his venue. Maybe Freud remembered the famous Rabbinic dictum from his childhood: "Change one's place to change one's fate" (Talmud Rosh HaShaNah 16b). Freud obviously intended that the Rebbe should distance himself from the causes of his gloom and doom. This advice is consistent with the recommendations that Freud made to Bruno Walter around 1904. At the time Walter was Gustav Mahler's young assistant conductor at the Vienna Court Opera. Suddenly Walter was afflicted with a paralysis of the right arm, for which he was advised to consult Sigmund Freud. After seeing him, Freud told him to go for a holiday in Sicily (Sabbadini, 1997, p. 191). Nevertheless, the paralysis persisted. Freud then told his patient to forget about the problem and to resume conducting. When Walter remonstrated that this would not do, Freud replied, "I will take that responsibility upon myself," whereupon Walter reestablished his career (Walter, 1947, p. 184).

Following Freud's instructions, the Rashab began to take long walks. He also visited many different synagogues and met a variety of people, many of whom did not know who he really was. During this time his son recollects a fascinating aside. The Rebbe always regretted that his father, the Maharash, did not spend time with him telling stories of his predecessors and other *tzaddikim* (righteous men). But while he was in Vienna, the Rebbe began to have dreams in which his father appeared and told him Hassidic stories. During the long walks that Freud had advised, he, in turn, related these stories to his son, Yosef Yitzhak, who accompanied him (Y. Y. Schneersohn, op. cit., p. 89).

Freud also directed that the Rashab should "be in good surroundings where others could learn from him and tell him how much they appreciated his scholarship, so that his spirits will lift" (M. M. Schneerson, 1997a, op. cit., diary entry, 24 May 1932). He emphasized that hassidim should try to elevate the spirit of the Rashab by studying intensely and by delving more deeply into his writings. Moreover, and this is an essential point, he said that his students (*talmidim*) should inform the Rebbe that they have done so. Then (akin to what he instructed Bruno Walter), he would be prepared to "give over" more of his teachings.

Freud was quite perceptive in his analysis of the Rashab's distress at the situation back home in Russia. *Tomchai Temimim*, the yeshiva he founded, was temporarily closed because Jewish informers, likely *mitnagdim*, had gone to the Czarist police and spread malicious rumors about the place. His son, who was in Vienna accompanying him, had been in prison in 1902, also because of spurious information given to the police. In consideration, Freud cautioned his patient to spend time in Vienna, away from the volatile situation in Russia and away from Russian Jews—some of whom may indeed have been informers.

A fascinating anecdote from the Rashab's diary notes sheds more light on this difficulty (Glitzenstein, 1972, p. 56). For the festive Purim holiday feast, many of his adherents traveled to Vienna to be with the Rashab. They came from Russia, Poland, and Hungary. In particular, the Russian Jews wanted to spend time alone with the Rebbe. But, aware of the scandalous ideas that some people had attributed to him, he refused. Then, about an hour later, the Rashab's assistant brought in a special delivery letter. His son opened the letter. It contained a report on the status of the *Tomchai Temimim Yeshiva* back in Russia. The document related that the yeshiva was functioning very well and that the students were deeply engaged in learning. Consequently the Rashab felt better and agreed to see the Russian Jews. The vignette confirms what Freud told the Rebbe: That he needed to hear good news.

These accounts complete what we know of the exchanges between the Rashab and Freud. Obviously a lot more went on which was not relayed in his diaries, or from his son, the Rayatz, or from others. Maybe, one day, when the Freud archives are more available, further information may be forthcoming from Freud's side. That would be very useful in developing a fuller picture about what transpired.

Recently some new information has emerged from the Lubavitch library. In June 2010 Rabbi Beryl Levine, the chief librarian, wrote a letter about the Rashab that was posted on a well-known Israeli blog site, *Bechadrei Chareidim* ("In the rooms of the ultra Orthodox").[9] It concerned a longstanding problem that the Rashab had with numbness in his left hand. Levine revealed a number of previously untranslated details of letters written by the Rebbe to his backers. These included Rabbi Isaiah Berlin, a wealthy cousin who paid for his entire trip and treatment and is a direct ancestor of the famous Oxford philosopher of the same name. According to Levine, the new material shows that the Rashab only went to Freud for electrical treatment for numbness in his hand and that the Rebbe benefited from this. Levine asserts that the Rashab did not go to Freud for psychological help, although they might have had some "discussions."[10]

But far from making things clearer, the focus on electrical stimulation seems to amplify the mystery of what took place. Freud's biographers state that he gave up the practice early in his career. According to Peter Gay (op. cit., p. 62): "He found the conventional treatments of neurasthenics—electrotherapy, which he also tried on his patients—far more unsatisfactory even than hypnotism, and in the early 1890s he 'shoved the electrical apparatus aside', with an obvious sigh of relief."

Roland Clark noted that despite some successes, Freud dropped electrotherapy by 1887 and the Freud scholar, Peter Swales, said he did not use it after 1892.[11] Nevertheless, it is possible that Freud may have continued to use electrotherapy for neurological issues, especially as it would have boosted his income.

It is also possible that the Rashab emphasized his physical condition (he suffered poor health all his life), because he did not want to reveal the extent of his emotional malaise to his supporters. This explanation has been plainly documented by his wife and his son, and indeed, himself.

The occasion for Beryl Levine's letter was an animated exchange among hassidim about an article that claimed that the Rashab had been treated by an early disciple of Freud, Wilhelm Stekel, for sexual difficulties. This appeared in the *AJS Review* (Association for Jewish Studies) in the spring of 2010 (pp. 1–31) by the American academic, Maya Katz.

Katz's article was itself based on a short chapter entitled "A Vocational Neurosis," in an early work by Stekel, *Conditions of Nervous Anxiety and their Treatment* (1908). In this account Stekel describes his analysis of a "tall, powerful, robust looking man," "a Rabbi by profession," who had suffered a severe emotional shock six years before. Since then he had become overcome by anxiety, especially when praying, often stuttered and stammered when talking in public, and manifested a wide variety of physical complaints, including "burning feelings in his arms and legs, and numbness of his left hand and arm." However, other parts of the left side of his body were affected by a "hyper-aesthesia," an excessive sensitivity to stimuli (ibid., pp. 211–212).

The "shock" was a violent quarrel with his eldest brother, who, after blowing the inheritance he received on the death of their father, demanded that the Rashab share the family heirlooms, valuable books and manuscripts, with him. Moreover, the brother, "who was a man of the world," and was "addicted to women," was continually taunting his younger brother with erotic images and suggestions.

Stekel's analysis was primarily based on three dreams. From these he deduced that his patient had engaged in a variety of sexual activities with his brother, and an elderly family retainer, and a pretty young woman, the housekeeper with whom he had lodged in the summer. He added that the patient was awash with sexual desires, that he was a hidden "Don Juan, whose phantasies would put even those of a Marquis de Sade in the shade" (ibid., pp. 215–216).

As with Breuer's intervention with "Anna O," Stekel averred that once "the rabbi" revealed that he had shaken the hand of his house-keeper, and had reproached himself for doing so, fearing the wrath of God, he experienced a deep emotional catharsis, and an "indescribable relief." Then, by the next day, "the anaesthesia of his hand and arm had entirely disappeared" (ibid., p. 218).

In her study, Maya Katz (op. cit., p. 1) identifies Stekel's patient with the Rashab because they were of a similar age and seem to have endured "an occupational neurosis" associated with career pressure. Moreover both experienced numbness of the left extremity, and had a conflict with an elder brother. Katz also quotes (pp. 7–8) from the paper which I co-authored about the Rashab describing his meetings with Freud, and concludes that Freud could have referred the Rashab to Stekel. The question arises, why would Freud have passed on an eminent patient, like the Rashab, to Stekel, who at the time was a junior colleague? Could it be that Freud was simply trying to get rid of a deeply spiritual and religious patient whom he found disturbing? But then why was this not recorded by the Rebbe Rayatz in his diaries, which mentioned several meetings with Freud?

There are many aspects of Stekel's account which indicate that "the rabbi" was not and could not have been the Rashab. The idea that the fifth leader of Lubavitch was so consumed by sexual desires that he could hardly carry out his rabbinic obligations and scholarship is unlikely.[12] The Rashab had already accomplished more than many men do in several lifetimes, and was soon to embark on one of his most profound works, *Ayin Beis* (1977+), a multi-dimensional study of the relations between the container and the contained, the infinite and the finite.[13]

In psychoanalytic terms the primary conflict in Stekel's patient was between his id and superego, between his libidinal desires and anti-libidinal or repressive forces. With the Rashab the primary conflict was between his ego and ego-ideal, that is, between how he saw himself and how he wanted to be. The basis for this struggle was his identifications with his predecessors, all the prior Rebbes, including the founder of Chabad, the "Alter Rebbe," Schneur Zalman.

In addition there are many other details which do not fit. Stekel's patient developed a pronounced and very obvious stammer and stutter. In her paper Maya Katz (op. cit., p. 15) emphasizes this point as further proof that Stekel's "rabbi" was the "Rashab." But the only reference that Katz cites to support her claim concerns R. Yosef Yitzhak, the Rashab's son, who recalls that his father prayed with great intensity, sometimes sobbing and crying out when he intoned *Shema Yisrael* (Hear O Israel) and *Hashem Elokeinu* (Lord our God). Far from a stammer, it would seem that what Katz calls a "symptom" is a state of God intoxication on the part of the Rashab, a state which few individuals would be able to attain. In fact, there is no record in Chabad of the Rashab having a stammer or stutter. Clearly, the Rashab did not have a speech defect.[14]

Stekel's rabbi had anesthesias and hyperesthesias over large parts of the left side of his body. The Rashab seems to have suffered a numbness solely on his left hand which persisted for many years and was only ameliorated by electrical stimulations. And, as to R. Zalman Aharon (the Raza), the Rashab's elder brother, far from their relations being acrimonious, in general, the Rashab had a good relationship with him, a man who was also a Hassidic scholar and great teacher in his own right.[15] Finally, the Rashab was married at the age of fourteen, not eighteen, and was far from robust. He did not have a daughter, as Stekel stated.

How can we account for these discrepancies? We can do so if we assume that the "patient" Stekel described is a composite picture built up from several different sources. These include an actual person (who may or may not have been a rabbi), bits of information which Freud formally or informally passed on (he could be remarkably indiscreet), and the products of Stekel's erotic imagination (Gay, op. cit., p. 187). Although Stekel did make notable contributions to the study of dream symbolism and helped Freud to establish the Wednesday Psychological Society in 1902 (later to become the Vienna Psychoanalytic Society), he alienated his colleagues by being "boastful and unscrupulous" (ibid., p. 213). After first exclaiming, "Freud was my Christ," Stekel became very rivalrous and tried to "out-Freud Freud" with sexual interpretations (ibid., p. 173). Often he would invent cases, known as "Stekel's Wednesday patients," in order to contest the prevailing topics and arguments at their weekly meetings (p. 213).[16] Eventually Freud denounced his former acolyte as a "desperate shameless liar" and forced his resignation from the society.[17]

Two extraordinary men met in 1903. While one came to seek help for depressive feelings from the other, it seems probable that both individuals gained from this encounter. Only a great person like the Rashab could allow himself (and indeed push himself) to obtain help in a consultation with another great man, Freud. Both were seekers of truth. Both needed to analyze themselves and their worlds to the utmost degree.

It must have been strange for Freud to meet a Hassidic Rebbe after having been brought up in surroundings that both exposed and alienated him from Judaism and Hassidism. By 1903, Freud had long left his home environment for a secular and professional world, had achieved success as a neurologist, and was in the process of developing psychoanalysis, which subsequent generations have seen as a new science, but also as a "new religion" of the mind. It is likely that the shock of meeting the Rashab must have brought Freud back to his roots, even for a brief time.

While Freud may have felt himself to be "completely estranged from the religion of his fathers," he is still one who "has never repudiated his people, who feels that he is in his essential nature a Jew and who has no desire to alter that nature" (Freud, 1912–13, p. xv). Thus Freud lived the life of a secular, skeptical Jewish intellectual, a preeminent figure in developing a profound understanding of the mind, the self, culture, and social reality. This was his revealed persona, or as the Rashab would say, the "garment" he wore while "being in-the-world." I also think there was a "covert Freud," who reveled in his meetings with the Rashab and utilized Hassidic ideas in his work, even if he chose to conceal the connections and disparaged their Jewish contents through jokes. The covert Freud found the Kabbalah of considerable interest (Schneider & Berke, op. cit., p. 58, fn. 24).

Hassidic teachings talk about the power of a person's soul, or *neshamah*, which, in psychological terms, is related to one's strength of character. Whether revealed or concealed, it is clear that Freud possessed an exceptional *neshamah* which allowed him to touch the heart and mind of the Rashab during a period of severe turmoil. This enabled the Rashab to activate his own healing potential, and overcome his sense of spiritual failure. Then his bitterness and depressive feelings became not an impediment, but an impetus to action.

When the *Diaries* of the late Lubavitcher Rebbe (Menachem Mendel Schneerson, 1997a, op. cit.) were published and Freud was revealed as the famous professor whom the Rashab had consulted, many hassidim were aghast that the Rebbe, a profound healer in his own right, had sought help from Freud, a secular Jew known for his anti-religious views. Yet others saw this as a sign of his greatness: That he knew when to seek help for himself, would go to the best professional available, and could do so without being prideful.

Although the Rashab did gain temporary relief from the numbness in his left hand, the effects on his mind, spirit, and relationships were striking. It appears that after discussions with Freud, he was able to think more clearly, engage his students more closely, and expound his greatest works.

CHAPTER TWO

A tale of two orphans

The Rebbe Rashab arrived in Vienna on 6 January 1903 in order to meet "the famous professor," Sigmund Freud. He was accompanied by his son, Yosef Yitzhak Schneersohn (the Rayatz) who was known for his deep devotion to his father. But before meeting Freud, a strange, unsettling series of events began to unfold, the details of which were related by the Rayatz, who was well known in the Lubavitch community for his phenomenal memory.[1]

The story begins at the hotel where they had checked in after a long journey. His son recounts:

> My father's way was that he used to take a rest on the sofa after lunch. He didn't lie down, and he didn't sit, but he would lean with one leg on the couch. He used to refer to this as *valgerinzich*, roaming around.
>
> Once after lunch when he was resting in this manner, he took a longer time than usual and I didn't know what to do. It looked like he was not in this world at all. He wasn't sleeping, he was lying on his side, his eyes were bulging and appeared very strange. I was afraid to wake him, but I was also afraid to leave him like this. So I

started to pace back and forth in the room in a noisy manner, hoping that maybe this would alert him, but it didn't make a difference. Then I started shaking the table, but it still didn't help.

Suddenly, after many hours, the Rebbe stirred and asked, what day is it today? Which *Sedra* (weekly portion of the Torah) is it? (My father used to learn with me every week the Hassidic commentary from that weekly portion).

I answered him that it was Wednesday and also told him which portion of the Torah reading it was. (Y. Y. Schneersohn, op. cit., p. 62)

The account continues with the Rayatz describing what happened when his father woke up. The Rashab looked very confused. He prepared himself to "*davin Maariv*," that is, recite the evening prayers, which he did for a very long time, like the evening service of Rosh Hashanah (the Jewish New Year). Moreover, during the course of these prayers he sang a *niggun* (Hassidic melody) of the Alter Rebbe. All this left his son "wondering" (surprised, amazed).

On the next morning the Rebbe asked him if they had any money, because when they traveled, his son held their funds. The truth was that their finances were quite tight, but since his father obviously needed some money, he went to a pawnbroker and raised a loan on his silver stick. (This was a walking cane, a present that the Rashab had given to his son and to which the Rayatz was very attached). Having received a sum of money, he gave it over to his father. Afterwards the Rebbe told him that he wanted to go to a number of places. His son understood that he was not meant to go with him, so he stayed in the hotel and the Rashab went out alone.

Somewhat later a delivery man came with a big box. He asked whether Schneersohn lived here, and the Rayatz answered yes. The man said he had a delivery for him and was instructed to bring it to the hotel. Attached there was a note in his father's handwriting, "Take this package and pay the man twenty-five crowns" (ibid., p. 62). During the course of the next few hours, several more packages came from other shops. The Rayatz was surprised, for he saw that they all came from stores specializing in women's and girls' apparel. He presumed that his father had bought gifts for his wife and three daughters.

Later in the evening, the Rashab returned to the hotel and told his son that he intended to make a trip, and that preparations should be made. Where to, he didn't say, except that they would need to take along a *tallit* (prayer shawl) and *tefillin* (phylacteries) implying that they would be away for more than a day. Then the Rayatz paid the hotel bill, packed their bags, and they went to the train station where his father told him to buy tickets to Pressburg (now Bratislava in Slovakia), which was some distance away. He continued:

> When we arrived at Pressburg, I wanted to hire a carriage at the train station, as we usually do, but my father said we would go by foot.
>
> So I took our bags and we went along. While we were walking down the street we met a young man, a yeshivah *bochur* (student) who was running and rushing.
>
> My father stopped him and asked him directions to a particular hotel and restaurant.
>
> But the young man said quickly, "I have no time. Go straight ahead and you can ask over there."
>
> My father replied: "Is this the way to behave? Is this the way you perform the *mitzvah* [commandment] of hospitality? Don't you see that we are strangers, and that we are walking from the train station?"
>
> When the young man heard this, he understood that he had not conducted himself properly. So he stopped and showed us where to go. In addition he told us that the owner of this hotel had just passed away. My father thanked the young man and we walked further. Soon we came to the hotel and we saw that there was a woman and three daughters *sitting shiva* (in ritual mourning). The servants at the hotel gave us a room, and we rested. Then my father said he would like to go and walk around the city a little bit.
>
> We went outside and came to a yeshiva (Jewish school) where there were a number of students sitting and learning. My father spoke to several of them, including the young man we had asked for directions. He was also there learning. Then my father got into a very complex Talmudic discussion (*pilpul*) with another *bochur* (student), whom he praised highly. (ibid., p. 63)[2]

The next morning, the Rashab paid a condolence call to the widow and her daughters. The girls were *sitting shiva* on the floor. According to his son, he spoke to them and comforted them. He added that he was just passing by and would be staying in town for one more day. He asked the widow if she could arrange for him to have kosher milk. So the two men remained in this town until the next evening, staying for a total of two whole days.

The Rashab visited the widow and her daughters a number of times. Once he went by himself. When they asked who he was, he replied that he was a distant relative. When the girls asked him whether he knew their father, he answered that the issue was not important.

The conversations skirted around various subjects until the Rebbe spoke to the woman about arranging marriages (*shiduchim*) for her two older daughters. The widow moaned about her desperate plight, especially now that her husband had passed away. She had little money and didn't think she could get appropriate matches. Clothes and other things were very expensive, and she didn't have the means to continue with the *shiduchim* that had already been proposed.

The Rashab comforted her and made suggestions. For the eldest daughter, Chayaleh Gela (in Hungarian: Katalin), he recommended the student with whom he had got into a very long, involved Talmudic discussion. For the second daughter, Faiga (in Hungarian: Foge), he recommended the young man whom he had scolded in the street. As for clothes (trousseaus), he said the widow shouldn't worry, because he had already brought with him two sets of bridal clothes, as well as everything else that the orphans needed. All of this cost a few hundred crowns, which was a very large sum in those days. Having arranged the two marriages, the Rebbe and his son left Pressburg and returned anonymously to Vienna.

The name of Chayaleh Gela'a husband was Joseph Neumann. Their marriage took place on 15 June 1903, after the Jewish holiday of Shavuot (Festival of Weeks), probably in Pressberg. The name of Faiga's husband was Yaisef Lefkowitch. Their marriage took place in Vienna before the Rashab and his son returned to Russia in April. It is possible that the Rebbe attended the wedding, although there is no record of this happening.

Five years later Yosef Yitzhak recounted that he was traveling near Pressburg and decided to make a detour to the city, specifically to see how the two orphans, whose marriages his father had arranged, were doing. He recalled he could only find the third (youngest) daughter, Nachama. She told him that she too had married and was happy, but that her two older sisters were extremely happy.[3] Of the two husbands,

Joseph Neumann was a rabbi in a nearby town and the other, Yaisef Lefkowitch, was the Rosh Yeshiva (director of a yeshiva, a very learned, prestigious position). Both families were living in very fortunate circumstances.

Yosef Yitzhak Schneersohn told this story at a *farbrengen* (Hassidic gathering), some years after he had followed his father as Rebbe. Afterwards someone asked: Who was the hotel keeper who had passed away? The Rayatz answered: His name was Rav Avraham Bick.

Rav Bick had been a well-known buyer and seller of Jewish books and manuscripts, and even had his own printing press. He was also an eminent *Talmid Hacham* (Torah scholar) and was the author of many books on Talmud, Midrash, and other exoteric and esoteric subjects. These included *Foundations of the Meetings Tent, Ripe Fruits of Spring, Known to Understanding, Fruits of the Earth, I Take My Work upon Myself,* and *The Right Arm of Moses*. One book in particular, *Bikurei Aviv* (Ripe Fruits of Spring), received the endorsements of many leading rabbis (R. N. Kahn, op. cit., pp. 162–163).[4]

As for Pressburg, it is also worth noting that the city was a renowned center of Jewish life. Indeed, at that time, it was much more important than Vienna. The leading Torah scholar was the Chatam Sofer, and many learned men, Hassidic and non-Hassidic lived there.

The Bick family had and continues to have an extraordinary pedigree. His wife Miriam (surname Reines) was the direct descendent of the first and only Jewish king of Poland. How this came about is a wonderful story and is well worth a brief digression to tell it. Miriam's ancestors could trace their roots to Jews who settled in the city of Katzenelnbogen in the Rhineland, Germany in 1312. Indeed, many of them took the name of this city as their surname (Rosenstein, 1976b, p. 1).[5] These Jews traveled widely and by the mid-1500s a certain Saul was born in Padua, Italy, to Rav Samuel Judah Katzebellenbogen. As a young man, Saul moved to Brisk (Lithuania) where he married and lived in poverty. Eventually he journeyed to Poland, where he became an illustrious and influential member of the Polish court because of his "remarkable abilities." In particular, he was helped by his connection with a Polish noble, Prince Nicholas Radziwell, who, while traveling abroad, had been loaned substantial sums by Saul's father. In return, Samuel Judah asked Prince Radziwell to look after his son. Upon returning home, Radziwell sought out Saul and was captivated by "the brilliance and depth of his intellect." So "[H]e showered him with gifts and appointments and praised him to the skies to other nobles" for his learning and wisdom (ibid., p. 5).[6]

Then, in December 1586, the king of Poland, Istvan Bathory, suddenly died. When such an event happened, it was the custom for all the nobles to gather together and elect a new king by a unanimous vote. The law was that all of this had to be accomplished in one day. But the nobles could not agree who should be king. So in order that the day would pass and the law would not be transgressed, they agreed to make Saul king for the day and the following night. He became known as Saul Wahl. Wahl means "chosen" or "elect" in the Polish vernacular. Immediately the nobles who crowned Saul shouted, "Long Live our Lord, the King." They loaded Saul with royal honors, and he reigned all that night (Rosenstein, 1976a, pp. 20–21).[7]

Although Saul's reign was not long he used it to good effect. The eminent Saul Wahl inscribed many new decrees and enactments for the welfare of the Jews. These included a law that anyone who murdered a Jew should suffer the death penalty just like anyone who murdered a Christian prince (ibid., p. 6).

In the ensuing ten generations the Reines family included many distinguished scholars and religious leaders, perhaps none more so than the brother of Miriam, Rabbi Yitzhak Yaakov Reines, who was born in Karlin (Lithuania) in 1839. From his youth he was a maverick who tried to integrate religious and secular knowledge, especially languages, logic, and mathematics. But Reines is best known for establishing the Mizrachi movement, which combined Theodore Herzl's political Zionism with Orthodox Judaism. He had the foresight to see this as an answer to the deadly waves of anti-Semitism sweeping Europe. But for doing so he was denounced by most of his colleagues and branded a heretic. Significantly, the first Zionist Congress was held in Pressburg in 1904. Now Yitzhak Yaakov is seen as a visionary and has been honored by having a whole neighborhood in Jerusalem, Neve Yaakov (Jacob's Oasis), named after him (ibid., pp. 415–416).[8]

Avraham and Miriam Bick themselves had five boys and three girls, and from them, a plethora of progeny. Many survived the Holocaust and became distinguished rabbis and academics in Israel, Europe, South Africa, and America. These include Yehudah Neumann, professor of meteorology, Jerusalem; Jacob Neumann, professor of criminology, Liverpool and Capetown, and author of many books on criminology as well as Jewish subjects; and Rabbi Yaakov Yitzhak Neumann, very well known as the Pupa Rov, and who, for decades, was the leader of the Belz Hassidic community in Montreal, Canada. His nephew, Miki Neumann, was one of the leading mathematicians in the United States. In addition to writing over 150 papers on matrix theory and linear algebra, he was chairman of the Department of Mathematics at the University of Connecticut. So, significant accomplishments, religious and worldly, have continued with each succeeding generation.[9]

It transpired that Avraham Bick died on the afternoon of 18 February 1903. He had been sick for at least a year, and we know from his letters that he was desperately worried about the *shiduchim* (arranged marriages) of his two eldest daughters and his lack of funds for dowries.[10]

The events described in Vienna, when the Rashab could not be woken by his son, also took place on 18 February 1903. The trip to Pressburg occurred a couple of days later, between 20 and 22 February.

The exceptional features of this entire story extend beyond the actions of the Rebbe to arrange marriages for two young girls in a far-off city after the death of their father. The key issue is what happened when the Rashab lay down after lunch and went into a trance-like, somnambulistic state, out of contact with the outside world. Although his son did try to awaken him, it was clear that the Rashab was in a world of his own, and impelled by a strange concatenation of forces.

Let us begin by to considering the incidents of the story without taking into account the person involved or the circumstances in which the events took place. Then the primary focus would be on the symptoms, or the peculiar experience and behavior, of a highly successful religious man undergoing a crisis in his life.

For some time the man appears to have become despondent about his work and relationships. He complains about his accomplishments, even though they have remained at a very high level. He recounts feelings of worthlessness and describes periods of emotional detachment. Concomitantly he is upset by a peculiar numbness in his left hand.

Yet the man retains a careful awareness of his condition and travels to a distant city with his son to seek help from a distinguished secular professor. Then, while waiting in a hotel many days before the appointment, he falls into a deep trance for several hours. Soon after waking up, he is confused about time and place. Later his condition changes. A prior lethargy turns into intense activity. He asks for sums of money beyond his means, goes on a shopping spree, and buys large quantities of ostensibly inappropriate woman's clothing. The following day he suddenly travels to another city whereupon he takes upon himself the task of arranging marriages for girls he has never met and giving them the clothes he has just bought.

From the narrow perspective of contemporary symptomatology and classification, this person could be seen as suffering from a bipolar affective state. This nosology would note a depressive phase of this condition, followed by a hypomanic episode. Nowadays the term hypomanic would be used, rather than manic because, although agitated and driven, the man had not totally lost touch with reality and was not psychotic. Certainly, one can discern a flight of ideas, disorientation, and an inability to know basic status information (time, place, person). And the whole episode seemed to manifest a vague delusional quality. However, since it was of extremely short duration, it would be difficult to diagnose a hypomanic or manic episode, which usually takes place over, at the least, four to seven days.

Another possibility is that the person concerned had suffered an organic, neurological event. Although we do not know for sure, the apparent "strangeness of his eyes" could have been due to fixed dilated pupils, which, accompanied by a semi-conscious period of confusion, would point in the direction of a temporal lobe epilepsy. This is a disorder characterized by periodic motor or sensory seizures and sometimes accompanied by a loss of consciousness (American Psychiatric Association, 1980, p. 38). Since this episode is a one-time occurrence, it would be hard to postulate a grand mal seizure. With regards to a petit mal seizure, this individual, whom we know is the Grand Rabbi of Lubavitch, the Rashab, did not remain in a confused state. In fact he accurately completed the evening prayers and sang a *niggun* (Hassidic melody) of considerable complexity. This feat of memory, and prosody, alone totally argues against an organic component. So the likelihood of an epileptic episode seems very remote.

It is much more plausible that the Rashab went into a deep meditative state indicative of an altered state of consciousness (ASC). Much has been written in the literature regarding the definition of an altered state of consciousness (Dennett, 1991; Tart, 1972). The individual who has experienced an altered state is often unaware of his surroundings during the trance-like period. Afterwards, the person may appear confused or disorientated. Moreover, he may be unable to summon up details of his surrounding environment. An ASC seems to be the most likely possibility that describes the Rashab's condition.

The Rashab was able to enter into such a profound meditative space in order to be in touch with the wellsprings of his spirituality. In religious terms we can talk of his communicating with God in order to seek His divine intervention. In Kabbalistic terms, this is a state of interaction with the upper worlds. The psychoanalyst, George Klein (1959), compared this experience to that of an artist who is able to enter an emotional state that transcends ordinary consciousness. Here there has been a departure from mundane awareness to one that allows for an emotional, latent unification with the hidden. Therefore it is appropriate to utilize the term "mystical" to describe the altered state of consciousness of the Rashab.

In his pioneering study, *The Varieties of Religious Experience* (1901), the American psychologist and philosopher, William James, defined four characteristics of mystical states of consciousness:

- It defies expression ... no adequate report of its contents can be given in words ... its quality must be directly experienced; it cannot be imparted or transferred to others.
- Mystical states ... [are] also states of knowledge. They are states of insight ... they are illuminations, revelations ...
- Mystical states cannot be sustained for long.
- The mystic feels as if his own will were in abeyance, and indeed sometimes as if he were grasped and held by a superior power. (p. 293)

Essentially mysticism is the attempt to establish a conscious relation with the Absolute. This definition denotes the juxtaposition of mysticism, altered states of consciousness, and a reaching towards a Higher Reality (see Underhill, 1912, p. 97). Yet, it is difficult to attempt to understand a mystical experience or altered state of consciousness because, as James pointed out, the experience cannot be encompassed in words, nor is it objectively quantifiable. This was one of the problems facing Sigmund Freud when he was asked about his understanding of paranormal, mental, or psychic phenomena beyond normal experience. Initially he was very skeptical and disparaged anything that suggested occultism, spiritualism, and religion. Thus, even when he and his heir apparent, Carl Jung, were on good terms, Freud thought that Jung was too "gullible about occult phenomena and was infatuated with oriental religions" (Gay, op. cit., p. 238).

Freud, the scientist, saw himself as a defender of the eighteenth-century Enlightenment and a leader of the battle against mystical ideas. As he had earlier pointed out to his close colleague, Carl Abraham, "In general, it is easier for us Jews, since we lack the mystical element" (ibid., p. 205). Freud was constantly on guard that psychoanalysis should be seen as "scientific" and not be discredited for promoting superstition. Jung, however, was very critical of Freud's position, and accused Freud of "narrowness and bias" as well as "a sectarian spirit of intolerance and fanaticism" (ibid., p. 238).

This exchange took place in 1909 and was one of the factors that led to the split between the two men. But a decade later Freud seems to have mellowed and exclaimed, "I am not one of those who dismiss *a priori* the study of so-called occult psychic phenomena as unscientific, discreditable and dangerous" (ibid., p. 276). By this time Freud had become interested in telepathy, mental communication not involving the usual sensory channels. Moreover, he semi-seriously told Abraham that his daughter, Anna, possessed "telepathic sensitivity" (ibid., p. 443).

Freud wrote two papers specifically about telepathic communication. In one, "Dreams and Telepathy," he considered the possibility that telepathy could occur while dreaming (1922a, pp. 197–220). Although he tried to remain "strictly impartial" about the subject, Freud did conclude that it was "incontestable" that "sleep creates favorable conditions for telepathy" (p. 219).

In the second paper, "Psycho-Analysis and Telepathy," Freud presented several cases, including a prophecy by a fortune-teller, where he believed that "thought-transference" by "unknown methods" may have taken place (1941d, pp. 175–193).[11] Although he remained an "incorrigible mechanist and materialist," he found telepathy "fascinating." He compared his "favorable prejudice in favor of telepathy" to be "a private affair like my Jewishness and passion for smoking" (Gay, op. cit., p. 445). Ten years on, during an interview with Romain Rolland, the French dramatist and noted mystic, Freud denied that he had become credulous in his old age. He replied, "I don't think so. Merely all my life I have learned to accept new facts, humbly, readily. I believe that telepathy is a psychical event in one man causing a similar psychical event in another man" (Clark, op. cit., p. 496).

One such man was the Rashab who possessed immense psychic powers to affect the lives both of his followers, and of others. From the standpoint of the Kabbalah, or Jewish mystical tradition, he was a *Mekubal*, a person who could directly receive the *Ruach HaKodesh*, the spiritual forces which sustain the world. So his experiences and actions occur on a multitude of levels, Godly as well as earthly.

As I have shown in the last chapter, the Rebbe's lowness and sadness were preludes to a process of self-refinement that led to a tremendous creative upsurge in the last two decades of his life. Similarly the events that surrounded his trip to Pressburg were a remarkable attempt to protect and enhance the lives of two girls at the deathbed request of their father.

In order to understand how the Rashab accomplished this task, it is important to consider who he was, a *tzaddik* or "righteous person," as well as what he could do and did, that is, enter into a very high spiritual state. *Tzaddik* is an honorific title earned by unusually gifted people who are extremely close to God and who can intercede in trying to changing the fate of the world.

The idea of the *tzaddik* as an interlocutor, acting as an active agent mediating between man and God, is a concept unique to the Hassidic movement of the eighteenth century. The *tzaddik* would have a following of people who would ask for worldly as well as spiritual advice. Thus, they might request his prayers for the healing of bodily illnesses or plead for his blessings for an adequate livelihood or for a good marriage and children. The followers of the *tzaddik* were fanatical in their devotion to him. They emphasized the saintliness of their Rebbe, and not only on account of his scholarship, but especially because of his immense spiritual authority. As the verse in Proverbs 10:25 states: The *tzaddik* is the "foundation of the world" (Tanach, 1970, p. 1582).

In order to enter into a deep mystical states, a *tzaddik*, like the Rashab, could and would retreat and render himself unresponsive to the outside, mundane environment. After all, how could such a person, who is communicating with the upper worlds, be both in this world as well as in upper spheres? Did not one detract from the other? The contemporary Kabbalist, Moshe Idel likes to tell the story of the Great Maggid, Rabbi Dov Ber of Miedzyrec, who could induce the Divine Spirit by intensely concentrating his hand upon his eyebrow (Idel, 1995, p. 198). We also have records of renowned Kabbalists such as Rabbi Joseph Karo, the ARI (Rabbi Isaac Luria), the RaMCHaL (Rabbi Moshe Chaim Luzzatto), and the GRîA (The Gaon of Vilna), all of whom described their ability to communicate with spiritual forefathers and foremothers, prophets, and angels, during periods of ecstatic meditation (Glazer & Kallus, 2011).

They also had the capacity for telepathic reception and transmission, which encompassed an entity called the astral body or psychic body. This is a conceptualization that spans many cultures and millennia. It refers to a spiritual or dream body which can leave the physical world and travel to "higher" non-physical realms beyond the boundaries of time and space. Nowadays the astral body is widely seen as the carrier of out-of-the-body experiences and is often associated with near-death, dream, or drug-induced states. Mystics postulate an astral or out-of-the-body plane through which this "body" can travel. Such an event is called "astral projection."[12]

Gershom Scholem, the preeminent Israeli philosopher and historian, was the first professor of Jewish mysticism at the Hebrew University. Referring to the astral body, he inquired (1991, p. 252), what is the nature of this ethereal element? Apparently, it does not participate in the soul's wanderings, yet it is noted in the *Zohar* and other esoteric writings as man's *tselem*. He wonders whether the *tselem* (astral body) is a Kabbalistic version of the doctrine of the self as the deepest spiritual essence within man. Or, he muses, is it a version of the idea of an astral or psychic body within man, which constitutes a third, independent entity mediating between body and soul? (p. 252).

Similarly we can consider, does astral projection occur when the *tzaddik* extends himself spiritually in order to communicate with God on behalf of his followers. This experience renders the *tzaddik* momentarily detached from everyday reality in order to communicate with the "higher" spiritual worlds.

The transcendent powers of the Rashab were well known, although in practice he used them very sparingly (Schneider & Berke, op. cit., pp. 4, 17). His mystical abilities can be subsumed under the rubric of paranormal powers. This is a general term which includes telepathy, precognition, clairvoyance, astral projection, and psychokinesis. From this standpoint we can assume that the trance the Rebbe manifested soon after his arrival in Vienna was related to events that had occurred or were about to occur in Pressburg, and about which he was able to foretell. In fact, when the young student told the Rebbe that the owner of the inn had just passed away, his son, the Rayatz, commented: "This worked out to be exactly the time that my father was resting that afternoon, when he went into a trance."

Perhaps the Rashab realized the death of the innkeeper directly during the course of this episode. This would account for what his son observed. The Rebbe certainly seemed to be aware of what had happened, an awareness which led him to urgently purchase two trousseaus prior to leaving for Pressburg. It would also be consistent with the Rebbe's capacity as a *Mekubal*, a person who possesses a unique sensitivity to receive spiritual or paranormal inflows.

Dr. Peter Fenwick, a leading expert on paranormal and near-death experiences, with whom I have discussed this episode, has suggested that the Rebbe's trance state may not have been a simple example of his receiving or tuning-in to the passing of Rav Bick (Fenwick, 2000; Fenwick & Fenwick, 1995). On the contrary it may represent a much more active attempt on the part of Rav Bick to reach the Rebbe by projecting his *tselem* or astral body to get help for his daughters. In the year before his death Rav Bick was preoccupied with arranging marriages for them. He also must have known about the Rebbe, although we have no direct evidence that he had been in contact with him. However, we do know that he had been in communication with other Hassidic leaders, in particular, the Sadeh Ger Rebbe and the Sanzer Rebbe (Y. Y. Neumann, 1997, op. cit., 4th article).

Such "reaching out" when one is close to death is a not uncommon form of paranormal event. It has been termed "a deathbed coincidence," and can involve a prolonged altered state of consciousness on the part of both sender (projector) and receiver (Osis & Haraldsson, 1997).

Whether the episode represents such a near-to-death phenomenon or not, the Rebbe's refusal to take a carriage at the train station and his meeting with the two *bochurim* (students) all seem part of an unfolding of relationships which he had foreseen and which would lead to two successful marriages.

Like a chess grandmaster, we can speculate that the Rashab was able to see five, ten, fifteen, sequences in advance, spiritually and temporally, all of which leads to further questions. Why was the deceased father, Rabbi Avraham Bick, special, so that the Rebbe felt his passing and intervened in his family's future? I have pointed out that many members of his extended family survived the Holocaust. And several of them, especially the descendants of Joseph and Chaya Gela have made major contributions to Jewish thought as well as secular knowledge. One wonders what influence future members of the family will have on the world, on history, on the Jewish people.

The late Rabbi Yaakov Yitzhak Neumann, the son of Chaya Gela, has written: "We don't know what connection the Rashab had with my grandfather (Rabbi Avraham Bick). But I do know that my grandfather came from Russia to Pressburg and was a famous man who visited many Torah giants and published several books. He must have met the *tzaddik*, the Rashab, and from Heaven it was shown to him (i.e., the Rashab) that there were orphans" (Y. Y. Neumann, 2000, personal communications, 21 May, 24 July).

The late Lubavitcher Rebbe, Menachem Mendel Schneerson, has discerned (1997b) the deepest mystical meaning of the Rashab's visit to Pressburg during a *farbrengen* (Hassidic gathering) in 1962. For him it was akin to the mysterious trips that the founder of Hassidism, the Baal Shem Tov used to make to help Jews throughout Europe. He refers to the *Book of Lamentations* 5:3, where it says when the second Temple was destroyed and the Jews were exiled, "We were orphans from our Fathers, and our Mothers were like widows" (Tanach, op. cit., p. 1727).

Indeed, at the turn of the twentieth century, it can be said that Jews were living in a state of disconnection from their roots and from each other. It was a time of great conflict between the hassidim and *mitnagdim* (non-Chassids) and other religious and non-religious Jews. The work of the Rashab, as he understood it, had to do with comforting "the mourners" (the disconnected) and with arranging the marriage of "the orphans" (the Jewish people) with their divine source.

For Rav Menachem Mendel Schneerson, the whole episode was a metaphor, as well as the concrete embodiment, of this process. Thus, the fact that the Rashab went into a trance during the *Maariv* (evening) prayer, had to do with a going into the darkness of exile. When he emerged, it was to buy fine clothes, representing the adorning of the Jewish people with beauty and bringing out "their true essence." And the marriage did not just have to do with two girls, but with the need for all Jews to reconnect with their essential being, spiritual and secular.

It is very hard to grasp transcendental phenomena, such as the Rashab experienced, or ultramundane revelations, such as Rav Menachem Mendel Schneerson expounded. The reasons for this situation have to do with the metaphysical foundations of our science, which determines that there is no consciousness beyond the brain and the scope of our senses. As Rick Tarnas points out in *Passion of the Western Mind* (1991), we continue to live by the primary beliefs refined by Galileo Galilei (1564–1642) in the sixteenth century and Isaac Newton, a generation later.[13] Their "reality" consisted of an outside "objective world" comprised of matter and energy which could be clearly observed and quantified. Freud, the scientist, held a similar world view. For him the world of the occult could not be seen or measured. So he remained highly suspicious of the paranormal phenomena that colleagues like Carl Jung or Sandor Ferenczi described. He thought that they might be perpetrating conjuring tricks and chicanery or ridiculous assertions such as the idea that fruit jam fills the center of the earth (1933a, Lecture XXX, p. 32). Freud was worried that claims of the occult would bring psychoanalysis into disrepute, since both were dealing with subjective states that lay beyond ostensible proof (pp. 31–36).

But Freud, the scientist, also believed that it was important to keep an open mind. As we have considered, he refused to dismiss events like telepathy just because they could not be rationally explained or understood. He thought it was important to respect the unknown. So Freud can also be seen as the harbinger of a "postmodern metaphysic" which itself has been strongly influenced by recent advances in quantum physics. These ideas suggest that everything and anything is possible, and even probable.

CHAPTER THREE

The Jewish mystical traditions

Psychoanalysis and Kabbalah are theories about the nature of existence. They are also meditations, really methods for restoring shattered lives. These are lives which have been separated from their source. The particular domain of psychoanalysis is the head and the heart, that is, "the self," the totality of an individual's mind and emotions. I refer to a person confirmed in his subjectivity, as agent of his thoughts and feelings, and confirmed in his objectivity, the object of his own activity and focus of his consciousness.

In contrast the domain of Kabbalah, the Jewish mystical tradition, is the soul, a person's holy, timeless essence. I refer to an entity which is both elevated, that is, exists in spiritual realms, and is part of a whole, the primordial source, God.

Needless to say, such a capsule definition is limited and limiting. It does not take into account many other facets of psychoanalysis or Kabbalah. Thus, psychoanalysis, as currently practiced, is not just concerned with an individual man, woman, or child. On the contrary, it strives to see this person in relation to his family and friends. And to complicate matters even more, it considers each person to be a dynamic nucleus of relationships. Essentially he is a center of energies, a world in and of himself, containing and being contained by a myriad of other swirling worlds.

Kabbalah also focuses upon worlds and worlds within worlds. So a further way of looking at both psychoanalysis and Kabbalah, a further refinement, is that these two disciplines aim to explore the obvious and the esoteric, the conscious and unconscious aspects of existence. But they especially aim to reveal that which is mysterious and profoundly concealed.

As you can see, my introduction stresses the similarities, rather than the differences between psychoanalysis and Kabbalah. This is because I think that psychoanalysis is essentially a secular branch of Kabbalah, or to put it another way, psychoanalysis is secular Kabbalah.

Some decades ago Dr. David Bakan, who was professor of psychology at the University of Chicago, published a fascinating study of the origins of psychoanalysis entitled, *Sigmund Freud and the Jewish Mystical Tradition* (op. cit.). Bakan stated:

> ... the contributions of Freud are to be understood largely as a contemporary version of, and a contemporary contribution to, the history of Jewish mysticism. Freud, consciously or unconsciously, secularized Jewish mysticism; and psychoanalysis can intelligently be viewed as such a secularization. (p. 25)

In a similar vein, the noted British psychoanalyst, Wilfred Bion, emphasized, "I use the Kabbalah as a framework for psychoanalysis" (Eigen, 2012, op. cit., p. x).[1] In this study I shall consider psychoanalysis from the standpoint of Sigmund Freud, his associate, Melanie Klein, and their successors.

I intend to show that their personal origins, concerns, and methods are intimately rooted in Jewish religious and mystical traditions. To do so I shall concentrate on some of the fundamental features of their work. Each of these has long been recognized as an outstanding innovator and important contributor to our understanding of human nature. For Freud this includes "free associations," his basic methodology, and his theory of unconscious processes, the view that reality has both a manifest and latent content. For Klein I shall focus on two of her basic concepts, the container and the contained, and reparation.

There are some striking similarities in the lives of Freud and Klein which can account for their direct and indirect connections with Judaism and Kabbalah. Freud was born in Freiberg, Moravia (now

Pribor, Czech Republic) in 1856, but moved at an early age to Vienna where he spent almost his entire life in the company of Jewish friends, colleagues, and family. Significantly, both his parents came from Galicia, a region of Poland that was "saturated" with Jewish mysticism, especially Hassidism. Indeed, Freud explicitly acknowledged that his father, Jakob, came from a Hassidic environment (Krüll, op. cit., p. 90). Moreover, as I previously noted, both his paternal grandfather, Shlomo, and great-grandfather, Ephraim, were hassidim (ibid., see Table 3, Jakob Freud family tree).

Freud was familiar with Jewish mystical texts. Bakan described a meeting he had with Chayyim Bloch, a Lithuanian rabbi and distinguished student of Judaism, Kabbalah, and Hassidism. His mentor was Joseph Bloch (no relation) who himself was a mystic and a leader of the fight against anti-Semitism in Vienna. Joseph Bloch encouraged Chayyim to translate the works of Chaim Vital, the foremost disciple of Rabbi Isaac Luria (the ARI), the great sixteenth-century Kabbalist and preeminent progenitor of Jewish mysticism. Luria himself did not leave a written record of his ideas, but Chaim Vital expounded them in great detail. So it is through his writings that Lurianic Kabbalah entered the mainstream of Jewish thought.

Chayyim Bloch found the translation difficult and the topics somewhat distasteful. But he persisted as long as Joseph Bloch was alive. When the latter died, he withdrew from the project. Later he had a dream in which his mentor brandished a finger in front of his face and admonished him for not finishing the work on Vital. The dream encouraged Bloch to complete the book, but he still remained uncertain about it. This led him to seek out and show the study to Freud, whom he thought would find it of interest. This was indeed the case. After reading it, Freud exclaimed, "This is gold!" (Bakan, op. cit., p. xix). Furthermore, he agreed to write a foreword and volunteered his help in getting the book published. Then Freud gave Bloch his manuscript of *Moses and Monotheism* to read. After perusing it Bloch was horrified. He considered it an anti-Semitic tract and told Freud so in no uncertain terms. Freud, in turn, was infuriated and stormed out of the room.[2]

Bloch related that he didn't know what to do, to leave or stay, so as not to appear "impolite." He decided to stay for awhile and used the time to look over Freud's library. In it he saw several books on Kabbalah in German and a French edition of the *Zohar*, the principal text of Jewish mysticism (Bakan, op. cit., pp xix–xx).[3]

Bloch's meeting with Freud was unusual, but Freud's interest in Jewish camaraderie and concepts was not exceptional. For years he attended and participated in fortnightly meetings of a B'nai B'rith lodge. And as I will document in a forthcoming chapter, Freud held deep discussions on Kabbalah with Rabbi Alexandre Safran, the chief rabbi of Geneva.

Melanie Klein was born in Vienna in 1882 and lived her formative years there. Many consider her to be Freud's foremost follower. Klein greatly extended his work by expanding the field of child analysis as well as by pioneering the psychoanalysis of psychotic patients. Like Freud, Klein had a notable Jewish pedigree. Her father came from an Orthodox Jewish family and her mother was the daughter of a rabbi. Although she was not observant or formally religious, she did have a Jewish upbringing and in adult life Klein maintained a fondness for the festival of Yom Kippur, the Day of Atonement (Grosskurth, 1987, p. 13). As we shall see, these backgrounds clearly influenced their accomplishments.

Freud and Klein were healers. Their primary focus was damaged selves, that is, people who were mentally, emotionally, and socially broken or, to use the prevailing medical metaphor, "sick." Freud turned to the psychological realm because he found that the symptoms of mental illness could not be explained or treated physically. Instead he found that by utilizing a special relationship, one where his patients were able to speak freely about whatever occurred to them, their symptoms diminished or disappeared and their lives became less chaotic. The quality of listening was a very important element in this "free association" process. Later analysts called it "listening with the third ear." It is a listening which is very attentive, nonjudgmental, and highly sensitive to nuances of thought and feeling.

Freud's methods are astonishingly similar to those developed by the early Kabbalists, notably the thirteenth-century Spanish Kabbalist, Rabbi Abraham Abulafia. Abulafia strove to "unseal the soul, to untie the knots which bind it" (Bakan, op. cit., p. 76). Basically he developed a theory of repression and a means to deal with the effects of repression six centuries before Freud (pp. 75–80).

First, Abulafia emphasized the "mystical logic" of letters, the logic of "God's real world" which for Freud became the logic of the unconscious, especially as elaborated by linguistic processes (Freud, 1910e). Second, he described a form of free association which he called "jumping and skipping." The twentieth-century philosopher and founder of the modern, academic study of Kabbalah, Gershom Scholem, commented that this technique was:

> ... a very remarkable method of using associations as a way of meditation ... Every "jump" opens a new sphere ... Within this sphere, the mind may freely associate. The "jumping" unites, therefore, elements of free and guided association and is said to assure quite extraordinary results as far as the "widening of the consciousness" of the initiate is concerned. The "jumping" brings to light hidden processes of the mind ... (Scholem, 1941, pp. 135–136)

This exercise allowed Freud to peel back layer upon layer of disturbance, to penetrate anxiously concealed thoughts and feelings, and to initiate understanding, first in himself, then in his patients. The transformation from sick to sane took place when the concealed became revealed, when the unconscious became conscious, and his patients were able to "know" themselves. Essentially he discovered a process of demystification and dealienation facilitated by the spontaneous association of thoughts and feelings. Or to put it another way, through encouraging his patients to free associate, Freud was able to initiate a process of derepression. What does this mean?

Freud saw that people lived in two spheres simultaneously. One is the conscious level. He called conscious thoughts and actions the manifest content of our lives. The other is the unconscious level. This is not a static, but a dynamic interplay of experiences which he called the latent content. Freud saw that it is an ongoing effort to keep things latent or unconscious. Indeed, much of one's life may be devoted to this effort, while the outer manifestations of such struggles often emerge as "symptoms." But what are symptoms? Are they not simply bits and pieces of behavior, well worn responses, that sit astride our personality like so many garments? Usually no one considers them to be indications of illness, unless they become too painful to wear, or too disturbing to others. And much of this pain has to do with the inner conflicts which keep a person from being at one with himself and his source.

Making the unconscious, conscious enables people to become less conflicted with themselves. It helps them to gain peace and wholeness, or what in Hebrew is called *Shalom* and *Shalem*. Essentially it enables men and women to regain choice as to what "clothes" they need to carry and which they can shed. And it determines to what extent the light of their innermost being can permeate and nourish their lives, as well as the community in which they live.

The study of the Torah (the first five books of the Bible) involves an almost identical process. I refer to the interplay between *Nigleh*, the revealed Torah, and *Nistar*, the hidden Torah. Traditionally, Jews, and especially those initiated into Kabbalah, believe that the Torah is the word of God. These words contain but also conceal His radiance or illumination. By penetrating the outer layers or overt meanings of the words, Kabbalists believe that it is possible to gain a direct contact with God, and therefore, the source of all existence (Steinsaltz, 1988).

The *Zohar*, or Book of Illumination, is the principal text of Kabbalah. Ostensibly the work of Rabbi Simeon Bar Yohai in the second century, in academic circles it is now generally attributed, in whole or in part, to the thirteenth-century Spanish Kabbalist, Rabbi Moses de Leon (Bakan, op. cit., p. 83).

The book consists of a detailed commentary on the Torah in order to distinguish between what is manifest and what is latent, and to reveal the basic wellsprings of universal truth.[4] In the Torah chapter on *Be-Ha'alothekha* ("When you light ..."), from *Be-Midbar* (the Book of Numbers), the *Zohar* explains:

> Thus had the Torah not clothed herself in garments of this world the world could not endure it. The stories of the Torah are thus only her outer garments, and whoever looks upon those garments as being the Torah itself, woe to that man ... Observe this. The garments worn by a man are the most visible part of him, and senseless people looking at the man do not seem to see more in him than the garments. But in truth the pride of the garments is the body of the man, and the pride of the body is the soul. Similarly the Torah has a body made up of the precepts of the Torah, called *gufe torah* (main principles of the Torah), and that body is enveloped in garments made up of worldly narrations.
>
> The senseless people see only the garment, the mere narrations; those who are somewhat wiser penetrate as far as the body. But the really wise, the servants of the most high King, those who stood on Mount Sinai, penetrate right through to the soul, the root principle

of all, namely, to the real Torah. (*Zohar*, vol. 5, 1934, p. 211; also cited
by Bakan, op. cit., p. 247)

As Bakan points out and this passage reveals, the development of
Freudian psychoanalysis has meant that Kabbalistic forms of interpretation can be used to understand the profoundly human dilemma of
being alive. I refer to the almost universal fate of being imbued with life
force and simultaneously suffering from a self divided and cut off or
alienated from itself and from others.

The Kleinian contribution relates to the difficulty of containing man's
instinctual forces, and all their derivatives; or, from another angle,
holding what the Kabbalists would call the primary radiance of God.
Now, together with Klein's views, I want to consider the creation of the
world, from the standpoint of Lurianic Kabbalah. It is a development
of the work of Rabbi Isaac Luria, who lived and taught in Safed in the
sixteenth century. Through his insights, the *Zohar* (also known as the
Book of Splendor) has become more generally accessible.

According to the Lurianic understanding, when God created the
world, he withdrew his light into a single point. He thereby forged a primary nothingness or vacuum that became "the fertile teeming grounds
of creation." Today this "vacated space" is what quantum physicists
might call "a pregnant vacuum," replete with virtual particles which go
in and out of existence in billionths of a second.

The process of vacating a space overfilled with energy is known by
the term, *tzimtsum. Tzimtsum* denotes the act of withdrawal or contraction or concealment of divine radiance. After the initial *tzimtsum*,
this course of events reversed. Then light flowed back into the world
(being built) in the form of a very fine thread (called the *kav*). This event
denotes the act of emanation. And from this thread ten vessels were created from the radiant threads. In the Bible, Psalm 104 demonstrates how
this occurred: "He draws forth Light as a garment" (Tehillim [Psalms],
2001, p. 126).[5]

It is said that this light continued to pour into the vacuum left by the
original contraction and concealment. It, in turn, led to the creation of
containers or vessels (called *sephirot*) to contain the illuminations. So
we can see that the initial *tzimtsum* (contraction) was necessary in order
for these structures to exist. Otherwise everything would be annihilated
by the power of the energies released in the initial "big bang." Similarly,

the *tzimtsum* enabled part of the radiant threads to be held by and to establish the contents of the vessels. Thus, the containers also gave rise to the contained and gave shape and character to the contents.

The "higher" vessels and their contents, according to Luria, had to do with man's intellectual faculties, while the "lower" ones had to do with emotions and emotionality. As the emanations progressed, the former "higher," intellectual vessels remained strong and were able to contain the energies that poured into them. But the "lower," emotional vessels could not hold or limit the emanations that entered them. So they shattered. In Kabbalah the resultant explosion is known as the *shevirath ha-kelim*, the breaking of the vessel.

When this happened, the lower vessels and their energies, that is, the emotional containers and their contents, disintegrated. The result was a multitude of fragments or shards containing bits of the original light of creation. These fragments together with their embedded light are known as shells (*klippot*) and are responsible for the existence of evil. Evil therefore can be seen as the manifestation of uncontainable disintegrative forces, something which turns substance into chaos (known as *tohu*) (Gottlieb, 1989, pp. 17–18). This phenomenon is closely related to the Kleinian concept of primary envy.

The ensuing fragmentation led to the "exile of the *Shekinah*," the feminine, maternal aspect of God's presence. The whole point of existence is to free the light trapped in the shells, to undo this exile and to reestablish the unification of existence, the unity of the mundane with the divine.

Similarly, when a child is born, the unity between the child and his mother is broken. Then the child struggles to contain the primary impulses, which Freud called Eros and Thanatos, and which Klein recognized as the Life Impulse and the Death Impulse. Essentially we can consider the Life Impulse as the impetus to form and structure. This is negative entropy. Concurrently the Death Impulse is the impetus to randomize objects and events. This is entropy itself, the reversion to disorder.

Klein pointed out that the neonate finds it very hard to cope with these powerful impulses. In order to protect himself from terrible internal tension (experienced as incipient death) he splits or shatters his mind and being. Concomitantly, he tries to deal with the tension by evacuating, literally projecting, large parts of himself outwards, into others, even into inanimate objects. As a result, his outer world becomes full of bad persecuting bits and pieces, while his inner self becomes emptier and emptier. Then, in order to deal with the emptiness, he may take back or introject many of the bad bits. All these actions lead to an internal world which is highly threatening. Klein called this state of affairs, the paranoid-schizoid position. The term denotes a dynamic configuration of persecutory fears; annihilative and disintegrative defenses (splitting, projection, denial) and "part objects", or what I call "part people," that is, relationships that stick at or revert to a function: such as feeding or cleaning, rather than being part of a complete, autonomous human being.

How does the child overcome this dreadful situation? How does he reestablish his container and containing capacity? How can the bad bits become less toxic, more containable? Kabbalists would say that we can undo the broken vessel and subsequent exile, by establishing and reestablishing a close relationship with God. In the same vein Melanie Klein and her colleagues would argue that the child can become a functioning container of his own impulses (and thereby life forces), by establishing and reestablishing close relationships with those who love and care for him, especially his mother.

This process has been very well described by Dr. Hanna Segal, who is one of Melanie Klein's leading disciples: Segal comments on what happens during a good mother–child relationship, and, by direct implication, a good therapist-patient relationship:

> When an infant has an intolerable anxiety, he deals with it by projecting it into the mother. The mother's response is to acknowledge this anxiety and do whatever is necessary to relieve the infant's distress. The infant's perception is that he has projected something intolerable into his object, but the object was capable of containing it and dealing with it. He can then reintroject (take back into himself) not only the original anxiety, but an anxiety modified by having been contained. He also reintrojects an object (that is, a representation of a person) capable of containing and dealing with anxiety. The containment of the anxiety by an internal object (representation of a person) capable of understanding is the beginning of mental stability. (1986, pp. 134–135)

It is worth asking, what happens if the child is not blessed with a containing parent, or the patient with a containing therapist? Invariably he will try to project more and more of his bad feelings, somewhere, anywhere. And even more ominously, he may do this deliberately and maliciously. But, malicious projection is an operational definition of envy (Berke, 2012, pp. 158–161). Therefore, a failure of containment will lead to the explosion of envy, the evil impulse (in Kabbalah known as the *yetzah harah*) into the world (p. 205). A world full of bits and pieces of envious hatred is identical to broken bits of the primary vessels, each replete with embedded chaos. Fascinatingly, the Chinese world for chaos, *luan*, also means envy.

The opposite of chaos is order. A strong container and containing function is a prerequisite for such order, which is closely connected with peace and wholeness, *Shalom* and *Shalem*. Klein discerned that the time for accomplishing this goes back to the first year of life, as early as four to five months of age. Then the child begins to realize that the mother he loves and the mother he hates are the same person. This initiates what she called the depressive position.

The depressive position, when the child becomes more concerned with preserving another, rather than preserving himself, is a psychological milestone. It marks the onset of mental and emotional integration. It means that the child is able to face reality, whatever he feels inside himself or sees outside himself. Moreover, it means that he is able to take responsibility for what he does, good and bad; and is able to acknowledge and contain a wide variety of experiences: love and hate, guilt and despair.

The onset of the depressive position signals the growing capacity of the child to be a container of his own impulses. If the elucidation of this dynamic milestone is one of Klein's major contributions, perhaps her greatest is the concept of reparation. Reparation is the means of repairing an inner world shattered under the pressure of destructive impulses and an outer world of damaged relationships, people, and things. Reparation is a goal and the moving to this goal. According to Klein, reparation is never complete, rather it is an active process of striving toward completeness, whether of the head or heart or entire being. It is intimately related to the Kabbalistic concept of *Tikkun*.

The noted Israeli poet and Kabbalist, Pinchas Sadeh (1929–1994), has described what the development, *Tikkun Ha-Lev*, or Restoration of the Heart, has meant for him:

> This evening, while I was still engrossed in thought on a certain topic, a thought entered my mind regarding "repair of the heart."

A few years ago, when I edited a book of the writings of Rabbi Nachman of Breslov, I chose to call it *Tikkun Ha-Lev*, repair of the heart. I thought that the meaning of the name, simple in itself, was absolutely clear to me. But I am thinking that perhaps only now its meaning is becoming clear to me.

... time, fate, life and death—all these powerful forces prevent the possibility of repairing that which is broken. If so, what is possible? What remains for man to do, after all? What can save and rescue the things that are smashed? Maybe only—and even this only through tremendous effort, through difficult struggle, through great pain—this repairing the heart. In other words, repairing the heart, which was broken when all those things were broken. (Berke, 1996, p. 857)[6]

Melanie Klein struggled to define the depressive position at a time when she was grief-stricken from the death of her eldest son in a mountaineering accident. It is not too far-fetched to think that this effort was her way of trying to mend a broken heart. The resultant *tikkun* (repair) led to a powerful and extremely important concept.

We all know a popular children's rhyme which expresses similar fears and needs:

> Humpty Dumpty sat on a wall.
> Humpty Dumpty had a great fall.
> All the King's horses and all the King's men,
> Couldn't put Humpty Dumpty together again.
> (ibid., p. 857)

The despair in this refrain echoes with that of Pinchas Sadeh about the difficulty, even impossibility, of effecting a repair.

I think the sentiments are so moving because they are so elemental. How can one put together a loved one, or loved ones, after we have hurt them? And how strong are our reparative capacities? Are they really equal to our life forces, when, to quote the Scottish psychiatrist, R. D. Laing, "the dreadful has already happened"? These issues are especially relevant with Humpty Dumpty. For he is not an ordinary creature. Rather he embodies the cosmic egg, the archetypal container and contents of all life (see Cirlot, 1962, p. 90).

As in Kabbalah, Klein sets out to describe how to overcome fragmentation and loss, evil and exile. Only the terms of reference are different. Klein is concerned with the self, and this self in relation to others. To her, exile may mean separation from mother. For Kabbalists, evil also means fragmentation, disintegration, and ultimately death. Exile means separation from God.

The struggle to overcome the destructive forces in man and society was a continual theme in the work of Wilfred Bion, a colleague of Hanna Segal, and one of Klein's most eminent followers. Bion, who was president of the British Psychoanalytical Society from 1962 to 1965, was an influential maverick who "… demanded not that his patients get better, but that they pursue Truth" (Phillips, 1994, p. 136).

CHAPTER FOUR

Bion and Kabbalah

Wilfred Bion, a tank commander in World War I, brushed with death countless times, emerging from the war unscathed physically but emotionally distraught. His wartime experiences led him to a lifelong fascination with psychic catastrophe, whether evinced by shell shock or psychosis.[1] Bion queried how one can contain the uncontainable, a puzzle which preoccupies Kabbalah, as well as his writings.

This thought resonates with the work of Michael Eigen, a New York psychoanalyst and author, who has written a study of *Kabbalah and Psychoanalysis* (2012). In his work he describes many areas of convergence between the two disciplines, and in particular, with Bion's ideas. Eigen notes that Lurianic Kabbalah and Bion's books are expressly concerned with catastrophe (breaking of the vessels) and faith (whether in God, or in the "psychoanalytic attitude"). This is a profound belief that goodness will emerge by plumbing the dark, painful parts of the self. Moreover, both teachings focus on the known and unknown: on ontology (being) and the transformation of being; on the mind, and feelings, and on the beyond feelings, the essence of existence.

In a "Bionesque" way, Eigen loves to quote a statement by the British astrophysicist, Sir Arthur Eddington, about the nature of the

49

universe: "Something unknown is doing we don't know what" (Eigen, 2012, op. cit., p. 18). Perhaps these words contain the connection between the Lurianic idea of God, something "unnameable, inconceivable, unimaginable and unrepresentable, the infinite of infinities," and Bion's idea of "O", signifying unknown, ultimate reality. The paradox is that "O" may be unknowable but both Bion and Kabbalists have sought to "know" the unknown by approaching it with a state of mind without memory, expectation, intellect, or desire.

Essentially Bion realized that one can only approach the mystery of another human being, especially one broken by suffering, through self abnegation—absolute "egolessness." This is a well-known truth among mystics. An individual can only reach the Godhead (the Infinite, the Divine) by attaining what Kabbalists call *bitul*, a state of egolessness. Then one can be like a neutrino passing through the sun, or like an analyst who can tolerate psychosis. Such a person has shed his narcissism and carries no emotional charge, just like a neutrino which carries no electrical charge and can traverse objects without friction.

I am reminded of my first teacher, John Thompson, who was professor of "existential psychoanalysis" at the Albert Einstein College of Medicine (AECM) in New York during the 1960s. Milton Rosenbaum, the founder and chairman of the Department of Psychiatry at AECM, related that he hired Thompson because "I saw him as a very special person. He had a spiritual side—a philosopher, writer, poet" (Weindling, 2010, p. 282).

Thompson would sit still and silent with his catatonic patients six days a week for months, even years on end, until a brief movement indicated that they were willing to engage with him. One such man exploded with powerful waves of his arms, after Thompson remarked on a minute gesture: "Don't give me that shit! Don't give me that shit!" (Thompson, personal communication, March 1963). Thompson, in turn, took some paper and put a pencil in his hand. The man then began to draw thin, tortured, but well-constructed figures in the manner of the Swiss artist Alberto Giacometti. He later recalled his experience:

> How I loved my sainted doctor as he spoke of his life, spoke of my psyche only as it emerged in drawings, paintings. Oh, he knew me beyond words and touched me with the grace I had always sought. He had been intimate with Albert Camus, Pope John and Cardinal

Montini before his elevation, he was the psychiatrist in T. S. Eliot's
Cocktail Party, the psychiatrist at the Nuremberg Trials … How
he healed me without a word about my past. (Weindling, op. cit.,
p. 289)[2]

Thompson's patient subsequently became a successful draftsman and
sculptor. It was with this account in mind that I responded to Mary
Barnes, a former nurse, who used her feces to paint breasts and wombs
on the walls of Kingsley Hall, a community where we were both resi-
dent in 1965.[3] The stench was unbearable and Mary was on the verge of
being thrown out. Her "smell space" had taken over the whole building. To avoid her ungraceful exit, I gave her large black crayons and
sheets of paper and urged Mary to use them. Her first efforts were
like primitive cave paintings—light, mobile outlines of archetypal
figures—Madonna and Child, Jesus and Mary, and babies inside babies
inside mother (Barnes & Berke, 1972a, pp. 236–238).[4] Mary eventually
established herself as a skilled painter and mystic.[5]

Both vignettes demonstrate the transformative effects of containing relationships. Then rage-filled fragments of feelings can reemerge
as cohesive creations. They also illustrate another common thread
between psychoanalysis and Kabbalah, that is, intense emotionality.
This can be so strong that it carries with it constant catastrophic threats
of disintegration. That is why Thompson's patient remained catatonic
for years. It was the one way he could keep himself intact. Mary often
used a similar technique. She could keep herself motionless for weeks
or months at a time. But, in addition, she tried to get rid of her angry
blackness, which she called "IT" by evacuating it in the form of smells
and stools. These were concretizations of what Bion hypothesized were
"beta-elements," raw bits of emotions and sensations, which could not
be used for thinking, but for projecting into others in order to control or
destroy them. Bion pointed out that:

Beta-elements are not amenable to use in dream thoughts but are
suited for use in projective identification. They are influential in
producing acting out. These are objects that can be evacuated or
used for a kind of thinking that depends on manipulation of what
are felt to be things in themselves as if to substitute such manipulations for words or ideas. (1962, pp. 6–7)

"Beta-elements" are extremely persecuting both to those who suffer them and to those who are the target of them. But, when tempered by benevolent reality (containment, truth, love), they can be "metabolized," and become what Bion called "alpha-elements," experiences available for consciousness. He described the process by which this happens as "alpha-function." For him, alpha-function serves to "digest" beta-elements and make them available for thinking.

> … alpha-function makes the sense impressions of emotional experience available for conscious and dream thought. The patient who cannot dream [i.e., no alpha-function] cannot go to sleep and cannot wake up. (ibid., pp. 6–7)

Bion's beta-elements are remarkably similar to the shards or fragments (*klippot*) caused by the shattering of the vessels of creation (*shevirat ha-kelim*). This happens when the vessels cannot contain the powerful emotions inside themselves. The ensuing shards (broken shells, sparks) are like bits and pieces of destructiveness. And as I have pointed out, they can turn something (substance) into nothing (chaos). This is catastrophic both for individuals (baby destroying mother in phantasy) and the world (consider the current plethora of end-of-the-world movies).

For Kabbalists the answer is to "raise the sparks." This concept has several components. One, like Humpty Dumpty, involves fitting broken bits together. Another has to do with reintegrating them as part of the "Tree of Life" (*Etz Chaim*).

The "Tree of Life" is a composite structure of the ten basic *sephirot* (vessels, the containers as well as their contents) and the way that they relate to each other. Eigen comments that the Kabbalistic Tree of Life "is one of the greatest spiritual light shows you can find, filled with nothingness and luminous fireworks." It is "… drenched in fecundity and [may be] represented by neural networks generating [myriads of] patterns" (Eigen, 2014, p. 55). Kabbalists also see it as the outline of a person. According to the schema of Moshe Cordovero (1522–1570), the Safed Kabbalist who was the predecessor of Isaac Luria, the top three sephirot denote the intellectual faculties of God: wisdom (*chochmah*), understanding (*binah*), and knowledge (*daat*).

The lower six sephirot denote the emotional attributes of God: kindness (*chesed*), severity (*geverah*), beauty (*tiferet*), victory or eternity (*netzach*), submission (*hod*), and foundation (or sexuality) (*yesod*). The lowest *sephirah* is the feminine principle which is paradoxically called kingship (*malchut*) and equals the receptive quality of God (the *shekinah*). Literally it means orifice or repository. This vessel is intimately linked to the highest *sephirah* (to do with will or volition) which is known as the crown (*keter*). Significantly, each of these vessels (*sephirot*, the container and the contained) is akin to a hologram, with the part equalling the whole. This means that each *sephirah* is itself a complete tree, and the part of that tree is a complete tree, and so forth, endlessly.

From the standpoint of the body, the crown is the skull; wisdom— the brain; understanding—the heart; kindness—the right arm; severity—the left arm; beauty—the torso; victory and submission—the two thighs; and foundation—the toes.

Interestingly, Cordovero relates the vessel of kingship (the feminine principle, the *shekinah*) to the mouth. He also compares the vessels (*sephirot*) to a tree with arms and branches through which the divine energies (known as the *shefa*) flow and irrigate the whole of creation.[6] But, for all the anthropomorphisms, he cautions:

> Master of the Worlds [God], You are the cause of causes and producer of effects, who waters the Tree [which] is as the soul to the body … In you, however, there is no similitude or likeness to anything within or without. (*Siddur Tehillat Hashem*, op. cit., p. 150)

Following from Cordovero's comments, it appears that the *sephirot* (divine vessels) are abstractions of human feelings taken to a "higher" level. By implication, a similar event happens during the "raising of the sparks," in order to overcome desolation and despair. First the broken bits fit together. Then they find their place among the emotional vessels (*sephirot*). Ultimately the shards move to an "advanced" state of wisdom, understanding, knowledge, and the beyond. In so doing the shards shed their nasty natures and become a force for good—contemplation and spiritual ascent.

This process is similar to the journey that Bion has portrayed, the movement from "beta-functioning" to "alpha-functioning," from a mind overwhelmed by "beta-waves" to one calmed by "alpha-waves." These waves emulate the electrical activity of the brain first discovered by the German neurologist, Hans Berger. He is most famous for his invention of the electroencephalogram (EEG). Berger found that beta rhythms had a frequency of 18–30 cycles per second. They were often chaotic and were associated with intense anxiety. In contrast Berger noted that alpha rhythms were slower, 8–12 cycles per second, and more regular. He correlated these waves with tranquility, REM sleep, and dreaming.

In the 1960s a whole industry was developed using biofeedback techniques to help transform people's brain patterns from beta states into alpha states. The latter was also connected with mystical meditative practices common to a variety of religious traditions. From a Kabbalistic viewpoint Rabbi Aryeh Kaplan has written about how to expand consciousness and achieve unification with the Divine in his book, *Meditation and Kabbalah* (1989).

The quest for unification is the ultimate element which links Kabbalah and psychoanalysis. In Judaism this is a spiritual pursuit preeminently expressed by the prayer in the daily liturgy: *Shema Yisroel Adonai Elohaynu Adonai Echad.* Usually translated as, "Hear, O Israel, the Lord our God the Lord is One," it also conveys the more urgent message, "Listen God, You are One, You are the Everything and the Everywhere, There is Nothing Besides You" (Siddur Tehillat Hashem, op. cit., p. 16).

The next paragraph of the prayer begins: *"V'ahav'tah et Adonai Elohechah b'chol l'vav'chah, uv'chol naf'sh'chah uv'chol m'odechah"* (ibid., p. 16). This means: "You shall love the Lord your God with all your heart, with all your soul, and with all your might." In other words, you should be deeply and passionately attached to the Everything and the Everywhere with every ounce of your being, especially your emotions and intellect and will. This is the goal of all mystics and explains why the Rebbe Rashab was so devastated when he thought that his intellect and emotions, his head and his heart, were disconnected and divided. For him this was far more than a split in himself. It was a spiritual disaster. He felt he had become detached from God, his spiritual source, his raison d'etre.

Essentially the Rebbe suffered a split in his self which coincided with a slivering of his soul. This prevented him from being at one with himself or with others. The reasons for this are not hard to discern. The year 1902 was the twentieth anniversary of the death of his father as well as the obligation to take on the burden of "Rebbeship." Meanwhile, he was beset by strife with his fellow Jews (non-hassidim) on one hand, and the Czarist state (police, legal authorities) on the other. As a result, one of his primary projects, the creation of a Hassidic yeshiva, *Tomchei Temimim*, was at risk of closure. Hence the Rashab's desperate cries,

"Where am I? Where do I turn? What should I say?" (Y. Y. Schneersohn, op. cit., p. 42).

Freud's great accomplishment was to help the Rebbe rebuild bridges between himself and himself, between his emotions and his intellect and his will. But is this not the task of psychoanalysis in general, "to raise the sparks," to enable an individual to overcome a self divided, and to regain connections both within and beyond the self? In the next chapters I shall further refine the nature of "the self" and "the soul" as well as the bonds between them.

CHAPTER FIVE

On the nature of the self: and its relationship with the soul

The self and the soul are key protagonists of both the psychoanalytic and Kabbalistic worlds. Still, they are amorphous concepts, perhaps the self more so than the soul. So really: what is the "self"?. what is the "soul"?

The "self" is a paradox. It is a specific entity, but also an exercise in ambiguity. Although it pertains to psychological realms, the term encompasses a multitude of meanings, ranging from the interpersonal to the transpersonal. Most narrowly, the many definitions include identity and identifications, awareness and self-awareness, as well as a host of mental functions which Freud referred to as "the mental apparatus." Fundamentally, the self refers to a person confirmed in his own subjectivity and objectivity.

Heinz Kohut, the psychoanalyst whom many consider to be the progenitor of self-psychology, contends that the self is essentially "not knowable" (1977, p. 311). Before reaching this conclusion he reviewed various attempts to refine the term, ranging from personality structure to psychological center. Subsequently he described the constituents of the self: ambitions, ideals, talents, and skills. A secure self is a cohesive whole. The converse lacks cohesion and remains a fragmented, chaotic mess. Ultimately Kohut refused to assign a specific, that is, inflexible definition to the "self." While he may not have believed that the self is ineffable, he did think that the term may be best left undefined.

Jungian or analytical psychology provides a broader conception. It sees the self as "the unifying principle within the human psyche." Thus, for Carl Jung, who for a while was Freud's designated successor, the self is both the center and the container of individual consciousness (Samuels, 1986, p. 135). An implication of this concept is that the self can be seen as a holographic representation of the universe. Such a view is not too dissimilar from the Kabbalistic ideas of the "soul," which as we shall soon discuss, range from the animal to the divine. These formulations begin with a human essence embodied in physical form and conclude with a state of absolute unity with the Infinite.

More down to earth, I recall the day I realized that I existed. It was a brilliant summer's morning in Newark, New Jersey. I was fourteen or maybe fifteen years old, and was ambling down Osborne Terrace, the street where I lived. I happened to notice the sky. It was bright blue, and the clouds, proud bundles of white, seemed to be dawdling in the air. I stopped and looked, very intently, as if transfixed. Suddenly I realized that I existed, and that there was an "I" who was also a "me." For the first time in my life I had a profound sense of myself, as a being, as a doer, as a separate and independent entity. I felt very relieved and alive. For as long as I could remember, I had seen myself, and was seen by other members of my family, as an extension of my mother. Now I knew this was not the case. I was delighted. Years later I learned that my understanding was what the psychologist, Abraham Maslow (1970), called "a peak experience."

That day I discovered my self. But what was this self that I had discovered? Well, in the first place, it had to do with a sense of my own identity. I existed in the world. I was a unique, but also solitary being in time (over many generations), and in space (with family and friends). Thus this event was the beginning of an awareness of myself as a separate player in the complicated business of human relationships. Such an awareness coincides with the perspective of the philosopher, Dan Dennett. He stressed that the self is "the center of narrative gravity" around which all our memories and life-stories revolve (quoted by the psychologist Richard Bentall, 2003, p. 199).

This description carries two major implications. One is that when a person has a clear sense of his own identity, he feels established in his own subjectivity. He understands that he is the agent of his own thoughts, feelings, and experiences which began with and end with himself. In other words, this individual becomes the vessel that contains the light of his own being.

Second, when he feels confirmed in his objectivity, he becomes aware of himself as object, the object of his own praxis, of his own mental and physical activities. In this respect the psychologist, William James (1890) defined consciousness as "the awareness of being aware." Here "awareness" is the activity and "being aware" is the focus, or the object of the activity. Similarly, to be the object of one's own activity can best be conceived as being the focus of one's own consciousness. We commonly express this experience by hyphenated words: self-awareness (as happened on the summer's day when I became aware of myself as an object of my own awareness); self-consciousness (a somewhat embarrassing sense that someone else is aware of oneself); self-esteem; self-image; self-love; self-preservation; self-punishment; self-reproach; and so on.

So it all seems very simple. The self has to do with an enclosed subjectivity (I becoming an "I"), and an enclosed objectivity (an "I" becoming a "me"). And it refers to identity, one's sense or personal awareness of extending over myriad relationships. But the concept also has to do with ontology. Ontology refers to one's being in the world. This often gets lost when thinking of "I-ness" or "me-ness."

Ontology raises fundamental problems of existence. How can I become an "I," and how can I become a "me"? Or, another way to pose this question is: what gives life meaning, and, more specifically, what gives meaning to one's life?

Such questions bring one closer to the realms of Kabbalah, and the issues which the Kabbalists have addressed over two millennia.

But first let us consider how psychoanalytic thought has touched bits and pieces of these concerns in some very interesting ways.

For a considerable time, analysts did not talk about the self. Freud himself did not use the term. Instead they talked about an "I" related to identity, more specifically the ego. Self became synonymous with the I, and generated considerable confusion. Was the self an I, an ego, an inflated identity as in narcissistic aggrandizement, the mind or what?

Later Freud used the term "ego" to refer to the thinking apparatus of the mind. According to his "structural model," he distinguished between the ego, the id, and the superego.[1] Consequently, the ego became the part of the mind to do with thinking, and grasping or understanding inner and outer reality. So after a while, the central self became synonymous with mind, and also with parts of the mind.

But Freud's terminology has to be approached with some circumspection. As Bruno Bettelheim has pointed out (1983, p. 40), his translators skewed his words toward the medical or scientific in order to gain acceptance for him, especially in the United States. "The ego" is a rather cold technical rendering of "*das Ich*," with its many layers of emotional undertones. Similar problems arise conveying the meaning of "*das Es*" and "*das Über-Ich*" (usually rendered as the id and the superego). Neither of these words equals the self. Nonetheless, when discussing superego function, such as in depression, the psychoanalyst, Charles Rycroft notes that hyphenated words such as self-punishment, self-reproach, self-accusation, and self-blame have been commonly used to indicate the object or target of self-hatred (1972, pp. 149–150).

In the 1930s ego-psychology became the dominant school of psychoanalysis in the United States. Its major proponents included Heinz Hartman, Ernst Kris, R. M. Loewenstein, David Rapaport, and Erik Erikson. Again the concept of self was bypassed in favor of the ego and its development. So instead of trying to see individuals as a whole, how they existed in and for themselves and in and for others, these practitioners narrowed their attention to a part of the mind, which they pursued with a rational, mechanistic rigor. Moreover, their thinking was highly influenced by models of social adaptation.

In many respects ego-psychology is not a psychodynamic theory. However, it did emphasize the importance of context in determining the unfolding of the ego, or in a larger sense, the self. As the psychologist, Richard Bentall, points out, when constructing a self, the child internalizes historically and culturally determined values (op. cit., p. 200).

The implication is that the concept of self varies from time to time and place to place. Thus in the contemporary United States we can and do refer to an "individualistic self," while in countries like Japan the emphasis is on a "collectivistic self," where a person cannot conceive of himself outside of a large social group.

The counterpart to ego-psychology is object relations theory which was developed by Melanie Klein and her colleagues. Here the term "self" became a much more mobile term (other than ego), and was used to describe the relational aspects of Klein's theories. This includes all the processes of separating good from bad, inner from outer, introjection from projection. Yes, Klein often used "the self" synonymously with "the ego," but this is a much broader ego to do with functions, defense mechanisms, and ways of coping with anxiety.

The psychoanalyst, Robert Hinshelwood, asserts in his *A Dictionary of Kleinian Thought*, that "the ego" stands for a part of the mind that can be objectively described, that is, from the outside. Then "the self" is even more complicated. It is the product of multiple introjections, projections and identifications. This self has to be approached from the standpoint of a person's own experiences. Of necessity, this way of looking at the self refers to an individual as subject, someone who is the initiator and container of his own feelings, phantasies, and internal interactions, or psychic relationships (1991, p. 285).

In a similar vein, the doyen of the Chicago School of Psychoanalysis, Heinz Kohut developed a concept of self relations which went beyond the bounds of self as the focus of itself (as in self-awareness) and self as the focus of an outside observer. For him the self was the instigator of relationships. This is a relating self, an entity which engages with others, both inwardly and outwardly, intrapsychically and interpersonally.

Over several decades, the term "self" gradually enlarged its meaning. From first denoting a static mental structure, it began to encompass the idea of a dynamic interrelating personality, a signified and signifier. This is certainly the case when considering the role of the self in the work of the existentialist psychoanalyst, Rollo May. May focused on ontology, the self as a center of being-in-the world. According to May, the self shares four basic ontological characteristics, that is, qualities of being (May, Angel, & Ellenberger, 1958, pp. 61–65). First, it is a center of personal existence (quite different from being egotistical or self-centered). Second, man, by which we mean humankind, mankind and womankind, continually strives to affirm this center. Third, he utilizes this center to engage other people. And fourth, the self is a center of consciousness. For man this refers to self-awareness, of himself as subject, and of others as object.

I would add a fifth criteria of "beingness." Man seeks to preserve his center, even to the extent of hiding it from himself. This has a lot to do with the creation of a false self system which we will detail later on in the chapter. Interestingly, by the 1960s an American anthropologist, Carlos Castaneda, helped to solidify the idea of a personal "center," as well as the concepts of "centralness" and "centeredness," through his best-selling books about Don Juan, a Mexican brujo or warlock and shaman (1968). He claimed that in order to protect oneself from death, disease, and injury, and assure personal safety, a person always has to find his place of power. Specifically, Don Juan taught that somewhere, in every room, there was such a place. But to find it a person had to be absolutely centered in his own being. Therefore power became equated with finding one's personal center of balance, and affirming the epicenter of the self.

Likewise, the *Zohar*, which is the central text of Kabbalah, discusses at length the importance of "centering." If one is "off" in any way, it emphasizes the need to tilt that person to a more "right" or "left" position. The modern term for this is "off center." Such directionality has a basic meaning as in describing an overly physical or emotional person, someone who is too warm or too cold or, for that matter, too active or too passive. Hence the significance of finding the "just right" center of balance.

This central "selfness" provides the starting point for personal relationships. Without such a point, relationships are impossible. Otherwise people engage in partial relationships, or pseudo relationships, or non-relationship relationships. At worse, relationships become extremely threatening. Why? Because the focus of one's existence is missing. Instead people remain in danger of being engulfed or overwhelmed by others' reality. At best, one's self is an entity in continuous relations with other selves as part of a people-related, or as Kleinians assert, an object-related world.

The consequence of possessing a stable personal center means that an individual can and does inhabit a universe of relationships. And not just one such universe, but several, depending on whether we are considering wider social networks, or intrapsychic domains. Moreover, a person can expand these universes through a state of expanding consciousness where one's core self becomes the creator of symbols and abstractions. Then, people, and things, trees, leaves, stars, grains of sand, and even oneself, they all gain a plethora of new meanings. This idea coincides with the findings of the "logo-therapist," Victor Frankl, himself a direct descendent of the Talmudic scholar, Rashi, and the Kabbalist, Rabbi Judah Loew of Prague. He taught (1984) that the nature of existence has to do with gaining meaning through existence, that is, by living life thoroughly.

From another angle, analytical or Jungian psychologists refer to the center of the self as "the original state of organismic integration," the place within oneself where one's personal being, one's innate self, and one's archetypal potential meet. At different points in a spectrum of "being," Jung distinguishes between the self, the soul, and the spirit. But in practice he often uses these terms synonymously (Samuels, op. cit., pp. 136–137).

At one end of this spectrum, Jung expanded the concept of self to include both conscious and unconscious consciousness or experience. This is in contrast to the ego which he, as did Freud, reserved for the conscious mind. Jung also saw the self as a mediator of opposites within a human's central personality. This implies that there is a "good self" and a "bad self," and "a coordinating self," a part of one's being which orchestrates relations between the two polarities.

Intriguingly, analytic psychologists have tended to tilt the term toward the negative. Thus they speak of the "shadow side of the self," the negative part of the personality, that which a person has no wish to be, the sum of all one's unpleasant qualities. These represent the inferior, worthless, dangerous, primitive aspects of one's nature, something dark which needs to be kept in the dark, hidden like an internalised "evil other." This "shadow side" is like the Kabbalistic concept of the *sitra achra*, meaning "the other side." This is the force for evil that exists within every person. Why evil? Because it is disconnected from godliness, and is therefore unrestrained in passions and appetites.

In contrast, the soul can be seen as one's primary, undifferentiated potential. It is the central invigorating core of one's existence. Used almost identically in Jungian psychology with "the psyche," the soul is a non-material, archetypal essence which can connect one's experience with all experience, one's being with all "beingness," whether animate or inanimate. In other words, it is that part of the spectrum which integrates inner reality with larger realities, the particular with the universal, personal consciousness with cosmic consciousness, Jung applied the word "spirit" to the non-material, ineffable component of being. But spirit differs from soul, because a soul may be incarnate or non-incarnated, but one's spirit is incorporeal, ethereal, and detached from the body. It is much more like the Kabbalistic entity of the *tselem*, an astral body or astral projection, like an apparition or shade. A spirit cannot be specified or encompassed by definition or description. It is formless, imageless, spaceless, and endless. Moreover, it can exist independently from an embodied being.

According to the Jungian analyst, Andrew Samuels, belief in the spirit world does not necessarily include belief in the soul. But spirit may be personified in visionaries or prophets. In many respects Jungians see spirit as the essential or basic unifying principle of the universe. This view brings us back full circle to the idea of the self. Jungians say that the self conveys the total interconnectivity of everything and is a holistic conception of man. This picture appears to conflict with the alleged determinist, reductionist drama of Freudian psychoanalysis. It may come as a surprise that such a view is misleading. In his book, *Freud and Man's Soul*, Bruno Bettelheim demonstrates that "psycho-analysis" essentially means soul-study or soul-investigation (1983, op. cit., p. 12).

In German the emphasis is on the first word, psyche, that is, soul, not mind. But in English the emphasis is on the second word, analysis, with all its scientific, systematic associations. Freud was a superb word-smith, a master of literary German. It is often said that if he had not developed psychoanalysis, he could have become a great novelist like Goethe. He used words very precisely. As the Nobel laureate, Herman Hesse, stated: "Freud convinces both through his very high human and very high literary qualities. [His language] … is beautifully concise and exact in its definitions" (ibid., p. 8).

If Freud had chosen to refer to the intellect or mind, he would have used the precise German word, *geistig*, meaning, mental. On the con-trary, he wrote psyche or *Seele*, both of which mean soul. But they tend to be mistranslated in English as "mind." Thus Freud wrote in his early paper, "Psychische Behandlung (Seelenbehandlung)" (Treatment of the Soul):

> "Psyche" is a Greek word and its translation is "soul". One could thus think that what is meant is treatment of the morbid phenom-ena in the life of the soul. But this is not the meaning of this term. Psychical treatment wishes to signify, rather, treatment originating in the soul, treatment—of psychic or bodily disorders—by meas-ures which influence above all and immediately the soul of man. (pp. 73–74)

Compare this statement, as translated by Bettelheim, with the way it appears in the English, *Standard Edition*. Here the title is given as "Psy-chical (or Mental) Treatment," and the passage is translated by Strachey as follows:

"Psyche," is a Greek word which may be translated "mind." Thus, "psychical treatment" means "mental treatment." The term might accordingly be supposed to signify "treatment of the pathological phenomena of mental life." This, however, is not its meaning. "Psychical treatment" denotes, rather, treatment taking its start in the mind, treatment (whether of mental of physical disorders) by measures which operate in the first instance and immediately upon the human mind. (1890a, p. 283)

Why are these examples important? Because to explore the self and the soul, and the interplay between them, it is necessary to preserve the richness of human experience, its emotional resonances, its inexactness and ambiguity. Bettelheim suggests, and I would agree, that a psychoanalysis was not meant to be a dry intellectual exercise. Rather it was more akin to the writing of a great novel, the unfolding of a person's "*history*," and recovering of his narrative gravity.

So when Freud deployed *das Ich*, he was trying to convey far more than a part of the mind. He meant the "I," the whole of a person's subjectivity, and the "Me," the whole of a person's objectivity, the totality of his personality, his entire self. And when Freud deployed *das Psyche* and *die Seele* he meant far more than mind. He was trying to convey the full import of his holy, timeless essence, that which was most spiritual and worthy in him. As Bettelheim stressed, "Freud often spoke of the soul—of its nature and its structure, its development, its attributes, how it reveals itself in all we do and dream." He asserted that psychoanalysis is "a spiritual journey of self-discovery," or as we now understand, "soul-discovery" (Bettelheim, 1983, op. cit., p. 4).

How did Freud's intentions become distorted? Bettelheim concluded the distortions had to do with the wish of his English translators to make Freud's work more acceptable, by making it more "scientific." Consequently his technique appeared to become more and more abstract, more and more dehumanized. Instead of being concerned with man, it became concerned with mind. Then soul-study evolved into psychoanalysis, mind-analysis, from the incomplete translation of the word *Psyche*.

However, I think this is only partly true. The answer also lies in the complicated and contradictory personality of Freud and his followers. They needed and wanted to prove themselves as scientists and doctors, and to establish a new practice and paradigm of healing. And to do so, they had to operate in a world which was extremely hostile to their Jewish identities and backgrounds. Thus we can speak of a Freud *niglah* and *nistar*, revealed and concealed. The overt Freud reveled in the mind, its structure and typology, its repressions and cathexes. Concomitantly, it is possible, even probable, that the covert Freud took pleasure in the study of the soul, very much related to his hassidic roots, going back many generations.

CHAPTER SIX

On the nature of the soul: and its relationship with the self

In considering the nature of the soul I will explore it from the perspective of Hassidism and the Jewish mystical tradition because they are the roots from which Freud and so many of his followers emerged.[1] As I have previously described, the soul is a person's holy, timeless essence. I refer to an entity which is both elevated, that is, exists in spiritual realms, and is part of our primordial source and the endless everything. Therefore the soul is transcendental in nature and orientation. It yearns for knowledge of the most creative and sublime aspects of existence. Not only does it surpass the self, but the soul necessarily seeks to obliterate it in order to achieve union with the infinite, which in Kabbalah is called the *ayn sof* (the without end). And, by so doing, the soul acts to repair or rectify the chaotic threads of the universe.

The *Zohar* asserts there are many paths to soul-knowledge:

> One way is to contemplate the mystery of his Master. Another is to know one's self. Who am I? How was I created? Where do I come from? Where am I going? How is a body fixed to function? How must I give an account of myself before the Ruler of All? (Song of Songs, 18, in Drob, 2000b, p. 373)

Who is the Master? He is the primordial source, the everything and the everywhere, the Godhead. So knowledge of one's self and contemplation of one's soul go hand in hand. Both lead to an extraordinary capacity to "see" and comprehend the microcosm and the macrocosm, the deepest interior realities and the highest cosmic truths. Why is this the case? Simply, because men and women are made in God's image. By image I do not mean a picture of a supreme being, for no such picture could possibly exist. Rather we refer to the qualities or characteristics of the divine, which are called *sephirot*. These vessels are usually depicted as spheres and organized in the shape of a human figure or the image of a tree, the Tree of Life. Each sphere is a bundle of illumination as well as the vessel which contains this illumination, like a torus which holds an energized plasma. So, as I have explained in a previous chapter, the *sephirot* are both the containers of godly qualities and the qualities themselves: Will, wisdom, understanding, knowledge, kindness, severity, and right on through to the feminine principle, called kingdom. A soul task we all face is to identify the energies embedded in our own "trees" and raise them to their appropriate emotional and spiritual level. To do this is to bring about a repair (*tikkun*) in the fabric of the universe.

The Safed school of Kabbalists (led by Isaac Luria) also developed the idea that knowledge of the roots of one's own soul was essential to achieve a personal repair or, from another angle, soul-actualization. They believed that every individual could uplift his being by discovering, uncovering, and recovering the energies imprisoned in himself. The Kabbalists called this process, extraction (*birur*). It is comparable to the long, difficult efforts during psychoanalysis to rediscover one's own repressed thoughts and feelings.

However, as the psychologist Sanford Drob points out, there is a big difference between what contemporary psychoanalysis or popular psychology might understand as self-investigation and self-discovery, and what the Jewish mystics intended. For them, uncovering the roots of one's soul through meditative extraction (*birur*), and achieving a personal rectification, was like finding the missing bits and filling in the cracks in one's existence. It did not have to do with success, accomplishment, happiness, or pride. Quite the contrary: They strove to obliterate these desires and overcome all attempts at self-enhancement. What these mystics wanted was to explore and determine the nature of their own unique spiritual life-task. In their terms this meant realizing their "Godly soul" and transforming themselves into a conduit for transcendent values and supernal will.

Drob explains that a person who seeks guidance from a Kabbalistic master or hassidic Rebbe does not require psychological reconstruction (as in psychotherapy or psychoanalysis). He is much more concerned with finding a way to serve God, and his fellow men, according to his personality and circumstances. If he succeeds in this task, then he will gain personal satisfaction and fulfillment. This is "good," even more so when it originates in "evil." Quoting the Zohar (184a, vol. 4, p. 125) Drob adds:

> The perfection of all things is attained when good and evil are first of all commingled, and then become all good, for there is no good so perfect as that which issues out of evil. (ibid., p. 381)

The existence of two souls, black and white, good and evil, yin and yang, competing for predominance has long been a feature in narratives of human destiny. In his epic tale, *Faust*, the great German dramatist, Goethe, eloquently describes this struggle:

> Two souls, alas, are housed within my breast,
> And each will wrestle for the mastery there.
> The one has passions craving for crude love,
> And hugs a world where sweet senses rage;
> The other longs for pastures fair above,
> Leaving the mark for lofty heritage.
> (Donleavy & Shearer, 2008, p. 22)

Hassidic thought postulates two kinds of conflicting souls, an "animal soul" (*nefesh B'hamit*) and a "Godly soul" (*nefesh Elokit*).[2] Both are spiritual entities, but the animal soul tends to be much more corrupt and corrupting because it is surrounded by layers or shells of personal drives, volitions, and cravings. These shells or barriers are known as *klippot* (singular: *klippah*) and are closely connected in psychoanalysis with what D. W. Winnicott termed "the false self."

It is important to keep in mind that the animal soul, is not the same as the Freudian id. Yes, it is concerned with physical pleasures, but much more than this. It focuses on its own selfish, self-centered preoccupations. It is concerned with how they can be used to boost pride, ego, and ascendancy over others. In other words this soul carries an animalistic nature signifying narcissism. Therefore it is often referred to in the Hassidic literature as the "animal self," something dark and coarse, like a grub or worm.

The negative qualities of the animal soul are called "the other side" (the "*sitra achra*") and are closely identified with the evil inclination. This includes any transgression of the Ten Commandments, which inevitably includes multiple examples of envy and pride, greed and jealousy. These "sins" emanate from the "World of Chaos" and are akin to the chaotic state of being that occurs during a paranoid-schizoid state. Then one's mind and heart fragment and the ensuing fragments are life-threatening. Hence the central aim of both psychoanalysis and Kabbalah, which is to overcome intrapsychic and extrapsychic (spiritual) states of fragmentation. This process is akin to the movement from the paranoid-schizoid position to the depressive position, from chaos to inner integration.

But what if this movement does not happen? The Hassidic scholar, Rabbi Adin Steinsaltz, has described four kinds of evil which emanate from the animal soul according to the elements of fire, water, air, and earth (2003, pp. 61–63).

Fire encompasses pride and anger. The former concerns narcissistic aggrandizement or, in less technical terms, a swollen head, a puffed-up self, anything which falsely asserts one's preeminence over others (Berke, 2012, op. cit.).

Water involves lust, hedonistic pleasure, desire for the sake of desire, sex for its own sake. It is close to the Freudian idea of the id, a total self-centered sensuality.

Air conveys malicious gossip, boasting, boosting oneself with an expansive nothingness. Air actions are hot and insubstantial. But they take place in order to convince others that the "airhead" is bigger and better than they are.

Finally, earth is sloth and melancholy, any action or mood which pulls or weighs one down. Or, it can act on others to bring them down too. Sloth is malicious turgidness. Similarly melancholy, like depression, is a heavy world weariness, which paralyses the will and buries one's joie de vivre under tons of bile.

Each of these elemental responses: prideful preeminence, hedonistic pleasures, idle boasting, and turgid melancholy are forms of soul armoring. They are barriers (shells, husks, *klippot*) to both human and transcendent relationships. Even more so, they make people like "ironclad knights" in order to hide unrelenting self-indulgence. Yet, sometimes the armoring is not absolute. Then it is more like chain mail, that allows the intermingling of good and evil, rather than the rigid splitting into black and white. This, in turn, sets the stage for the emergence of complexity and ambiguity and a better balance of emotionality and spirituality.

The division of soul armoring into impermeable, semi-permeable, and porous states is roughly comparable to Freud's topographical theory of the mind, where the psychic divisions are unconscious, preconscious, and conscious. The porous shell, what Kabbalists call the *klippah nogah*, is akin to the preconscious. It is a barrier, but not a complete barrier to right action. It can be overcome or passed through by strong willpower, just as inaccessible elements of preconsciousness can be accessed by intense concentration.

The shells (soul barriers, *klippot*) are the spiritual analogues of Wilhelm Reich's "character armor" (1980), and D. W. Winnicott's "false self" (1960, p. 145). The latter are organized forms of concealment by which an individual seeks to protect himself or herself from overpowering erotic or destructive impulses. Experienced as very threatening, invasive demands, they may be felt as coming from within the self (oral, anal, genital excitement) or outside the self (an overstimulating, tantalizing parent). What is the threat? In the first place it may be a fear of fragmenting, a breaking of the mind-body container, because the bodily energies are too intense. Subsequently it is a fear of exposure and humiliation, of being shown up as less good than a relative or peer. In the latter instance a fragile self cannot cope with the anger and rage that close comparisons conjure up.

Such terrors lead a person to construct a secret life, based on avoidance and deceit in order to protect a "true" or "core" personality which would, if it could, be receptive to others. Sometimes the individual is aware that he or she is putting on "a false face," "a false front," or simply airs. More often than not, this person is not aware that his or her false front is a constructed personality based on multiple layers of denial and concealment. Inevitably he believes that this false self is the true self and vigorously resists any clarifications to the contrary.

Mary Barnes was an exception. She understood that her whole life was a living lie and concluded that the only way she could become real was to revert to infancy and grow up again. The return journey was messy and chaotic, but Mary managed to accomplish the task of reclaiming both her self and her soul.[3]

In her prior life as a nurse, Mary had worked long hours and spent enormous energy trying to please others. Later she realized that her life had became a total barrier to satisfying emotional or social relationships. The child analyst, D. W. Winnicott called this kind of falseness "the compliant self" (op. cit., p. 145). It is characterized by a lack of spontaneity and the need to fit in with and imitate others.

Winnicott suggested that a more extreme form of concealment lies with individuals who spend most of their lives both expressing and fighting a variety of physical and emotional symptoms. Perhaps most extreme are adults (or children) who immerse themselves in one aspect of their personalities to the exclusion of all else, such as intellectuals who seem to be all brain, or sportsmen who seem to be all body. At the same time these individuals may try to hide the brittleness of their lives by developing a "caretaker self" to hide all true feelings or by splitting themselves into different personalities. The net effect is to create inner emptinesses by the projection of threatening feelings (need, dependency, intimacy) into divers subselves or outwardly into others.

Yet, this is one part of the personality. The Kabbalah affirms that in every person there is a more direct expression of and yearning for spirituality. This is the Godly soul (*nefesh elokit*) which seeks to obliterate false, partial, or divided selves or souls in order to bring about a state of complete unity. This soul-expression is transcendental in nature and aim and is concerned with everything creative, sublime, and holy.

Man's Godly soul is that aspect of himself that lies beyond his biological or narcissistic needs. Spiritually oriented psychoanalysts like Eric Fromm, Victor Frankl, and Nina Coltart as well as Hassidic masters like the late Lubavitcher Rebbe, assert that the Godly soul is a clarion call from one's inner being, from one's "speaking silences," which impart every person with his deepest sense of meaning and fulfillment.

In contrast Freud appeared to extract meaning from life by systematizing irrationality. As Drob points out, he intended to create "a value free, purely secular psychology," and often referred to psychoanalysis as "a secular priesthood" (2000a, op. cit., p. 278).

The Godly soul, the *nefesh elokit* itself has a complex structure and can act as a hologram, where a part equals the whole. Kabbalists generally agreed that the *nefesh elokit* is divided into five levels. To begin there is *nefesh*, representing the physical dimension of spirituality. Then there is *ruach*, which corresponds with emotionality and is symbolized by the heart. Next is *neshamah*, which has to do with the intellect and is symbolized by the brain.

Chayah is the fourth spiritual level. Known as "the living soul," it is different, "higher" than the other three and conveys volition or divine will. Finally, *yechidah* signifies unification, the unity of all five levels with the Divine. Of course there are levels within levels. But most of them are complexities beyond the scope of this chapter.

The first three levels of the soul describe ascending (complicated, closer) forms of spirituality. These soul-dimensions also denote ascending levels of consciousness, from the ordinary to the transcendental. Mystics perceive these levels of transcendent awareness in terms of light or radiance. These dimensions, from *nefesh* to *neshamah*, denote the "inner light," degrees of soulfulness which a person can grasp and with which he can identity. They are akin to internal states of consciousness.

However, the radiance of *chayah* (volition) and *yechidah* (unification), the fourth and fifth levels of soul, lie external to the person concerned. They exist as "encompassing lights" and are said to exert their influence from outside, by surrounding or enveloping the individual. This may be because *chayah* and *yechidah* are so much "higher," that is, closer to the Godhead, and the intensity of their infinite radiance is endless and uncontainable.

Theoretically, through the action of the *chayah* soul it is possible for a person to complete the spiritual work of self-redemption. What does this mean? From a Jungian perspective it is the "realization of the shadow," while a Freudian might refer to it as "overcoming the web of repressions." In both spiritual and material terms we are talking about a process of overcoming conscious and unconscious chaos (*tohu*).

The seventeenth-century Kabbalist, Nathan of Gaza, referred to unconscious chaos (*tohu*) as "the thoughtless light" (Leet, 2003, pp. 276–277). For him redemption was the work of transforming unconscious chaos into consciousness and order, an outcome with which Freud would heartily concur. Essentially this involves restoring the evil impulses of the "other side" (the *sitra achrah*) to cosmic goodness and godliness. As Adin Steinsaltz points out, this is the intention of the *chayah* soul, to bring about a state of complete integration of man with himself and man with the source of his being.

Such a combination of the infinite and finite in one person introduces us to the fifth and most spiritually advanced level of soul, *yechidah*. It means unification, singularity, and oneness and describes a single, indivisible, transcendent entity. This ultimate level of the soul is a limitless light which surrounds physicality, emotionality, intellect, and will and imbues them with exceptional energies.

It is impossible to describe the *yechidah* soul, for it is closest to the infinite source of everything. To describe it is to enclose it with words, and that would be akin to enclosing infinity, an impossible contradiction. Because as soon as one tries to enclose infinity with the intellect it stops being infinite. Nonetheless, Kabbalists have tried over many centuries to penetrate the meaning of *yechidah*.

Rabbi Dov Ber, the second Rebbe of Lubavitch (the Mittler Rebbe) approached *yechidah* from the experience of extreme bliss or ecstasy. In this way *yechidah* can be aroused when the soul is totally and completely connected to the Godhead. He wrote in his essay, *On Ecstasy*:

> This is the category of essential binding and attachment ... of "surrounding and filling" ... the category of *yechidah* within him ... of the binding of his "essence," known as "cleaving," where the soul cleaves and is drawn automatically as a result of the divine "essence" in the soul herself ... It is this that is called actual divine ecstasy. (1963, pp. 64, 66–67)

As we can see, the essence of *yechidah* is attachment and connectivity. These describe two forms of oneness. The penultimate levels of unification allow for varied states of differentiation: Four lower souls, four worlds, four different directions. The utmost level of unification means that there is only oneness and nothing else.

But the question remains, how is it possible for material man to perceive an invisible and ineffable spiritual entity? The solution to this problem involves the "garments" which Rabbi Schneur Zalman (the "Alter Rebbe") asserted cover the soul (op. cit., p. 14). These garments are thought, speech, and action. Thought makes conscious the unconscious. Speech enwraps consciousness in words. And both speech and actions concretize experience. They communicate one's inner world to others. Together they represent different aspects of a person's personality. But personality is part of the self. So what Hassidic thought calls the garments of the soul, clearly signify the self.

Now we can see why the self and soul and are so closely connected. The soul vitalizes the self. It carries the inner essence of a person into the material world. Meanwhile the self provides a skin for the soul. It allows the radiant energies of the soul to manifest itself in actuality and effect the physical universe.

Perhaps Heinz Kohut provided the most moving connection between self and soul, and by extension, between psychoanalysis and Kabbalah, in his book, *The Restoration of the Self*. In the epilogue, he ponders the capacity of art and artists to depict the central dilemma of our age, how man can manage "to cure his crumbling self." Kohut confides that nowhere has he found a more accurate account of the yearning to restore a shattered self than in Eugene O'Neill's play, *The Great God Brown*. Toward the end, the central character, Brown, contemplates his wrecked life and tattered soul. Kohut concludes, through the words of Brown:

> Man is born broken. He lives by mending. The grace of God is glue.
> (op. cit., p. 287)

CHAPTER SEVEN

The replacement child

Sigmund Freud may have been a "godless Jew," as he often claimed, yet he possessed a pervasive Jewish soul. This was a *"yiddishah neshamah"* which he spent much of his life fighting and embracing, concealing and revealing, until he left the world at a moment of his own choice on Yom Kippur 1939.

Freud descended from a long line of *Galicianer* hassidim, many of them noted rabbis and scholars. Galicia is an enormous region of Eastern Europe ranging from Poland to the Ukraine. For centuries it was a self-enclosed center of Jewish tradition and mystery. This began to change in the 1800s when revolutionary currents reached the *shtetls* (Jewish villages) and the *haskalah* (Jewish enlightenment) burst forth. This, in turn, led to social and religious developments which aroused intense antagonisms among Jews who were desperate to slough off ancestral practices and others who were equally determined to maintain them. Long-established communities split into warring factions whereupon pitched battles repeatedly occurred. At the least families were torn apart by intergenerational denunciations.

As we shall see, Freud's family was no exception. It has been traced back a dozen generations by the German academic, Marianne Krüll, in her epic account, *Freud and His Father* (op. cit., pp. 233–235). Sigmund

77

himself was a replacement child. His birth closely followed the death of his grandfather (his father's father) after whom he was named.

The term "replacement child" generally refers to a child born after the death of a sibling and who is raised as a substitute for the child who had passed away. The replacement may then suffer emotional difficulties because of an inability to form a separate identity from the dead brother or sister. This situation arises from the entangled expectations and feelings that other family members harbor toward the deceased. But I think that replacements can follow the death of any family member, parent or child. This is particularly the case in Judaism where it is a duty for parents to name children after departed relatives in order to perpetuate their names. Accordingly, Jacob Freud gave the soul of his father (for it is thought that the name carries the soul) to his newborn son. He wrote (in Hebrew) in the Freud family Bible:

> My father, of blessed memory, Reb Shlomo, son of Reb Ephraim, went to the land of heaven, on the 16th of Adar [22 February 1856] and came to his resting place [was buried] on the 18th of Adar 5616 in Tysmenitz.
>
> My son, Shlomo Sigismund, long may he live, was born on the third day of the week [Tuesday] on the first of Iyaar 5616 [6 May 1856] and entered into the covenant [was circumcised] on the eighth of Iyaar. (Rice, 1990, pp. 33–34)[1]

The circumcision was the one ritual which Sigmund could not avoid. Otherwise he spent much of his maturity avoiding, denying, fighting, or railing against religious practices which he thought were overloaded with superstition. Thus, he almost called off his marriage to his fiancée, Martha, and pondered converting to Christianity, because her mother was a devout Jewess who insisted that her daughter go through a proper Jewish ceremony. Moreover, Freud insisted that Martha break with her mother's observances and agree to eat ham. He was determined to make a "heathen" out of her (Yerushalmi, 1991, op. cit., p. 11). And once they were married Freud insisted that his wife did not light candles on Friday night. She complied but the ban rankled with her for decades. After Freud died, Martha complained to the Oxford philosopher, Isaiah Berlin, "That *mamzer* [yiddish for bastard]. He even forbade me to light Sabbath candles." Whereupon she lit candles every Friday night for the rest of her life.[2]

This vignette reveals one aspect of Freud's relationship with his wife and to Judaism. On the other hand, Yosef Yerushalmi, the eminent historian and author of *Freud's Moses*, quotes from a letter that he wrote to Martha during their courtship. In it he assures her that:

> ... even if the form wherein the old Jews were happy no longer affords us any shelter, something of the core, of the essence of this meaningful and life-affirming Judaism will not be absent from our home. (ibid., p. 11)

As we can see, Freud's attitude to Judaism was complicated and contradictory. He hated the religious rites and rituals, but loved Jewish jokes and food and only felt comfortable among kindred friends, colleagues, and relatives. He championed science and rationality, yet pioneered a discipline rooted in Kabbalah and the exploration of subjective states. Not least he strongly identified with a Jewish *Weltanschauung* or worldview. This is clear when, in an unguarded moment, Freud wrote to the chief rabbi of Vienna, David Feuchtwang, (who was also a neighbor):

> Your words aroused a special echo in me, which I do not need to explain to you. In some places in my soul, in a very hidden corner, I am a fanatical Jew. I am very much astonished to discover myself as such in spite of all efforts to be unprejudiced and impartial. (Rice, op. cit., p. 25)[3]

How can we account for the striking discrepancies between Freud's public and private personas? In the first place we have to consider the historical circumstances during which Freud, his father, his grandparents, and his great-grandparents lived, and how this affected them.

Up until the mid-1800s, East European Jews led very restricted and precarious lives. In the huge Austro-Hungarian Empire, for example, they were barely tolerated and were treated as a public nuisance, like the *djimmis* in Arab lands, or untouchables in India. They had to pay the Bollete (essentially a tax upon Jews), could not live in the cities without a special permit which had to be renewed every six months, could not attend most schools, and were barred from all occupations except petty trading. They could not even get married without prior government approval (Yerushalmi, 1991, op. cit., p. 11).

But by the end of the century most Jews gained freedom of movement, of residence, and of occupation. Still the royal road to social acceptance and advancement was assimilation or conversion. Those who took these paths looked down upon their East European compatriots (the *Ostjuden*) as "primitive, uncultured and uneducated" and were deeply biased against them.

The Freud family were clearly *Ostjuden*. And they were religious, but they were far from being the ignorant, unkempt, superstitious yokels of popular prejudice. Jacob Freud, Sigmund's father, responded to the opportunities that had opened up by learning German and traveling freely on business. In so doing he extended the horizons that were available to his parents and broke the bounds of *shtetl* (village) culture. He was even married (for the third time) by a reform rabbi. All this helps to explain why his son's biographers, notably Ernest Jones, Peter Gay, and Ronald Clark, all assumed that Sigmund Freud was an assimilated Jew who had been born into an assimilated milieu (ibid., p. 9).

The reality was quite different. Freud's parents, Jacob and Amalie, remained religious Jews throughout their lives. Jacob, for example, knew the entire Passover Haggadah by heart. Freud's niece, Judith, recalls her grandfather reciting it at the family seder. She also remembers that he was a biblical scholar who spent long hours studying the Talmud in the original Aramaic (ibid., p. 10).

Sigmund himself fell in love with and chose to marry Martha Bernays, the daughter of a devout Jewish family. Her grandfather was Hacham Isaac Bernays, the chief rabbi of Hamburg. Although he did introduce German into the synagogue (a reform innovation), he was strictly observant as were Martha's parents. Her mother (Freud's mother-in-law), Emmeline, wore a *sheitel* (wig) and Martin Freud remembers that his grandmother always sang the Sabbath prayers "in a firm, melodious voice." Needless to say, she kept kosher,[4] and would not even have allowed herself a glass of water, if she visited a non-kosher household (Clark, op. cit.; Gay, op. cit.; Jones, 1953, 1955, 1957). Since she was a frequent guest at the Freud household, and, as Martin also noted, "was always determined to have her own way," it is probable that Martha also kept a kosher home, at least while her mother was alive.

The word "reform" is a key to understanding why the Freuds were considered to be assimilated Jews. To the modern mind, "reform" connotes a liberal, less stringent Judaism, easy to wear and to bear. This was not the case in the 1850s in Galicia. Then the term referred to a Judaism touched by the *Haskalah* (the enlightenment) and more available to the non-scholar, such as by reading prayers in the vernacular, or by traveling outside the confines of the *shtetl* (village). But the religious requirements and practices remained the same.

The rabbi who married Freud's parents, Isaac Noah Mannheimer, was a leader of the Jewish community in Vienna and an outspoken antagonist of the rigid, ultra-orthodox interpretation of *Halachah* (Jewish law). Among other things he wanted to modernize and beautify synagogue services. Therefore he was identified as "reform" by Freud's biographers. And his officiating at Jacob and Amalie's marriage was seen as conclusive proof that Sigmund was brought up in an assimilated household.

However, Mannheimer was a religious conservative. He did not approve of the innovations of the reformers which were based on promoting rationalism and discarding revelation and tradition. He was as much anti-reform as anti-orthodox. What he wanted was to reconcile traditional Judaism with new social developments (Rice, op. cit., pp. 4, 7, 11).

Officially Mannheimer held the title of "preacher." He was the only person empowered by the government to perform Jewish marriages. So it is more than likely that the choice of Mannheimer to conduct their wedding had little to do with assimilation and much more to do with the Freuds' wish to have their marriage made legitimate. As Yerushalmi declares, you may rest assured that the ceremony occurred in the traditional manner with "the glass being dutifully shattered under Jacob's foot in remembrance of the destruction of the ancient Temple in Jerusalem" (Yerushalmi, 1991, op. cit., p. 63).

As further "proof" that he came from a non-observant, assimilated family, and that he himself was totally non-religious, Sigmund repeatedly declared that he did not receive a Jewish upbringing and that he had practically no knowledge of Hebrew, Yiddish, or interest in Jewish customs. He asserted that although he was alienated from his traditions, he did maintain a sense of peoplehood as well as a strong identity with Jewish food, friends, and suffering. Essentially he could be seen as "a non-Jewish Jew," or what Yerushalmi calls, Judaeus Psychologicus, a Psychological Jew. This is a Jew whose Jewishness is devoid of all but the most vestigial content, who is ignorant of most Jewish texts. Moreover he is someone in whom "traits" take the place of substance, and rationality and independence of mind reign supreme (ibid., p. 56).

Thus, in 1925 Freud wrote to the editor of the Jewish Press Center in Zurich:

> ... I can say that I stand apart from the Jewish religion as from all other religions: that is to say, they are of great significance to me as a subject of scientific interest, but I have no part in them emotionally. On the other hand I have always had a strong feeling of solidarity with my fellow people, and have always encouraged it in my children as well. We have all remained in the Jewish denomination. (Rice, 1990, p. 41)

How did this happen? Freud claimed that his father allowed him to grow up without knowing anything about Jewish religion and culture. In a letter to A. A. Roback who had sent him a copy of his book, *Jewish Influences in Modern Thought*, Freud replied:

> I had such a non-Jewish upbringing that today I am not even able to read your dedication which is evidently in Hebrew characters. In later years I have often regretted this gap in my education. (ibid., p. 44)

In the same vein, during December 1930 Freud wrote to Yehuda Dvosis-Dvir, the Hebrew translator of *Totem and Taboo*:

> I hope that you will find [my foreword] satisfactory. It gives me extraordinary pleasure and satisfaction that some of my books will appear in the Hebrew language. My father spoke the holy language as well as German or even better. *He let me grow up in perfect ignorance on everything concerning Judaism*. Only as a mature man was I angry at him for it. But I felt my being Jewish earlier because of the effect of German anti-Semitism to which I was exposed during my days at the university. (ibid., p. 44; my emphasis)

Freud's statements contradict what has become known about his upbringing. He grew up in a Jewish home with all its customs and traditions. When he was a child his father taught him Hebrew and the Bible, and these studies continued for many years, both with his father and at school. The government decreed, for example, that religious instruction had to be included in the curriculum of primary school from age six and later at secondary school (*Gymnasium*) until graduation at age eighteen. The schedule of instructions for Freud's primary school classes has been found. It includes intensive Hebrew readings (the translation of prayers, writing, grammar) and Bible studies (the entire Old Testament) (see Rice, ibid., pp. 48–54; Yerushalmi, 1991, op. cit., pp. 68–69). This continued at the Gymnasium, but added the study of Talmud besides a deeper exploration of the books of the Prophets, Psalms, and Proverbs. Since Freud received the highest grades in his class and had to pass a very stiff exam at the end of the course, he must have achieved a considerable mastery of the subjects. Yet as an adult, he remained a master of dissimulation. As Yerushalmi points out, the truth can emerge in funny ways, both in terms of Freud's fondness for Jewish jokes and in his attachment to his beloved chow dog.

In June 1936, the writer, Arnold Zweig, sent him a copy of the *Wiener Illustrierte*, "with a picture of you with Zofie's puppies at your feet." Freud was incensed and replied: "My Jofie is a stickler for accuracy and does not like being called Zofie by you. Jo as in Jew." Yerushalmi adds: "Of all the languages which Freud knew or could have known there is only one in which the name makes sense. In Hebrew Yofi means— Beauty" (ibid., p. 70).

Freud's religion teacher at the Gymnasium was Samuel Hammerschlag. He was also the headmaster and principal instructor at the School of Religion (*Israelitische Kultusgemeinde*) having taken the leadership from Leopold Breuer, the father of Joseph with whom Freud collaborated on *Studies on Hysteria*. Over the years Hammerschlag was much more than a teacher. He became Freud's mentor and confidant, almost like a second father (Fichtner, 2010, pp. 1138–1141). The two families lived near each other and were so close that Freud named his daughter, Anna, after Hammerschlag's daughter, Anna, who had also been Freud's patient. It has been thought that Leopold Breuer and Samuel Hammerschlag were proponents of Reform Judaism, to demonstrate that through their influence Freud had become an assimilated Jew. Again a lot depends on the word "Reform," since both men were observant and believed in Divine Revelation. When Hammerschlag died in 1904 Freud wrote a particularly warm and laudatory obituary for two Viennese newspapers (Rice, op. cit., pp. 189–191).

Given Freud's religious background, it is fascinating that nothing has been written, or even mentioned in myriads of documents, about

Sigmund having had a bar mitzvah when he was thirteen. Of course, like some boys he may have objected so strongly that he never went through the ceremony. Or it might not have been a prevalent custom in Vienna at the time.

But I am told that this is not the case. In fact, given his parents' and grandparents' practices, and his studies with Samuel Hammerschlag, it is almost certain that a bar mitzvah did take place.

Freud was born on the first day of the Hebrew month of Iyar (6 May) in 1856. His thirteenth birthday was on the eleventh of Iyar (12 April 1869). This means that the *Sedra* (Torah reading) for the following Sabbath was *Tazria—Metzora*, which has to do with the terrible consequences of malicious gossip. Ernest Simon, the German Jewish educator and philosopher, has combed Freud's writings and has found a significant clue to support a bar mitzvah in his paper, "A Note on the Prehistory of the Technique of Analysis" (1920b, pp. 264ff.).[5] In it Freud discusses the great influence that the writer and satirist, Ludwig Borne, had on him.[6] He specifically refers to the 1863 three volume edition of Borne's collected works and recollects:

> ... in his fourteenth year [*im vierzehnten Jahr*; not as Strachey translated, "when he was fourteen"] he had been given Borne's works as a present, that he still possessed the book(s) now, fifty years later, the only one(s) he had retained from his childhood. (Simon, 1980, pp. 200ff.)

This paper was published almost exactly fifty years after Freud's thirteenth birthday. Simon noted that bar mitzvahs always occur during the "fourteenth year." He also claimed that he was able to convince Anna Freud that "this passage contains a screen memory of Freud's Bar Mitzvah, for '*nur zur Bar-Mitzwa bekam man Klassiker geschenkt*' (only for one's bar mitzvah does one receive classics as presents)" (Yerushalmi, 1991, op. cit., p. 132).[7]

Many factors contributed to Freud's denial of his knowledge of Hebrew, Yiddish, and Jewish rites and rituals. First, if not foremost, was his descent from a long line of *Galicianer* rabbis. I have already mentioned that in Vienna in the mid 1800s, *Yiddishkeit* was just coming out of the closet. But *Galicianers* were considered the worst of the worst: Unkempt, dirty, and poor, even if this description did not do justice to the Freud family, or to Sigmund himself. To be a *Galicianer*,

(East European Jew, *Ostjuden*) carried a strong stigma. Gentile Viennese as well as German speaking, middle and upper class Jews, looked down upon them and their customs and made every effort to avoid them (Gay, op. cit., p. 19). Sigmund even helped to create and perpetuate the Freud "family romance" that their ancestors originally came from Cologne and were German aristocrats (Rice, op. cit., p. 135). Probably he never came to terms with the fact that his mother spoke a Galician Yiddish and never mastered the German language.[8]

We know that Freud passionately wanted to advance both his career and marriage prospects. Therefore, he could hardly have been unaware that his chances for upward mobility were severely hindered both by being Jewish and for coming from an *Ostjuden* background. Among Viennese Jews there was a social hierarchy. At the top were Sephardi Jews who tended to be wealthy, long-settled descendants of immigrants from Amsterdam, Turkey, and before that, Spain and Portugal. They personified "old money." Then there were German Jews, strongly identified with the fatherland, followed by Litvaks, *mishnagdim* (anti-chassidim) from Latvia and Lithuania. At the bottom of the ladder there were the *Ostjuden* who, after the ghettos opened in the mid-nineteenth century, began to pour into Vienna.[9] Their arrival unleashed a flood of anti-Semitic hatred throughout the Austro-Hungarian empire.

Anti-Jewish riots and pogroms were commonplace, encouraged by the nobility and academic elite. The Archduchess Maria Teresa, for example, funded vicious anti-Semitic tirades in her newspaper, *Oesterreichischer Volksfreund* (Austrian Friend of the People), while professors like August Rohling (University of Prague) declaimed:

> The Jews are authorized *by their religion* to take advantage of all non-Jews, to ruin them physically and morally, to destroy their lives, honour and property, openly by force, as well as secretly and insidiously … so as to acquire power all over the world for their nation. (Bloch, 1923, p. 30 in Bakan, op. cit., pp. 27–28; emphasis in original)[10]

The "Jewish Question" was an obsession among right-wing politicians, in particular the notorious mayor of Vienna, Karl Lueger, who ran the city from 1897 until his death in 1910. Lueger was a populist rabble rouser, specializing in racism, demagoguery, xenophobia, and anti-Semitism. Adolf Hitler was a close friend and admirer. Paradoxically he counted Jews as friends and while he was mayor the Jewish population of Vienna greatly increased.[11] Freud loathed him. Once, in a letter to his friend and former collaborator, Wilhelm Fliess, about his struggles to stop smoking, he said that he "only overindulged one day for joy at Lueger's non-confirmation in office" (Freud, 1954, p. 245 in Bakan, op. cit., p. 31).

Freud's disillusion with his father can be traced to the period before his bar mitzvah when Jacob told him how he had been attacked by a anti-Semitic lout:

> When I was a young man I went for a walk one Saturday in the streets of your birthplace [Freiberg, Moravia]. I was well dressed, and had a new cap on my head. A Christian came up to me and with a single blow knocked off my cap into the mud and shouted, "Jew, get off the pavement." What did I do? I went into the road, and picked up my cap. (Freud, 1900a, p. 197; in Yerushalmi, 1991, op. cit., p. 40)

Freud was horrified by his father's craven response. He had hoped to hear about a heroic counterattack like those mounted by Hannibal against the Romans. As an adult he would become very angry and combative in the face of such incidents. He was not afraid to defy anti-Semitic passengers on a train nor did he hesitate to wade into a hostile crowd brandishing his cane (Freud, 1960, p. 136 in Yerushalmi, 1991, op. cit., p. 40). As a young doctor he applauded a colleague, Carl Kola, who had fought a duel and wounded a surgeon who had called him a "Jewish swine."

> Our friend is quite unharmed and his opponent got two deep gashes. We are all delighted, a proud day for us. We are going to give Kola a present as a lasting reminder of his victory. (ibid., p. 40)

But fin de siècle anti-Semitism in Vienna continued to grate against Freud in many ways, some subtle and some overt. It made it much more difficult for him to gain the academic appointments as well as the financial security which he craved. In consequence his teacher, the world famous physiologist, Ernest Brucke, advised him to forego an academic career and take up clinical practice, which he did reluctantly in 1882.[12]

At the same time a pressing issue was his wish to marry a slim, dark-haired young woman, Martha Bernays, whom he met at his sister's house and with whom he had instantly fallen in love (ibid., pp. 50–54). Martha came from a distinguished German-Sephardic family. Her grandfather, Isaac Bernays, the chief rabbi of Hamburg, was a prestigious person both in Jewish and non-Jewish circles. He was known as the "Hakkam of Hamburg" in order to emphasize his lofty position and his "alleged" origins as a Sephardic aristocrat. One of the Hakkam's sons, Berman Bernays, was Martha's father. He had been a wealthy businessman, although by the time she met Freud he had lost most of his money (Yerushalmi, 1991, op. cit., pp. 11, 47).[13] However, two of Berman's brothers, Martha's uncles, were successful academics. Jacob Bernays was a Classics and Hebrew scholar. Michael Bernays became a celebrated historian. In his twenties he converted to Christianity and was ostracized by the family for doing so.

After his conversion Michael was able to wine and dine with the Prussian "upper crust" including King Ludwig II of Bavaria (ibid., pp. 100–101).

Sigmund and Martha were engaged for four years. Freud's biographers assume that the prolonged period was the result of his wish to secure his finances before the marriage. This was only partly true. Apparently the real reason was that the Bernays family did not think that Freud, being a *Galicianer*, was good enough for their daughter, and, if the family had been in better straights, they would never have agreed to the match. Be that as it may, the Freuds were married on 14 September 1886 in a traditional manner. Freud recited the customary prayers in Hebrew. He was assisted by his bride's uncle, the banker, Elias Phillip, a devout Jew. The marriage ceremony itself was conducted by Dr. David Hannover, an Orthodox rabbi, in Wandsbek (one of the largest boroughs of Hamburg where the Bernays family lived) (ibid., p. 12).[14]

Because he disliked the ritual and was infuriated by their disapproval of him, Freud kept up a grudge against the Bernays the rest of his life. As they were strictly observant, his reaction to their rejection intensified his dislike of religious practices. In fact, Freud made a point of snubbing their customs by deliberately turning on lights during the Sabbath.[15]

The many faces of Freud account for his image as a ferociously striving, cutting edge innovator fighting to establish his ideas against contradictory currents in himself, and outside himself. Thus he was a "godless Jew" as well as a man who has "never repudiated his people, who feels that he is in his essential nature a Jew and who has no desire to alter that nature" (Yerushalmi, 1991, op. cit., p. 14). This was the case even though so many of his colleagues and compatriots had bought "the entrance ticket to professional advancement" by renouncing their faith. Freud added in the preface to the Hebrew translation of *Totem and Taboo* that "he could not now express that essence in words; but some day, no doubt, it will become accessible to the scientific mind" (1934b, p. xv in ibid., p. 14).

I think this essence did become accessible to Freud's mind when he replied to a query by Max Graf, father of his famous patient, "Little Hans." Graf asked whether, given the prevalence of anti-Semitism, would it not be better if he raised his son as a Christian? Freud retorted:

> If you do not let your son grow up as a Jew, you will deprive him of those sources of energy which cannot be replaced by anything else. He will have to struggle as a Jew, and you ought to develop in him all the energy that he will need for that struggle. (Graf, 1942, pp. 465–476 in ibid., p. 14)

Freud prepared himself for this struggle through his intellectual accomplishments and by refusing to accept, as he put it, others' lowly expectations of him. When he was at the University of Vienna Freud noted that, "above all I was expected to feel myself inferior and an alien because I was a Jew" (E. Freud, L. Freud, & Grubrich-Simitis, 1978, p. 79). And as we have seen, Freud could be very belligerent with his enemies, real or imagined. Yet, paradoxically, he could also maintain his self-esteem by "identifying with the aggressor," or at the least, the predominant culture. Significantly, in 1926, he declared: "My language is German. My culture, my attainments are German. I considered myself German intellectually ..." (Viereck, 1930, p. 30 in Yerushalmi, 1991, op. cit., p. 41). He kept this view for some time until he became fully aware of the anti-Semitic outrages going on in Germany and Austria. Then he felt "embarrassed" and decided to "suppress" these contentious thoughts (ibid., p. 41).

Freud's family came from Tysmenitz (pronounced tismenitz) in Galicia. In its time it was an important market town as well as a hub of Jewish learning and culture. It was also a center of contention between the *mitnagdim* (the strictly Orthodox) and the hassidim. When they were not exchanging insults, both groups feared and hated the *maskilim* (followers of "reform," the *Haskalah*) whom they considered to be heretics.[16]

Freud himself remarked that he came from a family of hassidim. Given that hassids are usually distinguished by their loyalty to a particular Rebbe (hassidic leader), it would be fascinating to know which Rebbe the Freuds followed. Shlomo Blond, who chronicled the history of Tysmenitz, has said that there were two main Hassidic groups in Tysmenitz (op. cit., pp. 42–58). One was of the disciples of Rebbe Yechiel Michel of Zlotchover. They were known as Zlotchover hassidim and were noted for being very quarrelsome.

Their competitors adhered to Rebbe Naftali Tzvi Horowitz of Ropshitz. He was an even greater Hassidic leader famous for emphasizing the power of prayer. But he too was in conflict with other Jews in the town about such issues as the use of steel knives in the ritual slaughter of animals and the preferential treatment of rich Jewish families whose boys avoided conscription. He especially disliked the changing customs brought about by the "enlightenment."[17]

It is not exactly clear where Freud's grandfather, Shlomo, a wealthy wool merchant, or great-grandfather, Ephraim, stood in these disputes. However, since they were pious Jews, it is likely that there were bitter arguments and acrimony in the family about Jacob's decision to break the boundaries of *shtetl* (village) life by learning German and living elsewhere.

I am describing a host of intergenerational hostilities let loose by the political and social upheavals of the nineteenth century. Of course these did not only affect Jews. But their impact on Jewish life was profound. The liberation of Jews from the *shtetl* blew apart the ties of family, community, and religious practice which had kept Jews intact for centuries. For many Jews this was a breath of fresh air. They did not have to worry about or abide by the strictures of the Torah or *Mitzvot* (religious commandments). They willing paid the price, conversion or assimilation, the "entrance ticket" to fame and fortune and social acceptance, as the great German-Jewish poet, Heinrich Heine, explained.

For someone as ambitious as Freud, the temptation to buy this ticket must have been very strong. Yet he did not do so. He held on to his "essence," "godless," but strongly Jewish. How did he manage this? He was a master at learning from and then conceptualizing, externalizing, and universalizing family feuds and his own inner strife. Much of this turmoil was the direct result of his being a "replacement child."

As explained, Sigmund, the son, was born just after the death of his grandfather, Shlomo, and was given his name. It is inevitable that, as he grew up, the young Freud would reoccupy his grandfather's position in the family. This meant he would be seen and treated as if he were his father's father. Any resentment and guilt that existed between Jacob and Shlomo about "the emancipation" would reemerge as intergenerational tensions between Jacob and Sigmund. Indeed, was there a religious battleground between the two men? Did it contribute to the formulation of the Oedipus complex for which Freud became famous? And, if so, who felt threatened by whom?

To answer these questions we have to consider the Oedipus myth in its entirety, not just the jealous wish of a boy to kill his father and marry his mother. The story began long before Oedipus was born. In ancient Greece, 750–300 BCE, there was the custom, called *paiderastia*, for older men to take pubescent boys as lovers (Berke, 2012, op. cit., pp. 12–13). The Danish psychoanalyst, Thorkil Vanggaard, points out that pederastic intercourse was a sacred act, publicly celebrated and steeped in solemnity and honor. The aim was "to make a boy into a man with strength, a sense of duty, eloquence, cleverness, generosity, courage and other 'noble' virtues" (1972, p. 75 in ibid., p. 13). This relationship continued until the boy showed the first growth of beard. Then a big party was held, like a bar mitzvah, to celebrate the boy's coming of age. Of course, all this was done with the encouragement and consent of the boy's family, from the moment he was taken by the older man till the time he returned home. The young man was given a special title, *klenos*, meaning famous. He was also accorded special privileges including distinguished dress and marks of public respect which he retained for life (Berke, 2012, op. cit., p. 14).

According to Greek legends, the father of Oedipus was Laius, king of Thebes. While visiting with Pelops, whose kingdom was in another part of Greece, Laius fell desperately in love with Pelops' beautiful son, Chrysippus, and took him as his lover, without asking Pelops' permission. This action broke all social bounds and violated sacred religious and moral conventions. Pelops was enraged and cursed Laius that his children and children's children would do likewise. Moreover Laius was warned by his soothsayer that a son would be born who would kill him.

Laius tried to avoid this fate by refusing to have further relations with his wife, Jocasta. But one night she got him drunk and slept with him. When the ensuing baby was born, Laius arranged for the infant to be abandoned on the side of a mountain with his ankles pierced by pins (hence the name Oedipus, meaning swollen foot). But the boy was rescued by a passing shepherd and brought to the childless king and queen of Corinth, who adopted him.

When Oedipus grew up he heard about the curse and fled Corinth because he loved his parents and wanted to protect them. Then the tale continues as we all know. He was assailed by a stranger on the road to Thebes. The man was Laius, his biological father. There was a fight and Oedipus killed him in self-defense. Upon arriving in Thebes, he found that the city was being terrorized by a monster who strangled and ate anyone who could not answer a certain riddle. Oedipus solved the riddle and was given the queen, Jocasta, as his reward. He did not realize that the woman was actually his mother. The subsequent marriage worked well. The couple produced four healthy children and Oedipus was a wise and capable ruler. The truth only emerged many years later, and only after a plague had hit the city. Far from being pleased or triumphant, Oedipus was horrified. He mutilated his eyes and fled into exile (ibid., pp. 15–18).[18]

The conventional view is that Oedipus was overwhelmed by remorseless libidinal impulses which led him to hate and kill his father and to desire and possess his mother. But, the myth also describes how Oedipus loved his parents (as he knew them) and tried to protect them. Thus, the "Oedipus complex" was only one part of a complex multigenerational drama during which a grandfather figure (generation 1) curses his son for "breaking all bounds" and then this man (generation 2) attempts to murder a baby boy (generation 3) whom he fears will kill (more likely, supersede) him.[19]

I think the corrosive currency in the relationship between Shlomo and Jacob, and Jacob and Sigmund, was not jealousy, but guilt. And this had to do with the breaking of the boundaries of *shtetl* culture. Very little is known about grandfather Shlomo except that he was a hassid and a pious man. Therefore his reality was the all pervasive realm of religious observance and study in conjunction with a close connection to his Rebbe. In this respect, one of his most important obligations was to pass on these traditions to his sons, and especially to his eldest son, Jacob.[20] When Jacob was touched by the winds of liberation, such as by traveling widely, whether for economic or social reasons, he necessarily transgressed some, maybe many, of the edicts which governed Tysmenitz life. We do not know specifically how his father reacted, but we can assume he was displeased and reprimanded his son. Jacob, in turn, must have felt lashed by guilt and hurt by the conflict with his father. Maybe this is why he continued to travel widely and eventually settled in Vienna, far away from Tysmenitz. Nevertheless, Jacob generally remained a devoted Jew.

Was there another source of Jacob's self-reproaches? Marianne Krüll brings up the issue of his sexuality in her book, *Freud and His Father*. She suggests that during his travels and while he was away from home, Jacob relieved himself by masturbation and engaging in extramarital liaisons. Moreover, she concludes that this was the dark secret which Sigmund refused to explore (op. cit., pp. 91, 100–101). Instead, with the demise of the seduction theory, he transferred responsibility for the neuroses from parents' perverse wishes toward their children to children's incestuous wishes toward their parents. Maybe this was true. There is no direct evidence one way or the other, except for the occasional tantalizing tidbit in Sigmund's dreams (ibid., pp. 111–114). Krüll does agree, however, that Jacob was overcome by deep feelings of guilt, to do with sloughing off "the yoke of Torah."

Certainly, Jacob spent a great deal of time and effort to teach his son the Bible and other aspects of Jewish law. By this means he was following the "Sayings of the Fathers," and more specifically, the teachings of his father, Shlomo, in "passing on the tradition." But I think that by his teachings, Jacob was also trying to assuage the shame and guilt he felt for "breaking the bounds" of *shtetl* (village) life.

Therefore, in addition to the traditions, Jacob could hardly avoid passing on his guilt back to his son, that is, the generation that came after him. Furthermore, it is likely that he acted to pass considerable guilt back to his own father, in the guise of the replacement child named Shlomo. The name Shlomo represented the generation that came before him. We can assume that in his mind Jacob transferred many wishes and assumptions about his father onto his son.

In general, when people are made to feel guilty, such as by not living up to expectations, they react with rage and revenge toward the source of the guilt. In this instance Sigmund returned the guilt by rebelling against God, the law, the observances, and any other aspect of organized religion, anything his father or grandfather held dear. Thus, in his book, *The Future of an Illusion* (1927c), he insisted that the idea of God was simply a superstitious projection of feelings about one's own father, and he described religion as "a childish illusion."[21] For his children, he refused to provide a Jewish education, although he did remark that he was pleased that they had all chosen Jewish partners. Yet, except for his daughter Sophie, who married a religious man, his children remained indifferent or antagonistic to *Yiddishkeit* (Jewish customs and observance). In subsequent generations they nearly all took on non-Jewish partners.

Did Jacob want to kill his son, as Laius intended with Oedipus? On the contrary, he took great pride in his son's accomplishments. Sigmund may not have become a *Torah Hacham*, a Jewish scholar, but he became a world renowned thinker and creator of a new discipline for understanding the mind and treating mental disorders. Furthermore, although Sigmund tried to conceal the connection, we have seen how much psychoanalysis is intimately related to another discipline which is uniquely Jewish, the Kabbalah.

Having ingested many of Jacob's guilt-ridden conflicts about grandfather Shlomo, Sigmund had his own guilty qualms about his relationship with his father, Jacob. He wanted to be his own person, and not take on the role of Jacob's ideal self, which even if he could, was itself a battleground between tradition and modernity. Sigmund rejected his *Galicianer* background. He wanted to be a scientist, a German, a man of the world. In other words he was extremely ambitious to surpass his father and other father figures like Josef Breuer, with whom he collaborated on his first book, *Studies on Hysteria* (1895d). Freud declared in *The Interpretation of Dreams*:

> An intimate friend and a hated enemy have always been necessary requirements for my emotional life. I always knew how to provide myself with both over and over. (1900a, op. cit., p. 483)

Freud concluded his relationship with Breuer on a very acrimonious note. The same happened with his friend and colleague Wilhelm Fliess (Gay, op. cit., pp. 55–58; Krüll, op. cit., p. 10). Could it be that a key to appreciating his struggles with friends and colleagues who became hated enemies was the confusion between paternal and fraternal relations. Sigmund had two half-brothers by his father's first marriage, Emanuel and Philipp. Both were twenty years older than him and were roughly the same age as his mother, Amalie, when she married his father. Little Sigmund liked Emanuel. But Philipp was more of a dangerous rival for his mother's love. As Marianne Krüll noted, "It was not his father who deprived him of his mother, but his big brother." Moreover, Ernest Jones, Freud's biographer, said that Freud himself remarked that Philipp was "his mother's mate, and whom he tearfully begged not to make his mother again pregnant" (1953, op. cit., p. 10f. in Krüll, op. cit., p. 125).

It would seem that as far as the oedipal triangle was concerned, half-brother Philipp was the real rival. And he was the arch villain in one of the central traumas in Sigmund's life when the boy was torn away from his "ugly, elderly, but clever" nursemaid, Resi Wittek. She cared for him as a child and they shared a close physical attraction. Freud himself recollected that his feelings toward Resi were warm and sensual. Then one day Philipp caught the woman stealing some money. He had her arrested and sent to prison.[22] For young Freud the sudden disappearance of his beloved nursemaid was an emotional catastrophe. Krüll thinks the separation contributed to a host of heart problems in his adult life, as well as his formulations about Thanatos and Eros, Death and Sexuality (ibid., p. 122). His anger toward his half-brother may also have contributed to Freud's vehement rejection of religion. Both Emanuel and Philipp were devout Jews.

Clearly, Freud redirected the hostility he felt toward his father and father figures, and brother and brother substitutes, to religious observance. In addition, the deprivation he suffered from his mother was a third reason for his negative attitude to religion. During a large part of his childhood, Amalie was emotionally and physically unavailable to him. Freud referred to himself as "the first-born son of a youthful mother" (ibid., p. 115). One could add, and he was born into a house of mourning with all the anxieties that this entailed.

Then, soon after his birth, his mother conceived a second son who emerged sixteen months after Sigmund. Significantly he was named Julius, probably after her beloved brother Julius. At that time he was very sick with tuberculosis. Six months later baby Julius died from enteritis, while TB took Amalie's brother, Julius, a month later at the age of twenty-one. Amalie herself survived TB, but only after spending long periods away from home convalescing in a sanatorium (ibid., pp. 116–117).

His mother had six further children after Julius. They included Anna, who married Eli Bernays, Martha's brother, and four further sisters, all of whom died in Nazi extermination camps.[23] Her children and grand-children describe her in less than flattering terms: "a classic Jewish matriarch, a tyrant, a tornado, impulsive, moody, strident, impatient and highly emotional" (ibid., pp. 116–117).

Like Freud's mother-in-law, Emmeline Bernays, Amalie came from a strictly observant background and remained that way throughout her very long life—she died at the age of ninety-five (Rice, op. cit., p. 4). Freud's attitude to his mother was a mixture of respect and rejection. He would visit her regularly on Sunday mornings, but suffer "attacks of indigestion" beforehand (Krüll, op. cit., p. 118). He was attracted to passionate, narcissistic women and his close colleague Sandor Ferenczi observed "a unilaterally androphile orientation" in his psychological system. This meant that Freud maintained a pronounced masculine tilt in his theories which Ferenczi claimed was due to his aversion to a "sexually demanding mother" (Roazen, 1963, pp. 35–36). So Freud's negative feelings toward his mother provided another reason for his intense dislike of religious rites and rituals.

How is it then that Freud fell in love with and married a religious Jewish girl? Given his great desire for professional and social advance-ment, it seems much more likely that Freud would have married an assimilated, or even a non-Jewish woman from a wealthy German-oriented Viennese family. That this did not happen reflected the division in his heart and mind between antagonism and affection. On the one hand he despised his mother's lower class, *Galicianer*, Yiddish speaking manner. And on the other he idealized her beauty and, as he saw it, her charm. The hostility he felt toward his mother he redirected to religion. His love he directed to Martha Bernays.

A similar split occurred with his father, Jacob, to whom he felt much closer than to his mother. Indeed, Sigmund openly identified with Joseph, the biblical Jacob's favored son and a great leader of the Jewish people. When his father died, Sigmund wrote

> I feel now as if I had been torn up by the roots …. [it is] the most important event, the most poignant loss of a man's life. (Clark, op. cit., pp. 160, 175)

At first glance this is a curious statement about a man who was the focus of so much guilt, doubt, and resentment. Thus when Freud knew his father was terminally ill, he went on holiday in Italy anyway and almost missed his funeral (Krüll, op. cit., pp. 40–42). Yet he also spoke very warmly about the "old man" who taught him about the Patriarchs and Moses and the Prophets for years in German and Hebrew from the family Bible. Called the Philippson Bible, it was profusely illustrated with Egyptian woodcuts and was another reason why his biographers thought Freud came from an assimilated background. Interestingly, Freud related in the revised edition of his *An Autobiographical Study* published in the 1930s:

> As I later came to realize the entire direction of my interest, my later interests, was determined by my early immersion in the Bible story almost as soon as I could read. (Ward, 1993, pp. 39–40)

Freud described his father as a man of "deep wisdom and imaginative lightheartedness, of dignity and demeanor." He added that his dad had "a sense of humor and a shrewd skepticism about the uncertain vicissitudes of life." Moreover, he often "pointed a moral by quoting a Jewish anecdote" (Krüll, op. cit., p. 109). He could be "grouchy" but was generally an "optimist." According to Ernest Jones, Freud used to identify with his father and even remarked that "he was the duplicate of his father physically and to some extent mentally" (ibid., p. 110).

These words convey the positive aspect of Freud's relationship with his father. Still, contrary to his vehement rejection of religious practice, Freud embraced Jewish ethnicity. He was a stomach Jew, he loved holiday delicacies; and a jocular Jew, he loved Jewish jokes. He was proud of his Jewish heritage and considered himself be a part of the extended Austro-Hungarian Jewish community. To this end Freud maintained a long-standing membership of the Viennese lodge of the International Order of the B'nai B'rith (Children of the Covenant) which he joined in September 1897, about a year after his father died. There he presented some of his most important papers and was able to relax in the company of his Jewish "brothers." Moreover, he gained much-needed support for his "controversial theories" and for his capacity to resist the anti-Semitic tirades going on around him (D. B. Klein, 1981, pp. ix–x, 8–9, 72–76).[24]

Freud also relished his connection with the *Israelitische Kultusgemeinde* (IKG) (Jewish Cultural Center). As a boy he attended its religious school and received the highest grades in his class. He continued his lifelong association with the IKG until he had to flee Vienna to escape the Nazis in 1938 (Rice, op. cit., p. 21). Meanwhile his Zionist sympathies led to his being named to the board of governors of the Hebrew University in Jerusalem. And he was delighted when his sons joined *Kadiimah*, the student Zionist organization. Later, in 1935, with Nazism rampant, and despite his distaste for Jewish nationalism, he wrote to *Keren Ha-Yesod*, a branch of the World Zionist Organization:

> I well know how great and blessed an instrument this foundation has become in its endeavor to establish a new home in the ancient land of our fathers. It is a sign of our invincible will to survive which has, until now, successfully defied two thousand years of severe oppression. Our youth will continue the struggle. (Yerushalmi, 1991, pp. 12–13)[25]

In the same spirit, Freud was moved to tears by a dream he had after seeing a play by the journalist and Zionist leader, Theodore Herzl, Das Neue Ghetto. In the dream Herzl appeared and described the perilous condition of the Jewish people, as well as the need to act immediately to save them. (Aberbach, 1980, p. 39).

Evidently, Freud felt very warmly about his father on many levels of Jewish experience. The question arises, what was Jacob's attitude to his son? At his birth Jacob wrote a long welcoming passage about the birth of "Shlomo Sigismund, long may he live" (Rice, op. cit., p. 34). He did not do this for any other of his children.

Far from competing with him or wishing him dead, Jacob was generally proud of his accomplishments, both scholastically and professionally. In honor of his son's thirty-fifth birthday, Jacob had the family's Philippson Bible rebound in leather. He presented it to him with an impassioned dedication written in Hebrew. This began, "My precious son Shlomo," and ended, "From your father who loves you with love eternal" (ibid., p. 37).[26] He only demurred at one point, when addressing the issue of religion.

CHAPTER EIGHT

Sigmund Freud and Rabbi Safran

Freud often spoke about the "warfare between science and religion" (Gay, op. cit., p. 533). The former was rational, logical, and progressive, while the latter was obsolete, backward, and mired in superstition. He repeatedly declared that "religion is the enemy" (ibid., p. 533). By religion he meant supernatural, magical, irrational thoughts and beliefs. Indeed, to show his disdain for superstition, he rented an apartment in an infamous building, the *Kaiserliches Stifungshaus,* just after he was married. The block was also known as the House of Atonement because it had been erected on the site of the old *Ring-Theater*, which had previously burned down with enormous loss of life. But even after it had been rebuilt, the place remained almost empty. Few people were willing to court bad luck by living in a "house of death." Years later Freud's sister Anna recalled: "My brother, far from sharing the general superstition, did not hesitate to establish himself there with his young wife, and his example quickly encouraged others." (*Clark*, op. cit., p. 89).

This event was considered so important, that a year later, after his daughter Mathilde was born, the Imperial Chancery sent Freud a letter congratulating him on being the father of the first baby to be born in the building (ibid., p. 89). To celebrate the occasion Freud was also made the gift of a vase from the Royal Porcelain Workshops.

In the ensuing years Freud completed several of his most important works including *Studies on Hysteria* (with Josef Breuer) and *The Interpretation of Dreams*. Moreover, it was a period when many distinguished individuals consulted him, such as the conductor, Bruno Walter, the composer Gustav Mahler, and of course, the fifth Lubavitcher Rebbe, Sholom Dov Ber Schneersohn, the Rashab. Although Freud focused increasingly on psychological rather than physical treatments, he continued to see himself as a scientist and detached observer of mental phenomena. Then, in 1906, Freud heard from a young Swiss psychiatrist, Carl Jung, who had become increasingly interested in the new discipline of psychoanalysis. They met a year later, after Jung had sent Freud a copy of his recently published *Diagnostic Association Studies*. Perhaps a more pressing reason was Jung's concern about his relationship with a passionate young Russian Jewish girl named Sabina Spielrein. She had been his patient at the Burgholzi Clinic in Zurich. Then she became his lover and his student. Eventually she became a close colleague who contributed many critical concepts to analytic thought including "the anima" (the direct analog of the Kabbalistic idea of the *shekinah*), "the death instinct," and the significance of the breast-baby connection, which Melanie Klein later developed.[1]

Spielrein desperately wanted to have a baby by Jung to be called Siegfried. In her mind the child represented the fusion of Jew and Aryan, Freud and Jung. This was not to be. Alternatively she hoped to act as an intermediary between the two men. This was also not to be, nor would Freud agree to accept her as an analysand (Yerushalmi, 1991, op. cit., p. 45).[2] Freud wrote to her:

> My wish is for you to be cured completely. I must confess ... that your fantasy about the birth of the Savior to a mixed union did not appeal to me at all. The Lord, in that anti-Jewish period, had him born from the superior Jewish race. But I know these are my prejudices. (ibid., p. 45)

A year later, upon learning that Spielrein was pregnant, Freud wrote to her:

> [Let's hope] ... that if the child [is] a boy, he will develop into a stalwart Zionist ... We are and remain Jews. The others will only

exploit us and will never understand and appreciate us. (ibid., p. 45; see also Carotenuto, 1982, p. 116ff.)

In the beginning of their relationship both Jung and Freud were charmed by each other. Jung appeared "tall, upright, clean-shaven, and with a bullethead of close cropped hair, like the very model of a Nordic Siegfried" (Clark, op. cit., p. 240). Martin, Freud's son, remarked that Jung "held himself more like a soldier than a man of science and medicine" (ibid., pp. 240–241). Meanwhile, there was Freud, twenty years older, a leader "anxious to recruit an army for battle" (M. Freud, 1957, p. 109 in Clark, op. cit., pp. 240–241). The two men talked for thirteen hours straight. Jung recollected:

> Freud was the first man of real importance I had encountered ... no one else could compare with Him ... I found him extremely intelligent, shrewd, and altogether remarkable ... But I could not swallow his so-called science positivism, his merely rational view of the psyche and his materialistic point of view ... Above all Freud's attitude to the spirit seemed to me highly questionable. For him everything was "repressed sexuality." (Jung, 1963, pp. 146–147 in Clark, op. cit., pp. 240–241)

Freud was not taken aback. He agreed with Jung. "Yes, so it is, [repressed sexuality] is just a curse of fate against which we are powerless to contend" (ibid., p.147). A further fate which Freud was determined to avoid was that his newborn discipline would be dismissed by psychiatry as a "Jewish science." That is why he was so eager that the Aryan son of a Swiss pastor would become his second-in-command. But many of Freud's friends and colleagues bitterly opposed his wish that Jung should succeed him. At the Second International Psycho-Analytical Congress at Nuremberg in 1910 they held a protest meeting against Jung being made permanent president of the Vienna Psychoanalytic Society. Freud retorted:

> Most of you are Jews, and therefore you are incompetent to win friends for the new teaching. Jews must be content with the modest role of preparing the ground. It is absolutely essential that I should form ties in the world of general science ... I am weary of being perpetually attacked. We are all in danger ... The Swiss will save

us—will save me, and all of you as well. (Wittels, 1924, p. 140 in
Bakan, op. cit., p. 58)

On another occasion Freud rebuked Karl Abraham, one of his closest
supporters, who also had severe reservations about Jung:

> Be assured, if my name were Oberhuber, my innovations would
> have found, despite it all, far less resistance ... Our Aryan com-
> rades are after all, quite indispensable to us; otherwise, psycho-
> analysis would fall victim to anti-Semitism. (Gay, op. cit., p. 205)[3]

Still, Freud worried to Abraham about the "hidden anti-Semitism of
the Swiss" and advised him to develop a "masochistic" streak, even
if this meant accepting certain slights and wrongdoing. Freud added,
"In general, it is easier for us Jews, since we lack the mystical element"
(ibid., p. 205).[4]

Eventually, however, the incongruities between Freud and Jung
spilled over into open hostility. If Freud was the Laial father, unwill-
ing to tolerate dissension about the incompatibility of science and
religion, then Jung was the oedipal son who had to go his own way
even if this meant attacking the source of many of his ideas. Jung
acknowledged that Freud had a unique ability to discover facts
about the mind, but he also accused him of lacking "critical reason
and common sense" (ibid., p. 238). Freud, in turn, criticized Jung for
hiding behind a "religious-libidinal cloud." He insisted that Jung
was "gullible about occult phenomena and infatuated with oriental
religions" (ibid., p. 238).

Yet, for all his devotion to scientific objectivity and skeptical inquiry,
Freud could be remarkably superstitious, especially concerning his own
mortality. He was haunted by the belief that he would die at the age of
fifty-one or maybe sixty-one or sixty-two. In fact, for years he was con-
vinced that he would die at the age of sixty-two because in 1899 he had
been assigned the telephone number 14362. Since he had published *The
Interpretation of Dreams* at the age of forty-three, he was terrified that
sixty-two was to be his death year (ibid., p. 58).

These considerations played a big part in his relationship with
Wilhelm Fliess who himself made extensive use of numerology in his
work. Numerology, or divination by numbers, is closely connected to
the Kabbalistic doctrine of *gematria*. This is the traditional Jewish system

of discerning the meaning of a word or phrase by adding the numerical value of the Hebrew letters, and finding the equivalent in other words or phrases. In Hebrew one can easily do this because each Hebrew letter is associated with a number, from one for *aleph* (the first letter of the alphabet) to 400 for *tav* (the last letter).[5] Thus, the word count for forty-three includes the Hebrew for "great," "high," and "mighty" (*gadol*) as well as "was appointed," "proven," or "demonstrated" (*hoh-chee-ach*), prophetic words for a future classic study of dreams and dreaming. However, one can understand Freud's fear of the number sixty-two. It has a very negative equivalence. It can denote "harlot" (*zonah*) and "be unclean" (*tahmoo*). Yet the following number, sixty-three, is even more ominous for it conveys "we are undone," (*ah-vad-noo*) and "be blotted out," "be wiped out" (*yee-mah-cheh*) (ibid., pp. 4, 30). The potential significance of these numbers led Freud to write to Jung on 16 April 1909 about his death date, contradicting his earlier statement about Jews "lacking the mystical element": "You will see in this another confirmation of the specifically Jewish nature of my mysticism" (McGuire, 1974, p. 219 in Clark, op. cit., p. 220).

Interestingly both Freud and his wife Martha believed that certain numbers were "bad" and other were "good." They particularly liked the number seventeen, because they became engaged on the seventeenth of the month. They thought it brought them good luck (Clark, op. cit., p. 220). Perhaps they also knew that the gematria for seventeen is "good" (*tov*).

Freud took great pride in being a rationalist, a scientist, an objective observer. In truth, he is best known for being a master of irrationality, or, to use the term I prefer, non-rationality (the unconscious, dreams, fantasy). And his greatest achievement, psychoanalysis, is essentially a method for exploring subjective and intersubjective states. It places a special emphasis on the symbolic expression of emotionality and sexuality, very much like the Kabbalah, the Jewish mystical tradition. On the surface the aims of these two disciplines appear to differ. Psychoanalysis is a means to overcome psychic conflicts and neurotic symptoms. It has to do with personal repair. The Kabbalah aims to unite man with God and bring about a messianic era of peace and harmony. It has to do with universal repair. But the two ideas are complementary. They act according to the maxim which the psychoanalyst, Frieda Fromm-Reichman loved to quote, "To redeem one person is to redeem the world."[6]

There are a surprising number of direct connections between Freud and the Kabbalah besides a similarity of themes. Thus, one of his favorite pastimes was playing the card game, Taroc. It originated in Italy in the fourteenth century and utilizes a seventy-eight card pack consisting of four suits plus the twenty-two tarot cards as trumps. The pictures of tarot, the King, the Queen, the Spirit, the Chariot, and so forth are intimately related to Kabbalistic iconography.[7] In his letters to Wilhelm Fliess, Freud remarked: "On Saturday evenings I indulge in an orgy of taroc, and I spend every other Tuesday evening among my Jewish brethren" (Freud, 1954, op. cit., p. 312 in Bakan, op. cit., p. 53).

We know that Freud met with Rabbi Chayyim Bloch and talked about a wide range of Jewish subjects. Bloch commented: "[During the course of the meeting] … we switched our conversation to a discussion of Hasidism and Kabbalah and Judaism in general, and he [Freud] showed himself to be a lover of his people …" (C. Bloch, 1950, p. 104 in Aron, op. cit., p. 290).

The closest link between Freud and the depths of his Jewish interests has recently come to light in the form of an exchange of letters between the Los Angeles psychoanalyst, Dr. Samuel Eisenstein, and the prominent Kabbalist and chief rabbi of Geneva, Rabbi Dr. Alexandre Safran. Their correspondence details several meetings that took place at Freud's request at his home in Vienna in 1934 to discuss "the relation between psychoanalysis and Judaism." They occurred after Freud attended a conference that Safran gave on Jewish thought. Their exchange demonstrates that Freud had a considerable fascination with and knowledge of Jewish religious texts.[8]

Alexandre Safran was born in Bacau, Romania, in 1910, and died in Geneva, Switzerland, in 2006. He had studied philosophy at Vienna University, in the years 1930–1933, receiving his doctorate in 1933. In 1940, he became the chief rabbi of Romania, the youngest chief rabbi in the world. During the Nazi era, he became very active with the Romanian Orthodox Church as well as the papal nuncio, in convincing the Romanian authorities to resist German demands for deportation of the Jews. Safran was instrumental in saving 57% of the pre-war Jewish population of over 800,000. Refusing to cooperate with the communist leadership after the war, he was forced into exile in Geneva, Switzerland. In 1948 he became chief rabbi of Geneva, where he remained until his death at age ninety-five. He wrote many books including major philosophical works on the Kabbalah including: *The Kabbalah: Law and Mysticism in the Jewish Tradition* (1977), *Israel in Time and Space: Essays on Basic Themes in Jewish Spiritual Thought* (1987), and *Wisdom of the Kabbalah* (1991).

Samuel Eisenstein was also born in Bacau, Romania, and emigrated to the United States after finishing his medical studies in Italy. Eisenstein was a training analyst and past president and dean of the Southern California Psychoanalytic Institute. In 1934 Eisenstein attended a lecture in Bacau given by Safran after completing his doctoral studies in Vienna. Years afterwards, in June 1956, Eisenstein wrote to Safran about this lecture. He recalled that Safran had talked about an encounter he had had with Freud while he was a student in Vienna. Eisenstein reminded the rabbi about this (see Appendices A and B):

> I remember you saying that you remarked to Prof. Freud that you felt there was some relation between Freud's Jewish background and his discovery of Psychoanalysis. I also vaguely recall you saying that he nodded or gave some sign of being receptive to your suggestion. (Eisenstein, Appendix B)

Eisenstein wanted Safran to write up his meetings with Freud for a paper to be published for the celebration of the 100th anniversary of Freud's birth.[9] In July 1956, Safran responded, in French, to Eisenstein's letter and said that he was unable to write the article that Eisenstein requested because of the pressure of work and time (see Appendices C and D). The rabbi remembered that the conversation with Freud centered upon the saying in the first book of the Bible, Genesis, Chapter Four, verse 7:

> If you do good, will there not be special privilege? And if you do not do good, sin is crouching at the door. It lusts after you, but you can dominate it. (Kaplan, 1981, p. 17)

He added in his own handwriting: "and its [the verse's] commentary in the Talmud [Tractate] Kiddouchin 30b." This Talmudic discussion deals with the concept of the instincts: how the evil desire can creep up on a man and how a person may be able to overcome it.[10]

The context for the biblical verse that Rabbi Safran taught Freud has to do with the expulsion of Adam and Eve from the Garden of Eden and the birth of their sons Cain and Abel. Abel became a shepherd and Cain a farmer. The narrative continues with Cain bringing an offering to God of some of his crops. In contrast Abel offers up to God his choice animals. God seemed delighted with Abel and his offering, but as for Cain and his offering, he did not seem to be interested. Cain became extremely angry and depressed. God then said to Cain: "Why are you so furious? Why are you depressed?" Soon afterwards Cain killed Abel, whereupon God asked Cain, "Where is your brother Abel?" Cain replied, "Am I my brother's keeper?" (ibid., p. 17).

In order to analyze the verse which the rabbi quoted, and to understand what Rabbi Safran was trying to teach Freud about goodness, sin, and lust, it is useful to consider two philosophical concepts of the French Jewish philosopher, Jacques Derrida.[11] They are "deconstruction" and "binary opposites." Deconstruction allows us to examine a text and decenter it. This means that, while a text may seem to be unified, clear, and logical, a closer reading may show us that the text contains contradictory meanings. The concept of binary opposites enables us to pursue a dialectical formulation of opposite terms or meanings. This refers to the Hegalian idea of the reconciliation of antithetical ideas or events. For Derrida the clash of meanings is intrinsic to the concept itself. When recognized, it is possible to clarify which of them is the predominant theme.

The verse from Genesis 4:7 consists of three parts. It is worthwhile to review these separately:

1. "If you do good, will there not be special privilege?"
2. "And if you do not do good, sin is crouching at the door."
3. "It lusts after you, but you can dominate it."

The three parts to the verse all deal with "action." Either one can do "good" or one can do "not good." And man has the power to dominate the "not good" which can lead to sin if not controlled. By decentering, we can concentrate on a central theme—the underlying instinct which can lead to "good" or to "not good." "Good" and "not good" are binary opposites. By focusing on what one can do, the power to change lies in the hands of man. Both instincts—the "good" and the "not good"—are, in reality, one: "good." Either it remains "good" or it can be turned into "not good." But it does not have to dominate you.

Significantly, in the Aramaic translation of the Bible, both instincts—the "good" and the "not good"—are really one: "not good." The translation of verse 4:7 states:

> If you do good actions, it [the "not good"] will leave you. If you don't do good actions, on the Day of Judgment, your bad actions will extract a penalty if you do not return. If you return [to good], it [your bad actions] will leave you.

Here the translator may have felt that the lust to receive punishment will always be there, and man needs to overcome this underlying evil tendency.[12]

It is likely Safran and Freud were exploring the binary instincts, the "good" and the "not good." The above analysis relates to the biblical verse from a basic textual analysis. The Talmudic discussion on this verse, noted in Safran's handwriting, is from Tractate Kiddushin 30b, as follows:

> So did the Holy One, blessed be He, speak unto Israel: My children! I created the Evil Desire but I also created the Torah, as its antidote. If you occupy yourselves with the Torah, you shall not be delivered into his hand, for it is said: If you do good, will there not be special privilege? But if you do not occupy yourselves with the Torah, you shall be delivered into his hand, as it is written: Sin is crouching at the door. Moreover, he is altogether preoccupied with you [to make you sin], as it is said: "It lusts after you." Yet, if you will, you can rule over him, as it is said: But you can dominate it.

When Sigmund Freud met Rabbi Safran in the early 1930s, the psycho-analytic theories of instincts and drives were well documented. For his part Freud was quite clear in his usage of the two German terms: *Instinkt* and *Trieb*. The former deals with an animalistic behavior. The latter, from the German *Trieben*, to push, refers to an internal pressure that leads to a certain feeling or action (Laplanche & Pontalis, 1973, pp. 214–217).

The encounter between Freud and Safran, as documented in Safran's letter to Eisenstein, reviewed the classic Jewish sources (biblical and Talmudic) for the *yetzer ha-tov* (the good inclination/drive) and the *yetzer ha-ra* (the evil inclination/drive). The Hebrew term for drive is *yetzer*.

It can be loosely translated as: impulse or inclination; an emotional impetus which excites the heart to have desires.

In order for Safran to continue with his discussion of these two inclinations/drives, he would have had to have shared with Freud more profound mystical and philosophical conceptions, particularly from the major Jewish mystical text, the *Zohar* (Book of Radiance/Splendor). In its modern translation (Matt, 2006) it states:

> The moment a human being comes into the world, the evil impulse appears along with him, inciting him constantly, as it is said: "At the opening sin crouches" (Genesis 4:7)—evil impulse [i.e., of the womb] ... This never leaves a person from the day he is born, forever, whereas the good impulse accompanies a person from the day he begins to purify himself. When is that? When he becomes thirteen years old [i.e., at his bar mitzvah]. (Vol. 3, p. 1)

And a second comment in the *Zohar* avows:

> Come and see how intensely a person is attacked, from the day that the Blessed Holy One endows him with a soul to exist in this world! For as soon as a human being emerges into the atmosphere, the evil impulse lies ready to conspire with him: "At the opening [i.e., at birth] crouches sin" (Genesis 4:7)—right then the evil impulse partners him ... because the evil impulse dwells within him, instantly luring him into evil ways. (ibid., Vol. 3, p. 85)

When does the *yetzer ha-tov*, the good inclination begin? The *Zohar* clearly establishes this at the age of thirteen—the age of majority, at the time of a boy's bar mitzvah. Yet, the great twelfth-century Jewish sage, Moses Maimonides (The Rambam) concluded that the good inclination/drive can be found only after the child's intellect develops (2006, p. 324, fn. 45).

In contrast, the *Aboth d'Rabbi Nachman*, an ethical treatise that is one of the fifteen minor tractates of the Talmud, insists: "... the evil inclination speaks, 'Since I am doomed in the world to come, I will drag the entire body with me to destruction'" (chapter 16, p. 15a).

Given Freud's extensive but disguised knowledge of Talmudic writings, one wonders whether he was aware of this passage and whether it could have been a prelude to Freud's ruminations about the death instinct. It is striking that Freud had given a lecture to his B'nai B'rith lodge in 1915, entitled: "We and Death." He had initially thought of calling the talk, "We Jews and Death," in order to show the extent to which Jews are affected by destructive drives and fears about death. At that time Freud was addressing a specifically Jewish audience on aggressive instincts. In his earlier work (such as in *Totem and Taboo* (1912–13)) he had already begun to think about the connection between aggression and the death impulse. Obviously, Freud's understanding of aggressive drives and death changed dramatically after the First World War.

> The psychoanalyst Robert Hinshelwood elucidated the issue in his *A Dictionary of Kleinian Thought*: "He [Freud] raised aggression to the same level of importance as the sexual drives—in a strange way: by imputing to the human being an innate aggressive drive against his or her own existence, the death instinct." (op. cit., pp. 327–328)

As Hinshelwood points out, Freud formally introduced the concept of the death instinct in *Beyond the Pleasure Principle* (1920g, op. cit., pp. 3–64). "He introduced a new dichotomy: between inherently opposed instincts. The libido, now including the ego-instincts (for survival and life) is opposed by a silent, hidden *death instinct* which demands dissolution and the opposite of life" (op. cit., p. 266).

Freud's consideration of love and hate, life and death, are completely compatible with the Talmudic and Kabbalistic sources I have cited. Although one cannot be sure of the exact exchange between Rabbi Safran and Freud, it is highly likely that Safran covered all the aspects of the evil and good inclinations or drives, and that their discussion included many of the primary sources that I have cited.

Freud's interest in meeting a rabbi and Kabbalist indicates that he wanted to learn more about his Jewish roots and their relationship with psychoanalysis. And he obviously hoped that this could occur without arousing anti-Semitic attacks or being put down as an *Ostjuden* or finding that the discipline he created had been dismissed as "a Jewish science."

In the last chapter I considered Freud's paternal background, from his great-grandfather, Ephraim, to grandfather, Shlomo, to father, Jacob. I showed how these men, and their extended relations, were deeply enmeshed in the Hassidic and Kabbalistic currents and conflicts that centered upon their Galician hometown of Tysmenitz. No less important is the story of Freud's mother, Amalie Nathansohn. She was a native of Brody, a city in Galicia that was even more famous than Tysmenitz for the many scholars and Hassidic masters who lived there, and for being steeped in mystical folklore. Amalie's great-grandfather was Samuel Charmaz a very distinguished "prince, leader, chief and rabbinical scholar."[13] And his son, Amalie's grandfather, was one of the greatest and richest Jewish merchants in Brody. Other relatives included rabbis and leaders of the community.

Plainly Sigmund Freud had a very rich Jewish inheritance which emanated from both his paternal and maternal sides. His awareness of this must have contributed to his comment to Ernest Jones, "Racial relationship brings you closer to my intellectual constitution" (Jones, 1955, op. cit., p. 48 in Aron, op. cit., p. 234). The key word here is "constitution," meaning the physical or mental makeup of a person. Freud's makeup was inherently Jewish, although he struggled with and against this most of his life. But there were occasions, such as in his famous address, "On Being of the Sons of the Covenant [B'naI B'rith]" delivered on 6 May 1926 on his seventieth birthday to a meeting of his B'nai Brith lodge, when he affirmed:

"... the irresistible attraction of Judaism and Jews" and "... of the clear consciousness of an inner identity, the intimacy that comes from the same psychic structure." (Freud, 1941e, p. 274 in Aron, op. cit., p. 291)

Here Freud linked the ideas of "irresistible attraction" and "inner identity" with "psychic structure" or mental makeup. But from where does this internal structure come? Earlier in the talk he denied that he had had a Jewish upbringing (which as I have shown, is not true). Nonetheless it had to come from somewhere. From Freud's point of view the answer was that it came from the genes, for Freud believed in the theory of Jean-Baptist Lamarck, the French naturalist (1744–1829), that acquired characteristics could be inherited. This idea, known as Lamarckism, helped Freud to explain how certain emotions or personality traits could pass from one generation to the next.[14] And if this were true for psychological factors, it would also account for his exceptional interest in Judaism, whether to study it, or to decry it.

Thus in 1922 he exclaimed to his close colleague, Sandor Ferenczi, that he had "strange secret longings" that rose up within him: "... perhaps from the heritage of my ancestors from the Orient and the Mediterranean, and for a life of quite another kind ...." (Gay, op. cit., p. 601)

Freud did not need to look so far to explain his secret longings. In his own terms they came from his upbringing in Galicia, with all its mysterious legends, and the special Jewish essence that was passed on to him from his many relations. As for his irresistible interest in meeting with Rabbi Safran, one could say, it was in his blood.

APPENDIX A

Letter from Dr. Samuel Eisenstein to Rabbi Dr. Alexandre Safran
(25 June 1956) (With permission from Rabbi Dr. Nathan Cardozo,
Jerusalem)

June 25, 1956

Dr. Alexander Safran
11, Rue Marignac
Geneve, Switzerland

Dear Dr. Safran:

It must be at least twenty years since we talked or wrote
to each other. I had your address from your brother, Josef,
in Israel and this is the reason for my letter:

Many years ago (it must have been in the early thirties) on
your return from Vienna you gave a lecture in Bacau which I
attended. Among other things, you talked about your encounter
with Freud while you were a student in Vienna. I remember you
saying that you remarked to Prof. Freud that you felt there was
some relation between Freud's Jewish background and his
discovery of Psychoanalysis. I also vaguely remember you saying
that he nodded or gave some sign of being receptive to your
suggestion.

The reason why I place so much importance to your encounter
with Freud I am sure is familiar to you. This year the world
celebrated the hundredth anniversary of his birth, and
celebrations have been taking place here in America and in
Europe. Hundreds of articles by people who knew him have been
and still are being published. Few though, have discussed
with Freud his Jewish background and its possible influences
on his work on Psychoanalysis. You were in a unique position
as a Rabbi to discuss this with him. It would be of
interest if you would put down on paper the circumstances of
your visit to him and what was discussed during that interview.
Also how the visit was arranged and what were your impressions
about it. I am sure thousands of people here and in Europe
would be interested to read it. If you feel that you want to
do it, you could put it down in the form of an article and I
am sure I could have one of the Psychoanalytical Journals
publish it. Something like "A Rabbi's Visit to Freud" or
any other title of your choosing. If you feel though that

112

your visit was too brief to warrant a longer descritpion,
please write to me in a letter what was discussed during that
visit and I shall try to find the best way to have it published
or placed in the Freud Archives in New York. I am practicing
Psychoanalysis in Los Angeles and I am sure I will have no
difficulty to arrange this.

My parents always remember you and your family with great
affection and your great Father is remembered by all of us
with much warmth and admiration. I have been told that you
recently lost your beloved mother. I remember her as a very
saintly woman. I am sure you and your family must have felt
keenly her death.

My wife and I are planning a trip to Europe and Israel in the
summer of 1957. Switzerland is not in our program but I certainly
look forward to meeting your brother Joseph in Israel. I have
heard of the great and courageous work you have done for the
Jewish Community in Rumenia during the last war when you were
Chief Rabbi of Bucharest.

I eagerly look forward to a reply from you. Please give my
best regards to your family. My parents ask me to give you
their warm regards also.

                                   Sincerely yours,

                                   Samuel Eisenstein, M.D.

SE:JL

APPENDIX B

Transcription of Eisenstein letter,

Dr. Alexander Safran   June 25, 1956
11, Rue Marignac
Geneve, Switzerland

Dear Dr. Safran,

It must be at least twenty years since we talked or wrote to each other. I had
your address from your brother Josef, in Israel and this is the reason for my
letter.

Many years ago (it must have been in the early Thirties) on your return
from Vienna you gave a lecture in Bacau which I attended. Among other
things, you talked about your encounter with Freud while you were a student in Vienna. I remember you saying that you remarked to Prof. Freud that
you felt there was some relation between Freud's Jewish background and
his discovery of Psychoanalysis. I also vaguely remember you saying that he
nodded or gave some sign of being receptive to your suggestion.

The reason why I place so much importance to your encounter with Freud
I am sure is familiar with you. This year the world celebrated the hundredth
anniversary of his birth, and celebrations have been taking place here in
America and in Europe. Hundreds of articles by people who knew him have

been and still are being published. Few though, have discussed with Freud his Jewish background and its possible influences on his work on Psycho-analysis. You were in a unique position as a Rabbi to discuss this with him. It would be [of] interest if you would put down on paper the circumstances of your visit to him and what was discussed during that interview. Also how the visit was arranged and what were your impressions about it. I am sure thousands of people here and in Europe would be interested to read it. If you feel that you want to do it, you could put it down in the form of an article and I am sure I could have one of the Psychoanalytical Journals publish it. Something like "A Rabbi's Visit to Freud" or any other title of your choosing. If you feel though that your visit was too brief to warrant longer description, please write to me in a letter what was discussed during that visit and I shall try to find the best way to have it published or placed in the Freud Archives in New York. I am practicing Psychoanalysis in Los Angeles and I am sure I will have no difficulty to arrange this.

My parents always remember you and your family with great affec-tion and your great father is remembered by all of us with much warmth and admiration. I have been told that you just lost your beloved mother. I remember her as a very saintly woman. I am sure you and your family have felt keenly her loss.

My wife and I are planning a trip to Europe and Israel in the summer of 1957. Switzerland is not in our program but I certainly look forward to meet-ing your brother Joseph in Israel. I have heard of the great and courageous work you have done for the Jewish Community in Romania during the last war when you were Chief Rabbi of Bucharest.

I eagerly look forward to a reply from you. Please give my best regards to your family. My parents ask me to give you their warm regards also.

Sincerely yours,
Samuel Eisenstein, M.D.

APPENDIX C

Copy of Rabbi Safran letter in French

Dʳ ALEXANDRE SAFRAN
GRAND RABBIN DE GENÈVE

אלכסנדר ספרן
רב הראשי לגנבה

Genève, le 11 Juillet 1956.

Monsieur Samuel EISENSTEIN M.D.
6135 Wilshire Boulevard
LOS ANGELES 48, California

Cher Docteur Eisenstein,

J'accuse réception de votre lettre du
25 Juin, dont je vous remercie cordialement. Vos nouvelles m'ont
fait grand plaisir ainsi que celles de votre famille et de vos chers
parents.

Mes engagements antérieurs pour des travaux
ne me laissent pas le temps de rédiger l'article que vous me deman-
dez. Cependant, je peux vous indiquer que ma conversation avec Freud
s'est déroulée surtout autour du verset 7 du chapitre 4 du livre
de la Genèse, que j'ai indiqué au début de mon long entretien
(et de son commentaire dans le Talmud: Kiddouchin, 30 b)
avec lui sur les rapports entre la psychanalise et le judaïsme, et
auquel il a pris un très grand intérêt.

Cet entretien a eu lieu chez le Professeur
Freud, sur son invitation, après avoir assisté à une conférence
que j'ai faite sur la pensée juive.

Veuillez croire, Cher Docteur, vous et
votre distinguée famille ainsique vos chers parents, à l'assurance
de mes sentiments dévoués.

Dr Alexandre SAFRAN
Grand Rabbin de Genève

116

APPENDIX D

Dr. Alexandre Safran
Grand Rabbi of Geneva

Geneva, the 11th of July 1956

Mr. Samuel EISENSTEIN M.D.
6135 Wilshire Boulevard
Los Angeles 48, California

Dear Doctor Eisenstein,

This is to acknowledge receipt of your letter dated 25th of June, for which I thank you cordially. Your news and those of your family and dear parents have given me great pleasure.

Because of prior engagements for work, I will not have enough time to write the article you requested. Nevertheless, I can tell you that in my conversation with Freud, we discussed the 7th verse of the 4th chapter of the book of Genesis (and of its commentary in the Talmud: Kiddouchin, 301), in which I indicated the link between psychoanalysis and Judaism, for which he expressed a vivid interest.

This conversation took place at Freud's home, on his invitation, after he attended a conference I gave on Jewish thought.

Please receive, dear Doctor, my warm wishes for yourself, your distinguished family and your dear parents.

Dr. Alexandre SAFRAN
Grand Rabbi of Geneva

CHAPTER NINE

On opposites

I n his *Introductory Lectures on Psycho-Analysis* Freud anticipated the ideas of Jacques Derrida about deconstruction and binary opposites. In particular he saw that to really understand what a person is trying to communicate, you have to plough through many contradictory levels of meaning. Freud explained:

> ... mental life is the arena and battle-ground for mutually opposing purposes or, to put it non-dynamically, that it consists of contradictions and pairs of contraries. Proof of the existence of a particular purpose is no argument against the existence of an opposite one; there is room for both. (1916–17, pp. 76–77)

Earlier, in his study of dreaming, Freud described how and why dream-thoughts may be turned into their opposites. This happens in order to filter powerful emotions to do with love, sex, aggression, and other fundamental feelings:

> In addition to allowing them [dream-thoughts] through or reducing them to nothing, [dream-work] can *turn them into*

> *their opposites.* We have already become acquainted with the
> interpretive rule according to which every element in a dream can,
> for purposes of interpretation, stand for its opposite just as easily
> as for itself ... We can never tell beforehand whether it stands for
> the one or for the other; only the context can decide. (1900a, op.
> cit., p. 471)

The story of Cain and Abel which Freud discussed with Rabbi Safran, as
well as his exploration of dream-processes demonstrate that opposites
can be used to accentuate, magnify, conceal, and even clarify conflicting ideas. These include slips of the tongue and slips of the pen (known
as parapraxes) or antithetical actions which may suddenly reveal a
person's truer and deeper intentions.

The psychoanalytical interest in contradictions is equally matched
by the Kabbalistic focus on opposites. In fact this is a central concern
of mystical contemplation, how to reconcile good and evil, light and
dark, spiritual and material, upper and lower. The *Bahir* (Book of Illumination), one of the oldest Kabbalistic texts, quotes from a verse from
Psalm 139:

> Even darkness is not dark to You. Night shines like day—light and
> darkness are the same. (Tehellim, 2001, p. 168)[1]

The verse attempts to explain God's presence in the world. He is both
immanent and transcendental, accessible and inaccessible, close at hand
and infinitely distant. That is the paradox. How can He be so near and
so far at the same time? The mystics demand to know, how can He hear
our prayers when He is surrounded by darkness? They try to answer
this question by a dialectical inquiry. There are always two opposing
ways of knowing. Both are inherently part of the object (what is being
considered) and the subject (the sage). Both exist as deep programmed
extremes to highlight the importance of a quality or an intention. It is
necessary to recognize such polar opposites in order for a new reality
to emerge. This involves the synthesis of previous perceptions and the
capacity to see things from a different angle.

The psychologist Sanford Drob has succinctly summarized this issue:
"The Lurianic theosophy [exposition of the Kabbalah according to Isaac
Luria] actually involves a dialectical play of opposites: Emanation and
contraction, revelation and concealment, breaking of the vessels and

restoration" (Drob, 2000b, pp. 84–85). For Luria opposite poles are part of the world order and are necessary for the world to strive for and to attain perfection.

Similarly, the Talmudic scholar and educator Eliyahu Dressler was a master at weaving Hassidic, Kabbalistic, and philosophical streams of thought. He was especially interested in the interplay between the soul and the self, how a spiritual entity can harness the striving of a person's material qualities to comprehend creation. Dressler observed:

> The world was created in [with] opposites. There is purpose that unites them and merges them. There is an electron (with a negative charge) and a proton (with a positive charge), and they both make up the atom. So too there is body and soul, this world and the next world [to come], upper and lower worlds, light and darkness, life and death, evil and good, spirituality and, revealed and hidden … Opposites generate the purpose: misfortune brings salvation, darkness brings light, this world brings the next world, death brings resurrection of the dead. The general rule is: from the hidden sprouts forth the revealed. (1943, pp. 17–18)[2]

As we can see, Jewish tradition emphasizes several reasons for using opposites including the process of giving and receiving. Mystics insist that these two energy flows are not only related, but are actually the same! By giving one receives. How is this possible? It happens by opening pathways that are constantly replenished and by fortifying them both spiritually and materially.

It is likely that Freud borrowed from the Kabbalah the concept of polar opposites such as of intellect or feeling. One pole does not have to negate the other. Rather a person can derive meaning from each pole, or by their synthesis, to arrive at a position that is relevant to his existence. Wilhelm Stekel, for example, argued that in emotional life, everything is "bipolar." In a paper titled "The Psychology of Doubt," which he delivered to the Vienna Psychoanalytic Society in January 1910, he noted (pp. 357–359) that sadism can mutate into masochism, cruelty into pity, and piety into blasphemy.[3]

Later Freud wrote: "Reversal of an instinct into its opposite resolves on closer examination into two different processes: a change from activity to passivity, and a reversal of its content" (1916–17, op. cit., p. 127). The reversal of content is like "the transformation of love into hate" (ibid., p. 123). I would add, or vice versa, hate into love. Either transformation follows the rule, "From the hidden sprouts forth the revealed" (Dressler, op. cit., p. 18).

Opposites become a way of transforming difficult desires into another format to reduce the anxiety associated with the original concern, notably, sexuality. The issue of sexuality and bisexuality was a topic frequently discussed by Freud, and Fliess and Ferenczi, among his early collaborators.[4] The idea of bisexuality is that "every human being is endowed constitutionally with both masculine and feminine sexual dispositions ..." (Laplanche & Pontalis, op. cit., pp. 52–53). Freud concluded:

> "The dominant sex of the person, that which is the more strongly developed, has repressed the mental representation of the subordinated sex into the unconscious." (1919a, pp. 200–201)

There is nothing more "opposite" than the two sexual gender roles: male and female. Earlier Freud had noted that while there were two gender roles, there was only one sexual organ that was important, the penis, and there were those who had it (males) and those who lacked it (females). Clearly he overlooked the significance of the breasts and womb.

The Kabbalah recognizes the primacy and equal importance of the male and the female. These are embodied in the *sephirotic tree* which I described in Chapter Three. The tenth *sephirah* (*Malchut*—kingship), is the feminine attribute of the Divine. *Malchut* is the power invested in man by God which receives and gives. Therefore, if this *sephirah* represents both receiving and giving, it functions as both a female and male representative of the Divine!

The Kabbalist, Aryeh Kaplan, tried to resolve the seemingly dichotomous way of seeing male and female, by explaining that there is not a weaker or inferior sex. Both are equal and important in one's development:

> ... when we look at ourselves in terms of our external relationships, we are looking at our masculine identity. When we look at our Self, our inner core, we are almost looking at a feminine entity.

This role sharing also helps us to understand the days of the week:

... all week long in our struggle to gain spirituality, we are on a male level, that is, a giving mode. However, on the Sabbath, we are on a female level because we can absorb the fruits of all we have done during the week. (1990, p. 75)

What Kaplan reflects is the Kabbalistic notion of the giver (symbolized by the male) and the receiver (symbolized by the female). Their roles are different, but complementary. One cannot do without the other. Again we are seeing the interplay of opposites.

Perhaps the paramount or primary example of giving and receiving is the relationship between mother and child. For the child the feeding, nourishing, giving mother equals her breasts. For the mother, the hungry, sucking, receiving child is his mouth. Breasts which feed, take away pain or discomfort, and provide adequate stimulation are "good breasts." Breasts which do not feed, or are not available when wanted, which do not relieve pain or discomfort, and are not stimulating are "bad breasts." Similarly, the mouth which sucks when hungry (but not too hard), which smiles when satisfied, and gurgles and chirps is the good child. But the mouth which refuses to suck, cries continuously (while leaving the mother painfully engorged), is the bad child. There is a constant interplay between good and bad, or between the "good" and "not good," as Rabbi Safran explained to Freud when they met.

The same breast can be good or not good depending on the context of the feeding situation. By this I mean whether the infant is thin skinned or thick skinned. A thick skinned baby can tolerate frustration better. He does not scream too much when mother (i.e., the breast) is not immediately available. And he can amuse himself for longer periods of time. But a thin skinned infant may find the same breast intolerable, if it does not feed the moment hunger occurs, or if he is prone to colic, or he wants to be bounced every moment. Then the good breast can quickly become not good, "bad" (the bad breast), or "evil," and arouse severe aggression.

From the point of view of his mother, an infant can change from good to bad ("bad baby") if he sucks poorly, cries too much, or does not respond to her attention. As Freud's successor, Melanie Klein and her colleagues, have documented, this process can also follow the flow of anxiety between the mother (who can be any feeding adult) and the infant (see Hinshelwood's "early anxiety situations", op. cit., pp. 112–121). For Klein the synthesis of good and bad was the infant's capacity to move from a part object to a whole object relationship with his parent. This occurs when the infant perceives and tolerates his mother as a person in her own right, instead of her being a slave (i.e., at the beck and call of her offspring). This point, in turn, heralds the development of what Klein called the "depressive position," when the infant becomes human (i.e., with a full range of feelings including love and hate, guilt and remorse) (ibid., pp. 138–157).

Freud, like Klein, was fascinated by opposites, all the more so when they occurred in the same word. First he turned to his work on dreams to try to understand these verbal contradictions. He recalled that in dreams opposite elements may represent the same idea or wish and that a negation can be an assertion. But Freud was not satisfied with his grasp of this material until he came across the work of the German philologist, Karl Abel (1837–1906). Freud's ideas on antithetical meanings are largely based on Abel's philological or linguistic analysis of ancient Egyptian vocabularies and usages. Freud was struck by Abel's thesis that, in the earliest development of language, words arise by denoting a difference between two contrary states: light/dark or near/far.[5]

It is a well-known phenomenon that in many different languages certain words that share the same spelling or pronunciation can have opposite meanings. Freud dwelled on these contradictions in his 1910 paper on "The Antithetical Meaning of Primal Words" (pp. 154–161). He pointed out that, in Latin, *altus* can mean high or deep and *sacer*, sacred or accursed. In German, *boden* indicates the highest as well the lowest thing in the house, while *mit* (with) originally came from the word, *mitohne*, which signified with or without (ibid., pp. 159–160). Further examples are legion. In English, one need look no further than our contemporary obsession with envy, which, in common parlance, yields admire and hate (Berke, 1988, pp. 31–32).

Since Freud's paper there has been little written that specifically addresses the issue of antithetical meanings. However, the object relations school of psychoanalysis has allowed us to greatly expand our understanding of this phenomenon by elaborating the concepts of phantasy, projection, introjection, and projective and introjective identification. These mental mechanisms help to explain why primary words can gain such lush, rich, and, indeed, contradictory meanings. In this chapter I intend to complement Freud's linguistic considerations by exploring certain psychological dimensions of language.

Interestingly, in his original discussion, Freud did not define what he meant by "primal words." Maybe he thought the term was self-evident. Previously, he had elaborated the principles of "primal scene" and "primary process." "Primal phantasies" and "primary narcissism" would follow soon after (Laplanche & Pontalis, op. cit., pp. 331–341). "Prime" or "primary" was certainly meant to convey something onto-logically early, deep, and intense. The term encompassed basic life events including birth, growth, procreation, and death, and reflected unconscious, rather than conscious psychic events. Evidently, primary words are the verbal symbolic equivalents or representations of fun-damental life processes and everything concerned with them. And like these life events themselves, these words are highly charged with emotion.

Perhaps the most primary of all primary words is "breast." It is a word that denotes far more than an anatomical entity. Really, it touches anything and everything that sustains the body, warms the heart, and calms the mind. Hence, "breast" lies at the very center of human desire, as well as hostility. Many languages convey some aspects of the compli-cated, convoluted, and contradictory significance of "breast," but to my knowledge none does so better than Hebrew, a central member of the Semitic group of languages.

The family of Semitic languages has its origin in the genealogi-cal accounting in the biblical book of Genesis. This is where the descendants of Noah's son Shem are listed "according to their fami-lies and languages, by their lands and nations." The family of Shem included Aram, Ashur, and Eber, whom we now know as the Arameans, Assyrians, and Hebrews (Kaplan, 1981, op. cit., ch. 6, v. 10 and ch. 10, vs. 21–31, pp. 27, 47, 49).

The Italian linguist, Sabatino Moscati (1922–1997), pointed out that the term "Semitic" was adopted by European scholars toward the end of the eighteenth century as a common designation for that group of peoples to which the Arameans, Assyrians, and Hebrews belong.[6] This group of languages is closely interrelated with many similarities in phonology, morphology, syntax, and vocabulary (Moscati, 1960, p. 23). They all seem to share a common origin based on a linguistic structure of stems and roots. The majority of stems in the Semitic lan-guages consist of three consonants. According to the Hebrew scholar, Yechezkel Kutscher (1909–1971), this stem may be either a verb or a noun. Generally the Semitic languages have both (Kutscher, 1966, p. 99).[7] The basic meaning of the word is expressed by these consonants, while the addition of vowels, and prefixes, infixes, and suffixes determines the word's precise sense and function (Moscati, op. cit., p. 25).

Hebrew and the Semitic languages, in general, use a three letter (triliteral) stem. There are instances of four letter or consonant stems (quadriliteral) or even (in the case of nouns) five letter consonant stems (quinquiliteral). However these are invariably extensions of triliteral stems (ibid., p. 102; see also Kutscher, 1982, p. 6). Some theoreticians think that in the evolutionary stage of Semitic languages, they had roots of only two letters. This was a biradical base called the *radix primaria bilitteralis*. Kutscher asserts that those biradical nouns which have survived relate "to the basic vocabulary of human life such as parts of the body, kinship [and] notions of time …" (ibid., p. 6).

The biliteral root for the Hebrew word for "breast" is SHahD (שַׁד). It is composed of two consonant letters, SH (*shin*, שׁ) and D (*daled*, ד). Significantly, all Hebrew nouns are gender-specific, masculine or feminine. SHahD (שַׁד) carries the masculine gender. How is this possible, since a breast is clearly a female organ? Perhaps this gender differentiation is an attempt to demonstrate that while the entity may be female, the function (feeding, caring, protecting) may be male or female. But again I don't think this is the entire answer. It is more likely that the gender indicates the phantasy of control and possession. Here it is the man who possesses the woman, mother, wife: both her breasts and her womb (which, in Hebrew, also carries the male gender). In this way we can begin to see how a phantasy can affect the structure of language, and the elaboration of mental processes.

Moreover, the breast, as an object and function, is highly desired and desirable. But if access is thwarted or envy is strong, then something which is the focus of intense positive feelings will turn into an object of fear and hatred. Hebrew clearly reflects this transformation or projective identification of negative impulses. By changing one vowel, SHahD (שַׁד) becomes SHaDe (שֵׁד), demon. As we can see, the written word looks exactly the same, but by changing the vowel from an "ah" sound (small line under the consonant SH) to an "ay" sound (two small horizontal dots under the consonant D) the meaning of the word in Hebrew is totally different.[8] A demon or SHaDe (שֵׁד) is an antagonist to life, an entity suffused with hate and cruelty. It is a bad, dangerous, painful breast that has taken the place of a good, nourishing, flourishing one.

However, this transformation not only indicates a change in the object, but a change in the subject. The person who desires the breast may also feel demonic. Instead of feeding in a loving way, he viciously attacks the very thing he had previously treasured. So the new word denotes a dual metamorphosis, in the object which appears demonic and threatening, and in the subject which feels demonic and threatening.

Melanie Klein has explained that under the impact of frustration and anxiety (more explicitly, greed and envy) the infant directs phantasized onslaughts against his mother's breast and body. One such attack ... "is the predominantly oral impulse to suck dry, bite up, scoop out and rob the mother's body of its contents ... The other [way] derives from anal and urethral impulses and implies expelling dangerous substances (excrements) out of the self [infant] and into the mother" (Klein, 1946, p. 8). The latter are like commando raids which aim to gain sadistic (that is, demonic) control and possession of her body.

The Hebrew language demonstrates a further way in which a powerful phantasy provokes the profound mutation of a root word. This phantasy itself may be induced by hunger, envy, excessive excitement, and frustration. It changes the communication by charging it with noxious feelings.

The second consonant of SHahD (שד) is the Hebrew character D (daled, ד). By doubling this consonant, the subject is able to transform both the meaning of the word and the part of speech. SHahD (שד) the noun, meaning breast, becomes SHah'DaD (שדד) the verb, meaning to rob violently, plunder, or despoil. Here we can see two degrees of transformation. First, there is the change from a word meaning life-sustaining to another signifying life-damaging (the result of greedy, envious attacks). Second, there is the change from a noun, a denotative particle of speech, to a verb, an action word. So, under the impetus of an aggressive phantasy a word denoting a soft body organ which feeds becomes an action word indicating the wish to invade, scoop out, and directly or collaterally destroy the desired, now hated, object.[9]

There are many other ramifications of such transformations. For example, from the verb we can drop one of the double letters and revert to the root noun, SH-D (שד). But by adding the quiescent letter *vav* (ו) the word becomes SHoDe (שוד) and denotes the fact of robbing, or a robbery.[10] Similarly, doubling the D (*daled*, ד) yields SHo'DayD (שודד), the person doing the robbery, the robber. Clearly, we can see how linguistic exchanges demonstrate the effects of an aggressive phantasy on the state of mind of a subject. So, SHahD (שַׁד), "the object," "the breast," easily becomes SHahDaD (שָׁדַד), the verb, to "rob or despoil"; SHoDe (שׁוֹד) the noun, "the robbery," the effect of the action; and finally SHo'DayD (שׁוֹדֵד), the robber, all from the same root.

These changes are consistent with the fact that during the basic unfolding of language every concept is "the twin of its contrary, how could it be communicated to other people who were trying to conceive it, other than by being measured against its contrary?" (Abel quoted by Freud, 1910e, p. 157). Indeed, we might well ask, how can an infant grasp a thought except by comparing it to its opposite?

Bion makes this very point when he considers how the idea of a breast first develops. In order to appreciate the good, tangible breast, one has to experience a bad, absent one. More abstractly, the good breast becomes the absence of absence as much as the presence of presence. Or, as Bion put it (op. cit., pp. 34–35), the infant can feel intensely satisfied by evacuating an absence, concretely felt as pain, death, hate, greed, and so forth. There is a startling accuracy in the way that the root SH-D (שד) conveys the twists and turns of presence and absence, good and bad, desire and rejection, love and hate.

We have previously pointed out that the biliteral root may have a letter added to it in order to turn it into a triliteral stem. If we add the quiescent letter *aleph* (א) to SHahD (שַׁד), we get ehSHeD (אֶשֶׁד), which means waterfall or cascade. This is the male form of the word and surely depicts the phantasy of ever-flowing milk pouring from a large, powerful breast, as if it were water roaring down a mountainside. The female form is ahSHay'Dah (אַשְׁדָה), which signifies the slope of the breast or the side of a mountain. In this instance the meaning of the word conforms to the actual shape of the organ as well as to its idealization as a hill or mountain.

Once again, small changes in linguistic structure can lead to major changes in meaning. Thus, these transformations can lead from a container to the contained, from the breast, and, by extension, mother's body, to the phantasized part-elements held within: father, mother and the fiery intercourse between them. What about part of the container itself? DahD (דַד) is formed by dropping the *shin* and doubling the D (daled, ד). DahD (דַד) specifically means the teat or nipple, but it can refer to the breast itself, or to the analog of the teat, a spout or tap.

Alternatively Hebrew can change the breast into a drawer by adding the letter *hay* (ה·) to the root SH-D (שד). This leads to SHee'Dah (שִׁדָה)

which means a chest of drawers, an excellent container. In contrast the word Sah'Deh uses the other form of the of the *shin* consonant, the *sin* (שׂ). Sah'Deh (שָׂדֶה) denotes a field, which is a source of food, like the breast, while its companion See'DooD (שִׂדוֹד) conveys the action of harrowing the soil, that is, preparing it to grow the food. The latter word is antithetical to SHee'DooD (שִׁדוּד) which has to do with robbing and despoiling.[11]

Before concluding this section it is worth exploring two other kinds of structural transformations of SHahD (שַׁד), reversing the letters and adding a third full consonant to the end of the root. The reverse of SHahD (שַׁד) is DahSH (דַּשׁ), a verb meaning to thresh. The noun is Deh'SHeh (דֶּשֶׁא) for grass. Grass, of course, is any of the various plants of the grass family usually used for food, fodder, or grazing. So the word is entirely consistent with the source of supply or the breast. The verb means to beat grain as from a husk; again this refers to the process of preparing the food. If one adds another consonant, "N" (*noon*, נ), you get Dah'SHane (דָּשֵׁן), which refers to the richness of food or soil; and Deh'SHen (דֶּשֶׁן), a chemical fertiliser (to enhance the yield of food); and Dee'SHane (דִּשֵׁן) the verb, to fertilise.[12] But are any antithetical words produced from these roots? The answer is yes. If one simply doubles DahSH (דַּשׁ) you get DeeSH'DooSH (דִּשְׁדּוּשׁ), meaning to trample, to crush and destroy.

Other consonants also contribute fascinating, but related changes in meaning when they are added to the root SHahD (שַׁד). For example, with the letter chaf (כ, ך) we get SHee'Daykh (שִׁדָּךְ). This word conveys the act of making a match or arranging a marriage for someone, the result of which is a SHe'Dooch (שִׁדּוּךְ), a "match." As Klein would aver, such matches are closely related to phantasies of what takes place in the breast, the parental intercourse, or match-making. The result is many babies, the boys and girls, the men and woman, the "internal objects," contained therein.[13]

Similarly, when the word includes the Hebrew consonant *raysh* (ר), it becomes SHee'Dayr (שִׁדָּר), which means to broadcast, while different vowels yield SHa'Dahr (שַׁדָּר), a broadcaster; and SHeh'Dehr (שֶׁדֶר), a message.[14] It is not too far-fetched to consider that on a basic level these words relate to an infant who is crying for the breast. These cries are his way of broadcasting a message about his distress. With good mothering, the SHa'Dahr (שַׁדָּר), the broadcaster, will be heard and will get the right response, the soft, warm, nourishing breast SHahD

(שד). However, what is the result when this does not happen, when the SHeh'Dehr (שֶׁדֶר), the message, has not been heard, and the SHahD (שד) the breast, is missing? Then, as far as the SHa'Dahr (שַׁדָר), the broadcaster, is concerned the breast has become SHah'Doof (שָׁדוּף), blighted. The absent breast SHa'Dahr (שַׁדָר), is no longer a wondrous ehSHeD (אֶשֶׁד), a waterfall, but rather a dry, withered, persecuting object, like a SHaDe (שד), a demon. The result might be that the frustrated child will himself turn from a good little boy or girl into a SHay'Doon (שֵׁדוֹן), an imp or little devil, attacking the breast rather than contentedly suckling from it.

The many semantic transformations that I have just described allow us to follow diverse conceptual developments of the primary object, the breast: good to bad, negative to positive and vice versa. Concomitantly, they also allow us to follow the basic states of mind of the infant (the subject) toward the breast (the object) including contrary or antithetical intentions.

The culmination of this process, the final ascent of the semiotic tree derived from SHahD (שד), the breast, leads to the word SHaD'i (שַׁדִי). In English SHaD'i (שַׁדִי) is usually translated as "the Almighty." But within the religious community this word is literally synonymous with God.[15]

Philologists are not in complete agreement about the etymology of SHaD'i (שַׁדִי). According to the *Encyclopaedia Judaica*, many scholars have linked it with the ancient Akkadian word "*sadu*," meaning mountain. This, in turn, would be a cognate of Sah'Deh (שָׂדֶה) or field (1972, p. 677). I have already commented on the relation of Sah'Deh (שָׂדֶה), a field, to SHahD (שד), a breast. The direct connection is through the proto-Semitic word, "*tad*," which relates to "rounded breasts" (ibid., p. 677). As can be seen with ahSHay'Dah (אַשְׁדָה), which signifies the slope of the breast or the side of a mountain, the association from breasts to hills to mountains is easy to make. Indeed, there is considerable evidence for this, not only from ancient but from modern sources too. I refer, in particular, to the social expressions of unconscious phantasies.

One of the most familiar mountains in Europe is called the Jungfrau, or young woman, and is located in Switzerland near Interlaken. Popular postcards depict the mountain as a voluptuous young maiden covered in climbers scaling her summit, a breast. If this were not clear enough, the Swiss have tunneled through the inside of the mountain and built a railway which goes almost to the top. What is at the top? A couple of restaurants, of course. Moreover, the Swiss have placed restaurants at the top of many other mountains as well.

The verbal associations of disturbed patients also demonstrate the strong connection between mountains and breasts. Bruno Bettelheim was struck by the extent that boys at his Orthogenic School in Chicago treated the breast as an extremely powerful object, something to be feared and desired. They repeatedly asked the following riddle: "What is the strongest thing in the world?" The answer was always, "A brassiere, because it holds two huge mountains and a milk factory" (1955, pp. 36–37).

The boys were deeply concerned with a powerful, almighty source of all things. This attitude reflects the state of mind of infants and adults who feel empty, weak, needy, inferior, chaotic and "grenvious."[16] Their method of dealing with these feelings is to idealize the primary object, whether the breast, or its symbolic equivalents such as parts of the person, clothing, clouds, nature, or sometimes, reality itself. This idealization may occur in many ways including *size*, as with *Playboy* magazine centerfolds or mountains; *number*, as multibreasted women like Diana of Ephesus; and *function*, as waterfalls and cornucopias.[17] Of course, this discussion need not refer to a disturbed child or adult. It readily encompasses the primordial mind, which perceives all examples of fecundity and fertility as deeply mysterious and frightening.

However, as Melanie Klein has pointed out, idealization of the object is a fragile means of concealing a deep sense of personal inadequacy, whether to do with the outside world or internal reality (M. Klein, 1940, p. 349). When this mechanism breaks down, envious hatred of the formerly idealized person or function invariably breaks through, as can be seen in the ingratitude which people show to providers, or in the despoliation of nature. And then, of course, the SHahD (שַׁד), breast, becomes a SHaDe (שֵׁד) or demon.

An alternative means of trying to deal with this problem is by identification with the idealized source. In other words, if people cannot have the breast, they become the breast. This is what Klein has termed the manic defense (1935, pp. 277–279). In this situation, instead of an omnipotent object, we find an omnipotent subject, whereby the person concerned behaves and may even experience himself as the Almighty SHaD'i (שַׁדִּי): totally self-sufficient, ever flowing, and the source of all things. (More likely this state is the source of severe narcissistic personality disorders.)

The manic or hypomanic defense is essentially a uroboric attempt to hijack SHaD'i (שַׁדַּי) and gain mastery and control of that which is beyond mastery and control. By uroboric I refer to the wish to suckle oneself from one's own breast and penis. The "uroboros" itself is a motif which appears in many different cultures and consists of a snake biting its own tail. As such, "It slays, weds and impregnates itself. It is a man and woman, begetting and conceiving, devouring and giving birth, active and passive, above and below, [all] at once" (E. Neumann, 1954, p. 10).

Significantly, the power of SHaD'i (שַׁדַּי) has been recognized for millennia. The Septuagint, the translation of the Bible from Hebrew into Greek (allegedly completed by seventy-two Jewish scholars in seventy-two days for Ptolemy ll of Egypt in the third century BCE), translated SHaD'i (שַׁדַּי) as *"pantokrator"* meaning "all-powerful," while the Vulgate (the Latin translation of the Bible prepared by St. Jerome in the fourth century CE) used the term *"omnipotens,"* which speaks for itself. According to the *Encyclopaedia Judaica*, these translations were themselves based on ancient rabbinic distinctions of SHa, or "who," and Dai, or "enough" (op. cit., p. 677). So essentially, SHaD'i (שַׁדַּי) means "He who is self-sufficient," and conveys the idea of a primary being who is the cause of himself.

A primary being who is the cause of himself is identical with God. Now it is possible to appreciate the penultimate transformation of the Hebrew word, SHahD (שַׁד). In the beginning SHahD (שַׁד) conveys the experience of the infant for whom his mother's breast is the source of all: sustenance, pleasure, stimulation, the relief of pain, and indeed, life itself. Meanwhile the converse, the absent breast, signifies emptiness, pain, and death.

Further developments of SHahD (שַׁד), the breast, describe the manic phantasy of omnipotent domination of this source. Indeed, the first source that the infant experiences and the first source that the manic person tries to emulate are both rooted in the physical world. SHaD'i (שַׁדַּי), however, denotes a conceptual leap beyond the physical. It describes, or attempts to describe, a different order of reality. In this respect, SHaD'i (שַׁדַּי) is more encompassing than SHahD (שַׁד), for SHaD'i (שַׁדַּי) signifies an essence, a something which is both of this world and far beyond it.

One might also speculate about the psychological ramifications of defining an integrated supernatural reality. Could it be that these theological insights reflect man's nascent efforts to convey the fundamental importance of achieving an integrated internal world?

A potential confirmation of this hypothesis comes from Stan Tenen, an American mathematician and linguist, who has been researching the origin and nature of the Hebrew alphabet for over three decades.[18] According to Tenen the "pre-Babel" significance of the Hebrew letter shin (שׁ) has to do with the "externalization of relational energy." Meanwhile daled (ד) relates to what happens at a *delta'* where the river *dilates* and is *diluted* as it divides and pours into the sea.[19] Consequently, the integration of both letters, SH and D, shin and daled, leads to SHahD (שַׁד) which dispenses this flow in physical terms while SHaD'i (שַׁדִי) does the same on a spiritual plane.

According to Tenen the English equivalent of such integration is "SaiD," "teeth pouring out," or, as we would say, "speech." This process is continually being opposed by SHay'Dim (שֵׁדִים) (the plural of SHaDe) or demons. What do these demons do? They cause a division of energy, structure, and activity. Moreover, such a demon or SHaDe (שֵׁד) is related to the English "shade," a shadow or darkness, which divides or blocks the radiance of the sun and causes an object to be cut off from its source.[19]

From an analytic perspective, I am describing the process of splitting. Essentially SHay'Dim (שֵׁדִים), demons, frighten people and perpetuate a state of internal darkness and division. The antithesis of this situation occurs when both SHahD (שַׁד) and SHaD'i (שַׁדִי) are able to dispense their respective energies, "love" and "spiritual grace." The ensuing "shine" and "sheen" (to quote Tenen) enables those who have been distraught to achieve SHah'lom (שָׁלוֹם), peace of mind and SHah'lame (שָׁלֵם), wholeness. In Hebrew this process of repairing a divided self is known as Ti'kkun (תִקוּן) and, as Frieda Fromm Reichman pointed out, it can renew the world.

It is not insignificant that this chapter should begin with the psycho-linguistic study of a primary word, SHahD (שַׁד) and should end with the semantic elaboration of a primary dilemma, the passing from a chaotic to a complete state of mind. The impetus for doing so stems from Freud's curiosity about "contraries and contradictions," and from our interest in complementing the linguistic analysis that Freud presented by exploring the psychological dimensions of language.

The point of convergence for those who would emphasize semantic considerations and those who would emphasize mental factors is the mind. How does the capacity for conceptualization develop? What are the mental processes that contribute to this? How does this relate to thinking and thought and the use of language? And what comes first, the process or the thought? I have tried to show, through investigating the root letters SH shin and D daled (ש + ד), how their grasp of mental processes have enriched the linguistic analyses of antithetical meanings.

It has been fascinating to follow the twists and turns of SHahD (שד) to see how so many complementary as well as contradictory words can be and have been created by adding, dropping, duplicating, or even reversing a consonant. These transformations are clearly in line with Freud's discussion of dream processes (1910e, op. cit., pp. 160–161) and Abel's focus on sound reversal and the reduplication of roots.

At the conclusion of his paper on "The Antithetical Meaning of Primal Words," Freud suspected that it would be easier to understand the language of dreams if "we knew more about the development of language." I think the same holds true for grasping the language of primary objects, like the breast. Precisely by recognizing the development of primary words is it possible to gain a closer, multidimensional appreciation of reality.[20]

CHAPTER TEN

Lowness of spirit

In 1904, Freud delivered a lecture before the *Wiener medizinisches Doktorenkollegium* entitled "On Psychotherapy" (1905a, pp. 257–270) In this address Freud tried to elucidate some of the pitfalls of treating patients with the method of psychotherapy. He made it clear that while the therapist may expect the patient to make him a present of his secrets, the therapist needs to allow time to take its course. He cannot drag the secret of a depression out of his patient (ibid., p. 262).

These secrets are intimately connected with the conflicts that exist in and between people. Freud focused on the clash of opposing desires and feelings to explain the emergence of clinical symptoms. As I demonstrated in the previous chapter, "On Opposites," the development of language can serve to mask and unmask many of these conflicting elements. Freud himself deployed a military metaphor, a battlefield, to show how the mind is often at war with and within itself.

The first Lubavitcher Rebbe, Schneur Zalman of Liadi (the "Alter Rebbe") also believed that the "animal soul" (*Nefesh B'hamit*), which has to do with physical pleasures, especially pride and self-inflation, and the "godly soul" (*Nefesh Elokit*), which has to do with transcendent experience, were at war with each other. He compared the physical body to a "small city," and said the two souls were like two kings, each trying to capture the city and dominate the populace (*Tanya*, op. cit., ch. 9, p. 37).[1]

The effects of this warfare tend to surface as a state of despondency, confusion, hopelessness, helplessness, sorrow, worry, and worthlessness. Whatever they are doing people exclaim they cannot carry on. Even worse, they tend to suffer a plethora of physical complaints, including fatigue, headaches, heartaches, in other words, severe malaise.

This constellation of symptoms encompasses some of the reasons why the fifth Lubavitcher Rebbe, the Rashab, consulted Freud in 1903. He felt he was nothing and had accomplished nothing. Clearly this was not the case. But he kept repeating, "Where am I? Where do I turn? What should I say?" (Y. Y. Schneersohn, op. cit., p. 42).

Freud asked the Rashab to give a detailed account of his daily routine, how and why he did what he did. The Rebbe elaborated the substantial demands that the head (the intellect) makes on the heart (the emotions, desires) in the Chassidic *Weltanschauung* or worldview. Freud correctly realized that for the Rebbe the basic connections between his head and his heart had been broken and needed to be repaired. His diagnosis was that "His head grasps what his heart cannot endure." Or, from another angle, the Rashab suffered deep despair because his feelings could not cope with what his mind perceived.

In the *Tanya* (Teachings) the Alter Rebbe distinguished four different manifestations of a low, downtrodden, depressed state of mind. First he described "lowness of spirit," what he called *nemichat ruach*. This condition commonly occurs when a person is unable to achieve what he would like to do. The contemporary dancer and choreographer, Michael Clark, has eloquently described the gloom of *nemichat ruach*: "Frankly, nothing's ever good enough, that's what drives me insane. I just keep scrapping and redoing it [the dance routine]. It's part of the training as a dancer, you're never good enough" (Jobey, 2013, p. 24).

Second, there is "contriteness of heart," or in Hebrew, *lev nishbar*. The experience is akin to an unfathomable dread, especially when an individual becomes aware of his personal or spiritual inadequacies and failings. *Lev nishbar* also describes a profound sadness when confronted by the realization that one is not fighting strongly enough against the evil impulse (the *yetzer harah*). The latter includes all the destructive wishes that interfere with the relationship between man and man, and man and God (*Tanya*, op. cit., chs. 29 & 30).

Then there is *atzvut* which signifies "sadness or melancholy." It is the closest to what we can recognize as a clinical depression. Indeed, *atzvut* is often translated as "black depression." The term literally means constricted. The Chassidic commentator, Levy Weinberg, points out that *atzvut* is a numbness that squeezes one's heart (emotional center) and blocks out all feelings. In consequence the heart is as "dull as a stone" and is "flat without vitality" (1987, p. 407). *Atzvut* projects despondency and deadness. It is an emanation of the *shade* (dark, demonic, evil) side of the self. In Hebrew related words convey sorrow, suffering, edginess, irritability, and nervous tension (ibid., p. 406).[2]

Besides *atzvut*, there is a fourth degree of depression known in Chassidus (chassidic thought) as *merrirut hanefesh*, which translates as "bitterness of the soul." This is state of deep remorse and fury about one's human or spiritual failings. It is a condition that does not necessarily lead to melancholia or the implosion of the self. It is a challenge to transform one's life. The bitterness and accompanying anger are all essential components of the process that can enable a person to extricate himself from despondency.

Unlike in conventional psychiatry, the *Tanya* emphasizes that bitterness (*merrirut hanefesh*) is one of two depressive states where a person is not necessarily stuck or blocked. The other is remorse (*lev nishbar*). *Nishbar* also means broken, so *lev nishbar* can be freely translated as brokenhearted. In this state a person may be sad, but also be someone who has chosen to face his personal losses and shortcomings. Consequently, both bitterness and remorse can be seen as calls to action.[3]

The term that described the Rashab was *nemichat ruach*, an expression which is analogous to low self-esteem. This term also denotes humility. A person suffering from lowness in spirit realizes that he has a long way to go to reach his goals. For Chassidim this is not self-pathology but rather an expression of humbleness. Ultimately these contrary conceptions of depressive or doleful feelings teach us that there are two main kinds of depression. One is rooted in physical and emotional states beclouded by mixtures of good and evil. This parallels the psychoanalytic concepts of envy and narcissism. It is close to our psychological understanding of depression—related to guilt, shame, and conflicts over need and dependency. The other kind of depression is spiritually inspired, and according to the *Tanya*, is not depression at all but rather like an emotional hiccup, a lowness about one's spiritual failings, a momentary sadness, which can then be used as an effective weapon against despair.

Freud's formulations of lowness of spirit and black depression are not dissimilar to his understanding of melancholia. A person rejects someone or something he has loved or liked (the "cathected object") and identifies with its negative representation (the "rejecting object"). As a result, he suffers severe self-reproach because he feels hostile toward someone or something that he had previously liked, and consequently feels overwhelmed with guilt. But to overcome the guilt, the person may try to merge with or become attached to his prior foci (Freud, 1917e, pp. 243–258; see also Gay, op. cit., pp. 372–377). This makes matters even worse. Then the subject dislikes or hates himself all the more, for taking into himself (introjecting) and becoming part of loved objects which have turned bad.

How can a person overcome this poisonous situation? In Freud's view he needs to disconnect the hated or "rejecting object" from its attachment with his ego (or his "self" or "soul"). Needless to say this is not easily done. But in order to minimize the risks of endless ruminations and self-denigrations, the hating or "rejecting self" has to become conscious of its anger toward the original source of hurt. The awareness of such anger, akin to bitterness (*merrirut*), will break the cycle.

Freud called anger at the lost love object "hate." He long realized that "aggression" was an essential component of an ostensibly loving relationship, and that all such relationships were ambivalent (ibid., p. 372). Interestingly, the Matabele tribes of Zimbabwe do not have separate words for "love" and "hate." They use one word which signifies love/hate or hate/love. Which emotion predominates depends on the inflection of the voice of the speaker.[4]

Freud's seminal paper on "Mourning and Melancholia" was written during the First World War. Hence he was acutely aware of the power of aggression in human relationships. He also saw the extent to which the melancholic directs sadistic rage for others back toward himself with unmitigated severity.

In the *Tanya* the Alter Rebbe advised that to overcome the self-abasement and self-punishment that occurs during a relentless bout of lowness of spirit (*nemichat ruach*), a person has to redirect his aggression into soul-searching and use it as a weapon against his evil inclination. Then, when he gets angry with his anger, he will be able to overcome his "stuckness" and constricting preoccupations. But not only that, the redirection will transform low spirits into joy, a joy that would not have been possible without the preceding depression (Weinberg, op. cit., p. 411).

It is instructive to consider the depressions that Freud suffered in the light of these four categories: lowness of spirits, remorse or grief, melancholia, and bitterness. In his paper on "Psychical (or Mental) Treatment" Freud noted that:

> It is a matter of common knowledge that extraordinary changes occur in the facial expression, in the circulation, in the excretions and in the state of tension of the voluntary muscles under the influence of fear, rage and mental pain ... less well known is that ... persistent affective [emotional] states of a distressing or "depressive" nature (as they are called), such as sorrow, worry or grief, reduce the state of nourishment of the whole body, cause the hair to turn white, the fat to disappear and the walls of the blood-vessels to undergo morbid changes. (1890a, op. cit., p. 287)[5]

Freud himself was afflicted by many similar physical ailments. These included recurrent cardiac arrhythmias, shortness of breath, chronic indigestion, headaches (especially before visiting his mother), and fainting spells (related to conflicts with colleagues). In one such episode after giving up smoking his beloved cigars for three weeks he wrote to his friend, Wilhelm Fliess:

> Then suddenly there came a severe cardiac oppression, greater than I had before giving up smoking. I had violent arrhythmias, with constant tension, pressure and burning in the heart area, burning pains down my left arm, some dyspnea—suspiciously moderate, as though organic—all occurring in attacks lasting continuously for two-thirds of the day, *accompanied by depression which took the form of visions of death and departure, in place of the normal frenzy of activity.* (Krüll, op. cit., p. 15; my emphasis)[6]

Freud's physician, Max Schur, has pointed out that his letter to Fliess contained a lot of "faults and slips," and that these were expressions of Freud's extremely ambivalent feelings toward his illness and, indeed, toward himself. In the same letter Freud remarked: "It is embarrassing for a medical man, who spends all the hours of the day struggling to gain an understanding of the neuroses, not to know whether he is suffering from a reasonable or a hypochondriacal depression" (1950a, op. cit., p. 82).

In addition Freud suffered off and on from a generalized malaise characterized by fatigue, weakness, irritation, dejection, indigestion, and flatulence which, in his time, was known as "neurasthenia." Nowadays this diagnosis has fallen into disuse, but it is clearly related to the contemporary condition called "chronic fatigue syndrome." In a letter of 10 February 1886 to his fiancée, Martha Bernays, he noted that he and his half-brother Emanuel and sister Rosa all had "a nicely developed tendency towards neurasthenia."[7]

He wondered why this happened, whether it had tangible causes or, as we can see from his comments to Fliess, whether it was "hypochondriacal," that is, originated in internal, usually unconscious, emotional conflicts. The answer, as we have seen in the previous chapters, was that he was assailed from all angles, intrapsychically and interpersonally, by intense family, social, and professional pressures. I refer to the intermittent friction between Freud and his parents, his half-brothers, his wife, and his wife's parents; his loathing of religious observance and fear of anti-Semitism; as well as the complications of maintaining a practice while establishing a new discipline. Freud responded with ferocious ambition which led to an array of mental and physical symptoms when frustrated. To a large extent he deployed his prodigious intellect and capacity for hard work to overcome severe self-doubts. But when these "solutions" did not suffice, he felt in such "low spirits" that he thought he might never emerge from his malaise.

The second category of depression from which Freud suffered was loss and remorse. Nonetheless, he appeared to overcome his upset after his nursemaid, Resi Wittek, was suddenly banished from the family, or when his mother, Amalie, came down with tuberculosis, and had to spend long periods away in the Carpathian Mountains, or after his teacher, Ernst Brücke, advised him against pursuing the academic career he craved. Nor was Freud grief stricken when his father, Jacob, passed away, an event which Freud called "the most decisive loss of a man's life" (Gay, op. cit., p. 89).

But there were two losses which did shake Freud to the depths of his heart. The first occurred in January 1920, when his daughter Sophie, on whom he had doted since she was little girl, with "her curled hair and wreaths of forget-me-nots on her head," suddenly succumbed to the virulent influenza that had been sweeping across Europe in the wake of the war. Freud commiserated with her husband, Max: "It is a senseless brutal act of fate which has taken our Sophie from us, something that one cannot wrack one's brain about, a blow under which we have to bow our heads, poor helpless human beings that we are" (Clark, op. cit., p. 401).

Freud said further to a friend, Kata Levy, a Hungarian former analysand: "I don't know whether cheerfulness will ever call on us again. My poor wife has been hit too hard." But he added that he had too much work "... to mourn my Sophie properly" (Gay, op. cit., p. 392).

An even worse loss occurred three years later when Sophie's youngest son, Heinele, died aged four from miliary tuberculosis. The boy had been visiting Vienna. The whole family adored him. Freud anguished, "[The boy] ... was an enchanting fellow, I have hardly ever loved a human being, certainly never a child, a much as him" (ibid., p. 421). Freud complained that life had lost all meaning for him and confessed that for the first time in his life he felt terribly depressed. Although he rarely cried, this time he wept profusely. The loss of little Heinele in June 1923 was one of the most painful events in his life. It left him with a broken heart (ibid., p. 422; see also E. Freud, L. Freud, & Grubrich-Simitis, op. cit., p. 27).

Freud's recollections about his grandson were remarkable because he had suffered from recurrent depressions since childhood. Perhaps he meant that this bout was the most severe, for it must have been exacerbated by distant memories of the deaths of his brother Julius and his uncle Julius in the spring of 1858. Although very young at the time, it is likely that these events affected him directly, and indirectly through his mother, Amalie. She became emotionally unavailable to him when her infant son and favorite sibling both fell sick and passed away within a month of each other. These losses were compounded when his nurse-maid was summarily dismissed and his mother herself spent long periods away recovering from TB. Too often important women in his infancy and childhood suddenly vanished.

So from mourning we move to melancholia. Again one can see how Freud used his own experience to make significant discoveries about unconscious processes. That was his genius! In this instance the presumed rage with abandoning women leads love to turn to hate, hate to guilt, and guilt to anguish and despair. For Freud a further implication was that men are more reliable than women, but all attachments (since his father was often on the road) are dangerous.

The effect is continuous warfare in zones of the interior between angels and demons, Eros and Thanatos, the impulse of love and the impetus to hate. From infancy to adulthood these battles engage the darkest recesses of the self and of the soul: envy, greed, jealousy, and narcissism. They raise elemental issues about life and death, despair and repair, and are fought over thoughts (conscious, preconscious, and unconscious), words (*SHaD* and *SHaDe*, the good breast and the bad breast), and actions (destructive or constructive). As with sex, Freud opened these areas for consideration. His followers did more. Analysts are still struggling with the consequences of trying to understand what most people do not want to accept.

Experientially, deep depression is much more intense than low spirits. To use a contemporary metaphor the former is hard programmed. The conflicting impulses have become part of the very structure of the self. In contrast low spirits reflect the program, but not necessarily the structure. So it is easier to change the program through changes in cognition. That being said, both states are hard to shift because both involve powerful projective and introjective processes that create distorted realities. The former tend to be violent evacuations, such as described by the nineteenth-century English philosopher, Francis Bacon, who saw: "... the ejaculation or irradiation [of the mind] emitteth some malign and poisonous spirit, which can take hold of the spirit of another" (1890, p. 64). The purpose of these "ejaculations! are twofold. One is defensive, to get rid of disturbing ideas or feelings. The other is offensive, to control others' insides, to attack and damage them out of envy and greed. Then the outside world, whether people, places, or things can become very dangerous and threatening. And also one's own inner world may be split into different territories, riddled with grudges, full of anger and guilt, anxiety, and shame.

The added name given to the terrible mood that follows such feelings is "endogenous." Why? Because it is a blackness that comes from within, and appears to be of unknown origin, as compared to lowness of spirits which can often be traced to specific events or ideas, and, therefore, is seen as "reactive." The truth is that both states are reactive. But the antecedents of a severe depression lie deeper, more repressed, and therefore harder to understand. These are the nasty bits of anger and rage which Freud realized could become critical elements attacking a person from the inside of the self. They are invariably part of an oppressive superego.

This situation contrasts with lowness of spirits where the internal criticisms are also exacting, but not as violent. They tend to be related to the "ego-ideal," the part of the self which demands that a person be more and do more with his life. Still, as the dancer, Michael Clark, pointed out, it can make you crazy, because "Nothing is ever good enough."[8]

Bitterness is the fourth kind of depressive malaise. It is the counterpoint to a constricting, shriveling, death-like descent into nothingness. Bitterness bursts with acid and acrimony. It is a vitality that demands revenge for real or imagined hurts. Freud himself was no stranger to bitter recriminations, especially when confronted with threats to his ideas or authority. These corroded his former friendships with Josef Breuer and Wilhelm Fliess. They also undermined his professional relations with Wilhelm Stekel, Alfred Adler, and Carl Jung, all of whom were members of Freud's inner circle.

Stekel was a founder member of the Wednesday Society which became the Vienna Psychoanalytical Society, as well as a founder and co-editor (along with Adler) of the journal, *Zentralblatt für Psychoanalyse*, where many of the basic concepts of psychoanalysis were first presented. Although initially an adherent of Freud, Stekel developed his own ideas about symbolism in dreams, psychic conflict, and technique, many of which conflicted with Freud's. He also was a major supporter of Adler in the bitter battle for influence and power in the society.

As the friction between them escalated, Freud became ever more dismissive of Stekel as a wayward character full of "moronic petty jealousies." In private he called Stekel an impudent liar, an "uneducable individual" … an intolerable "swine" (Gay, op. cit., p. 214). During this struggle Stekel compared himself to Freud saying that a dwarf on the shoulders of a giant could see farther than the giant. Freud retorted, "That may be true, but a louse on the head of an astronomer does not" (Clark, op. cit., pp. 314–315).

Eventually Stekel resigned from the Vienna Psychoanalytical Society, but refused to give up editorship of the *Zentralblatt*. Freud was incensed but the American publisher of the journal, Trigant Burrow, backed Stekel (ibid., p. 315). Freud licked his wounds then started a new publication: the *Internationale Zeitschrift für Psychoanalyse*, now known in

English as the *International Journal of Psychoanalysis*.[9] This vignette again demonstrates how a bitter dispute can become a call to action.

Adler, like Stekel, was initially welcomed into the psychoanalytic circles, before he was spewed out as a dangerous heretic. It was not just that his ideas clashed with Freud's, but his dress ("sloppy"), personal mannerisms ("tactless"), and therapeutic style were also totally different. Even worse, Adler disparaged Freud's emphasis on unconscious libidinal processes. He preferred to focus on conscious feelings of inferiority ("the inferiority complex") and discrepancies in power in social relations.

Freud was furious with what he saw as Adler's political manipulations within the Psychoanalytical Society. He wrote to Jung in 1910:

> [He] is a very decent and highly intelligent man, but he is paranoid … He is always claiming priority, putting new names on everything, complaining that he is disappearing under my shadow, and forcing me into the unwelcome role of the aging despot who prevents young men from getting ahead. They are also rude to me personally [referring to Adler and Stekel]. I'd gladly get rid of them both. (Clark, op. cit., p. 307)

Freud was despondent that Adler would remain a thorn in his side. Then he and his supporters found a way to precipitate a showdown with Adler by inviting him to explain his views at a meeting of the Vienna Society in 1911. These clearly deviated from the "right path," and Adler resigned from the society. He too was bitter about what happened, but felt encouraged to found his own school of "individual psychology" (ibid., pp. 308–309).

Freud himself remained unrepentant about the break. Years later he wrote of the "specific venomousness" of Adler and of his "uncontrolled craving for priority." When Adler suddenly died from a cerebral hemorrhage at a scientific meeting in Aberdeen, Freud was triumphant. He remarked to the writer, Arnold Zweig: "For a Jew boy out of a Viennese suburb, death in Aberdeen is … [a just reward] for having contradicted psychoanalysis" (ibid., p. 311).[10]

But the biggest, the most bitter conflict was with Carl Jung, because Freud had laid so many hopes on him as the "heir apparent" of psychoanalysis. I have already discussed the incompatibility of their views on science and religion. This split deepened as Jung began to reinterpret Freud's beliefs and, in particular, the preeminence of sexuality in his formulations. This made a titanic struggle between them inevitable, with Freud the older man, the commander-in-chief of the psychoanalytic movement, and Jung, his younger and very ambitious protégé. It is ironic that while Freud was said to "have sex on the brain," his sex life seems to have ended after he produced six children. On the other hand, Jung, who purported to be a "man of the spirit", had a long affair with Sabina Spielrein and other lovers. Evidently, Jung was no slouch on the couch. Freud himself touched upon the inconsistencies in Jung's public views: "Anyone who promises mankind liberation from the hardship of sex will be hailed as a hero, let him talk whatever nonsense he chooses" (ibid., p. 335).

There was one specific moment when Freud's engagement with Jung soured. He had traveled to Kreuzlingen, near Lake Constance, not an easy journey, to visit Ludwig Binswanger, a Swiss psychiatrist, who had become a close friend and was seriously ill. Jung lived relatively close by and could have easily arranged to meet him. But he did not. Freud felt snubbed and very hurt by this action, rather inaction, on the part of Jung. It greatly exacerbated the professional tensions that had been growing between them (ibid., p. 318). Two years later (1914) Freud published a polemic, "On the History of the Psycho-Analytic Movement" with the aim of showing that the theories of Adler and Jung were incompatible with psychoanalysis (ibid., p. 334; quoted by Clark from Freud, 1914d, p. 4).

Freud suspected that part of the problem between them was that Jung related to him as his father who had been a pastor in the Swiss Reformed Church. When Jung was taken by the work of the French philosopher, Henri Bergson, Freud snarled to Ernest Jones: "So you see, he [has] found another Jew for his father complex" (ibid., p. 335).[11]

It was not long before the inevitable rupture occurred. Freud bitterly complained to James Putnam, the Boston neurologist who was his most influential supporter in the States:

> I must protect myself against people who have called themselves my pupils for many years and who owe everything to my stimulus. Now I must accuse them and reject them. I am not a quarrelsome person [but] ... I am not in favor of sloppy compromises, nor would I sacrifice anything for the sake of an unproductive reconciliation. (ibid., p. 334)[12]

In a letter to Freud Jung also bitterly complained about the way he felt treated. In response Freud proposed to terminate their relationship. Afterwards both men were very upset and Jung came close to suffering a nervous breakdown (Krüll, op. cit., p. 192). Jung's letter of 18 December 1912 read:

> I would … point out that your technique of treating your pupils like patients is a *blunder*. In that way you produce either slavish sons or impudent puppies (Adler-Stekel and the whole insolent gang now throwing their weight about in Vienna). I am objective enough to see through your little trick. You go around sniffing out all the symptomatic actions in your vicinity, thus reducing everyone to the levels of sons and daughters who blushingly admit the existence of their faults. Meanwhile, you remain on top as the father, sitting pretty. For sheer obsequiousness nobody dares to pluck the prophet by the beard and inquire for once what you would say to a patient with a tendency to analyze the analyst instead of himself. You would certainly ask him: *"Who's got the neurosis?"* You know, of course, how far a patient gets with self-analysis: *not out of his neurosis*—just like you. If ever you should rid yourself entirely of your complexes and stop playing the father to your sons and instead of aiming continually at their weak spots took a good look at your own for a change, then I will mend my ways and at one stroke uproot the vice of being in two minds about you. (ibid., p. 192)

Even here, Jung wrote of being in "two minds," which indicated a part of himself which wanted to love and respect his mentor. But Freud was not open to this. Instead he "mourned" the loss of his close colleague, former friend and "heir," by writing the fourth section of *Totem and Taboo*, which elucidates the primeval horde (the sons) who kill and eat their violent and jealous father. Given the juxtaposition of these bitter exchanges, it is likely that the "horde" refers to Jung (Krüll, op. cit., p. 193).[13]

After the break Jung established a new venture which he called "analytical psychology," and which became internationally successful. He lectured widely and wrote many papers and books which elaborated now well-established concepts such as "archetypes," "complexes," "the collective unconscious," and "synchronicity." His "revenge" was that many of his ideas originated in his discussions with Freud, or for that matter, Sabina Spielrein, usually without crediting the source.[14] Jung also became overtly anti-Semitic with well-documented remarks about the difference between "Aryan psychology" and "Jewish psychology."[15]

Although shaken by Jung's departure, Freud was also delighted. Months later, in a letter to Abraham he declaimed: "So we are at last rid of them, the brutal, sanctimonious Jung and his disciples ... All my life I have been looking for friends who would not exploit and then betray me ..." (Clark, op. cit., p. 336).[16]

Because his relationships with colleagues could, and often did, become strained, Freud expected "treason" and "betrayal." Moreover, he tended to look on the dark side of things and held that evil outweighs goodness. To a large extent he used his prodigious intellect to help overcome such thoughts. But despairing moments continued to haunt him. With this in mind we can say that he created psychoanalysis to help cure his own low spirits and depression. In so doing he was generally successful.

Otherwise he used tobacco and cocaine to enhance his moods. A good cigar was a favorite pastime. He smoked upwards of twenty a day for years. There were occasional breaks of several months on doctors' orders, but he always returned to his smokes, even when his mouth was half eaten by cancer. His daughter Anna recalls that although he was generous with her, Freud hardly bought anything for himself except cigars (Gay, op. cit., p. 393).[17]

In 1884 Freud read that exhausted Bavarian soldiers became strong and capable of long marches after taking coca. Freud was fascinated by the report and ordered some to see if it worked for "nervous exhaustion." First he tried it on himself. In his monograph, "Über Coca", he reported:

> I took 0.05 g. of cocaïnum muriaticum in a 1% water solution when I was feeling slightly out of sorts with fatigue ... it has a bitter taste, which yields afterwards to a series of very pleasant aromatic flavors ... A few minutes after taking cocaine, one experiences a sudden exhilaration and feeling of lightness ... The psychic effect in doses of 0.05–0.10 g. consists of exhilaration and lasting euphoria ... One senses an increase of self-control and feels more vigorous and more capable of work. (Freud, 1884e, pp. 289–314)[18]

Freud was so pleased with the effects on himself that he was soon giving the coca to family, friends, colleagues, and patients. It seemed that he had found a magic potion to overcome life's miseries as he enthusiastically addressed his fiancée, Martha in a letter of 2 June 1884:

> Woe to you, my Princess, when I come. I will kiss you quite red and feed you till you are plump. And if you are forward, you shall see who is the stronger, a gentle little girl who doesn't eat enough or a big wild man who *has cocaine in his body*. In my last severe depression I took coca again and a small dose lifted me to the heights in a wonderful fashion. I am just now busy collecting the literature for a song of praise to this magical substance. (ibid., p. 59)

In an essay on the religious practices of South American Indians Freud was keen to mention that coca was "a gift from the gods, to satisfy the hungry, fortify the weary, and make the unfortunate forget their sorrows" (E. Jones, 1953, op. cit., p. 82 in Bakan, op. cit., p. 203). Consequently, he believed that cocaine could be useful in overcoming morphine addiction and introduced it to a close friend, Ernst von Fleischl-Marxow. He was a doctor who had become an addict after suffering excruciating nerve pain following an infection acquired while performing an autopsy. But Fleischl-Marxow developed a "cocaine psychosis" replete with "white snakes creeping over his skin." Sadly, he never recovered from his pain or opiate addiction (Markel, 2011, pp. 74–79). Apparently Freud was so guilt-ridden by his friend's descent into madness and his inability to help him that he kept a picture of him on the wall of his study for the rest of his life (ibid., p. 78).

Years later Freud confessed to Wilhelm Fliess that his consumption had gotten out of control. He found he needed more and more to have the same effect. He also started to smoke cigars again after a long period of abstinence (due to heart symptoms) (ibid., p. 174). Then, in 1896, with "superhuman" effort, he stopped using cocaine altogether (ibid., p. 226).

CHAPTER ELEVEN

Reparation

1896 was the year that Freud's father died, an event which he said was "the most decisive loss of a man's life" (Gay, op. cit., p. 88).[1] One might think that Freud's reaction to the passing of Jacob would be an increased use, a heightened dependence on "magical substances" like cocaine to get over his grief. Yet this was not the case. For Freud it was also a moment of liberation from his father's expectations. Not long afterwards he began his epic study, *The Interpretation of Dreams* and he formulated the Oedipus complex. Both constructions led directly to the development of psychoanalysis. This became the "healing potion" which excited and sustained him for the rest of his life.

Five years earlier Jacob Freud had given his son a handsome present for his thirty-fifth birthday. It was a copy of the family's Philippson Bible, rebound in leather, and inscribed in Hebrew with a warm message from Jacob to Shlomo (Sigmund).[2] It reads (in translation from Hebrew):

My precious son Shlomo
In the seventh of the years of your life the spirit of the Lord
first moved you
And spoke to you: Go, read in My book which I have written

149

And fountains of knowledge, discernment, and wisdom
will burst open before you.
Behold. It is the Book of Books, the well unearthed by sages,
From which our rulers drew knowledge and justice.
A vision of the Almighty have you beheld; many things have you
heard and accomplished,
Gliding on the wings of the wind [spirit?].
Since that time has the Book been sealed up with me like the
broken tablets in the Ark.
For the day on which your years amount to thirty five
Have I covered it with new leather.
Calling it: "Spring up, O well; greet it with song!"
And offering it to you as a remembrance,
A reminder of love
From your father
Who loves you with love eternal.

Jacob, son of Reb. Shlomo Freud[3]

This is the original Hebrew version in Jacob's handwriting:

Taken as a whole the inscription is a dedication and blessing for the son whom Jacob especially loved, like his biblical namesake who embraced Joseph, the interpreter of dreams, a man who rose from misfortune to become the the de facto ruler of Egypt. He was a hero with whom Sigmund closely identified. In a letter to his good friend and benefactor, Josef Paneth, he stated, "My own ego finds it very easy to hide behind people of that name, since Joseph was the name of a man famous in the Bible as an interpreter of dreams" (Rice, op. cit., p. 67).[4]

Jacob Freud's message is like a dream with each line loaded with biblical allusions (ibid., pp. 73–84). For example, his paragraph begins: "In the seventh of the years of your life." This refers to a passage in Genesis 47:28 whereby "Jacob lived seventeen years in the land of Egypt, so that the span of Jacob's life came to one hundred and forty-seven years" (*The Living Torah*, 1981, p. 241). The psychoanalyst, Emanuel Rice, who has elaborated every hidden nuance of the text, suggests that by utilizing the number seven here, Jacob is alluding to the age when his son first started to read the Old Testament (op. cit., pp. 75–76).

Sigmund would have realized the reference. He knew his Bible very well, having studied it closely with his father over many years. For him these verses carried a multitude of meanings. They were a "coat of many colors" hugging a brilliant son, but also pleading with him to return to his roots and forgiving him for his rebellious ways. The words were not threatening. They did not carry the hostility that the legendary Laius manifested to his newborn son. But they do invite Sigmund to renew the love for his father which he never really relinquished. Maybe this was the part of his self-analysis which Sigmund did not want to see. Far from wanting to kill his father and marry his mother, Oedipus fled Corinth, the city of his childhood and the domain of the only parents he knew, in order to protect them. The extreme moods and somatic symptoms that bedeviled Freud were hints that demons from whom he tried to flee still lay within himself. It is intriguing to think that Freud developed psychoanalysis as an ingenious way of meeting these beasties head on.

Similarly, Jacob's benediction was his way of trying to address the underlying tensions that existed between himself and his son. In Kabbalistic terms he intended to effect a *tikkun*, a renewal and repair of their kinship. Concomitantly, he aimed to reconcile himself with his own father (Sigmund's grandfather), also named Shlomo, and to restore the "Book" (the *Torah*, the Book of Life), and, indeed, his own life, that may have been broken (like "the tablets of the ark") by his straying from the path of rigorous observance.

Tikkun has to do with correction, restoration, and rejuvenation. It is the core concept, the raison d'etre of Kabbalah, and it coincides with the impetus for reparation, perhaps the most significant psychoanalytic formulation of Melanie Klein and her colleagues.

As in Kabbalah, Klein set out to describe how to overcome fragmentation and loss, evil and exile. But her terms of reference were different. Klein was concerned with the self in relation to "internal objects," internalized representations of significant persons, and to a lesser extent, "external objects," actual life important people. For her, exile meant separation from mother, while evil equaled death. For Kabbalists, however, evil means fragmentation of the soul and separation from God.

Reparation is the will, means, and action of repairing an inner world shattered under the pressure of destructive impulses and an outer world of damaged relationships, people, and things. Reparation, like *tikkun*, is both a goal and the movement toward this goal. According to Kleinian psychology, reparation is never complete, rather it is an active process of striving toward completeness, whether of the head or heart or entire being. It is intimately related to its Kabbalistic counterpart, which also is a constant ongoing process, but with a larger purpose, to unify the universe.

Essentially *tikkun* has to do with healing—physical, emotional, and spiritual. For man this has to do with healing the rifts within himself and between himself and others, in order to gain and regain *Shalame*—wholeness, and *Shalom*—peace of mind.

Concurrently, the Kabbalah teaches that when a person restores his self-balance, that is, restores the proper weight of his thoughts, feelings, and actions on a personal scale, he will simultaneously perform a *tikkun ha-olam*, a transformation of the cosmos. Therefore, what happens internally will happen externally, what happens on a micro scale will also happen on a macro scale. From this we learn that there is a continual interplay between the ultimate goal of creation, which is to bring completeness to the world (*tikkun ha-olam*), and the action or personal praxis that has to be taken to bring this about.

There is a striking complementarity between the concept of repairing the world (*tikkun ha-olam*), and psychoanalytic aims and actions. The analytic focus is on the internal object world of the patient. Melanie

Klein used the words, *Wiederherstellung*, meaning restoration, and *Wiedergutmachung*, meaning restitution, to describe this process of correction. However, these translations were soon superseded by "reparation," which is a refinement of the previous versions and includes the idea of repairing something as well as making reparation to someone.

According to Klein, the basic need, indeed the ongoing project of every person is to overcome early infantile sadism. She insisted that such savagery usually took the form of intense phantasies of tearing, devouring, and fragmenting mother's body. Subsequently, these impulses extend to father, and to siblings, as well as to all the relationships that occur among them, externally and internally. Even more terrifying, by "the laws of revenge," this sadism soon rebounds on the child, and his or her own body, mind, and relations. Hence the nightmares of early childhood are replete with the same monsters and demons, ghouls and goblins, who inhabit horror films.

In consequence Klein's concepts encompass not just the need and fact of repair, putting things back together again, but of "re-pair," reestablishing torn and broken relationships, especially the one between the parental couple. By implication this leads to the idea of repairing social as well as personal and interpersonal reality, the macro-social as well as the micro-personal.

But both the Jewish and psychoanalytic traditions agree that an important first step has to occur before a correction or repair can take place. We refer to the recognition of a wrong, whether between man and God or between man and man. In Judaism this step is called *teshuvah*, and is a formal process of taking responsibility for wrongdoing or sin. *Teshuvah* means repentance, but it also signifies return, a turning back toward one's primary source.

Neither the fact nor process of repentance is formalized in psychoanalysis. Rather this step appears to be noted as regret, remorse, sorrow, or, in general, a concern for a lost or damaged other or "object." This concern arises during the "depressive position" when a person, the subject, sees another as "a whole object," that is, as though he (or she) exists in his own right, with his own needs, problems, and desires. But I think that a basic aspect of the Kleinian view, and indeed, the whole idea of repentance can also be accommodated under Sigmund Freud's formulation of the "reality principle," and related "reality-testing" and "reality adaptation." Here "reality" denotes the point where a person is no longer under the sway of instinctual, narcissistic, and subjective desires or perceptions.

It is a major accomplishment when a child or adult is able and willing to perceive people or things as they are as well as see the connections between them. This denotes a state of mind which can acknowledge loss, injury or absence. Moreover, it can embrace ideas and processes such as beauty, nature, and cognition. This is the maturational moment when a person perceives a misfortune and accepts responsibility for his or her contribution to a damaged world.

Repentance (*teshuvah*) is the conscious, and, more important, the heartfelt acceptance of the dark side of oneself. Or, as the noted Talmudist, Rabbi Adin Even Yisroel (Steinsaltz) observes, it is the reaching into "the nadir of the abyss" (2002, p. 2). Only then, when a person has dug down to the very bottom of his soul, can the descent into badness and madness stop, and the ascent toward redemption begin.[5]

The possibility of return means that all who are fallen can be raised up and that all sins can be erased. This is the second and very important theme of repentance (*teshuvah*). A "bad man" can become a "good man" by realigning his spiritual as well as material energies. Indeed, in Judaism, the repentant sinner is known as the "Master of Return" and has a higher status than a righteous person who has never strayed.

The psychotherapist, Estelle Frankel, has adopted the analogy of the incense (*ketoret*) once used in the temple service in Jerusalem to point out that "sin" is not only an evil aspect of life, but also a necessary contributor toward the course of emotional realignment and growth (1994, pp. 5, 23–24, 104–105). The incense was made up from eleven basic ingredients. One of the most crucial of these was galbanum, a bitter, foul-smelling gum resin.[6] In itself galbanum is disgusting. But as part of the incense mixture, it adds passion and pungency. Sin is also repugnant. But like galbanum, when integrated into the totality of our personality, it can add strength and vigor.

Furthermore, Frankel points out that repentance occasioned by love gives people a second chance, another opportunity to rectify their existence. This follows the dictum described in the *Zohar* that it is possible to approach the shadow side of the soul in order to unblock and reclaim the light hidden within it. Similarly the essential tasks of psychoanalysis are to dis-cover, un-cover, and ultimately re-cover a love of life which lies hidden amid a morass of suffering and symptoms. I would not suggest, however, that the overt expression of *teshuvah* (repentance), as happens on the Jewish holiday of Yom Kippur, was part of Freud's therapeutic agenda. Even more so, because we know that he despised (or feared) formalized religious practices. Nonetheless it is important to consider the underlying influences that contributed to his psychic formulations.

I have already reviewed Freud's Hassidic background. The physicist, Tom Keve, documents in his study, *Triad: the Physicists, the Analysts, the Kabbalists*, the extent to which many of the founding fathers of psychoanalysis, including Joseph Breuer, Robert Breuer, Abraham Brill, Sandor Ferenczi (originally Fraenkel), Heinz Hartmann, and Lajos Levy were direct descendants of rabbis, Kabbalists, or purveyors of mystical texts (op. cit., pp. i–ix).

Phyllis Grosskurth, in her biography of Melanie Klein, notes that Klein had a formidable Jewish pedigree (op. cit., p. 13). Similarly, Frieda Fromm-Reichman was strongly influenced by an Orthodox Jewish upbringing and a Lurianic worldview, as expressed by the title of her biography, *To Redeem One Person is to Redeem the World* (Hornstein, op. cit.).

While psychoanalytic practice may explore penitence, contrition, remorse, or sorrow—different ways of recognizing and responding to wrongdoing, it seems to do so without a specific set of procedures or steps for finalizing repentance, such as described by Maimonides or as elaborated by later scholars. Psychoanalysis is more concerned with the mental anguish, the self-reproach, the self-blame, and especially, the sense of guilt that arises from internal conflict. According to Freud's structural model of the mind, the central conflict occurs between the id, the ego, and the superego. This has to do with sexuality and socialization: the internalization of parental injunctions, infringement of moral imperatives, and doubts about the worth or value of the self. The result may be a vague inner dread often synonymous with "neurotic anxiety," or a life dominated by endless rounds of "cops and robbers," pursuit and punishment.

In contrast to the structural theory, the psychological model of Melanie Klein emphasized the conflict between Thanatos and Eros, the forces of death and disintegration versus love and life. This parallels the Jewish mystical tradition which emphasizes a psychology of conflict featuring *tohu* (chaos, the without form, void) versus *bohu* (emptiness, but literally the "it is in it," reconciliation, integration) (Kaplan, 1990, op. cit., pp. 78–83). In conjunction with the creation of the *sephirot* (the divine characteristics), *tohu* has to do with the world of one-dimensional points which is roughly comparable to a state of part object relations.

Bohu pertains to a developmentally later world of multidimensional, interrelated streaks and is roughly comparable to a state of whole object relations. But the inability of the divine containers or *sephirot* (the word refers both to spiritual energies and the vessels which hold them) to integrate leads directly to the "Breaking of the Vessels," (*Shevirat Ha-Kelim*), and the disintegration of the universe. When these *vessels* reconstitute themselves, and they are able to engage with each other, then the universe can be recreated and life can be reestablished.

The Kabbalah constantly describes the dialectical clash between opposing thoughts, emotions, mental states, and personal values as well as the process of integrating and reintegrating them on "higher," more complex levels of being. In psychoanalysis or psychoanalytic psychotherapy the transference relationship is the way of accomplishing this task, of working though the carnage of an ambivalently lived life. The cut and thrust of projection and introjection, transference and countertransference between the patient and analyst, enable both parties to transcend all boundaries of time, space, and person. In such a relationship, the patient does not represent an angry child, but he is that child. The analyst does not represent an injured parent, he is that parent. Similarly, the present is the past, while the consultation room becomes the place, the space where everything has happened, but where every "thing" can be overcome.

The beauty of an analytic relationship is that it provides a second chance to put things right. Klein captured this possibility by her original choice of the term *Wiedergutmachung* which signifies restitution or reparation. In German the word can be subdivided into *wieder + gut + machung*. Literally this means second chance (again) + good + making or "the making good for a second time." One might say that such second, third, and more chances are backup mechanisms for getting through the depressive position, and becoming "human."

The nineteenth-century Hassidic master and prolific writer and thinker, Reb Tzadok Ha'Cohen of Lublin (1823–1900), emphasized the temporal aspects of the extra chance. When repentance takes place out of love (for family, for friends, for society), an individual can travel in time in order to reverse a wrongdoing, so that it appears that the event, and its effects, never happened. This view coincides with what the Alter Rebbe meant when he declared that a heartfelt repentance can reverse time and overturn a bad decree. It is also consistent with positive developments during the course of therapy or analysis. When the positive transference is activated, we can see that love in the present can obliterate pain of the past. These time flows are transferential and transactional. They move backwards and forwards like the intricate counterpoint of a Bach partita, and show that the process of repentance is only complete when past turmoil and hardships are mitigated by present warmth and affection.

Although I have been discussing the changes that repentance can bring about in and of itself, it is a necessary, but not a sufficient condition for effecting a correction or *tikkun* in a person, or in the world as a whole. For a man and woman, the first steps are a willingness to perceive reality and acknowledge the hurts that have happened. The second move involves a mellowing of the heart and feelings of remorse. But the third change involves specific actions designed to redress and elevate a fragmented self and chaotic world. I now wish to address this third element, from both the perspective of what needs to be corrected and the actions that have to be taken to bring forth and complete the realms of reparation.

Initially I considered the conundrum that Heinz Kohut repeatedly posed: how can man "cure his crumbling self?" Therefore, the first focus of the discussion of reparation/*tikkun* will be the individual in relation to himself. This is the world of self. Then I shall explore the individual in relation to others. This is the world of relationships. Finally I shall review everything else, animate and inanimate, the totality of existence which comprise "the world." In truth all of these areas as well as their creation, destruction, and recreation are interconnected.

The world of self begins inside the womb when the child-to-be exists as an undifferentiated being complete with potential for thoughts to be thought, feelings to be felt, and relationships to be lived. For a brief moment he or she is akin to a perfect cosmic egg, albeit waiting to be shattered under the impact of existence. Beset by bits and pieces of rudimentary experiences, hunger and frustration, tension and rage, the nascent self and infantile ego soon succumb to dissolution and chaos (*tohu*). Then the newborn baby reverts to a crumbled state where its mind and bodily sensations become broken and fragmented. Moreover, full of indigestible internal events, the infant evacuates these bits and pieces, what Bion called "beta elements," into his environment through cries, vomit, wind, feces, urine, and kindred products and activities. These remnants lodge (actually and symbolically) in everyone and everything around him which, in turn, appear dangerous and life-threatening.

Significantly, the Kabbalah describes a similar intermediate stage during the creation of reality. This is the "Universe of *Tohu*," when the vessels which reflect and contain the divine condition emerge as separate entities. But these vessels cannot interact with each other or hold the intense light or energies which flow into them. So the lower seven ones (lower in a spiritual sense) shatter and explode outwards, imbuing everything around them with shards or fragments of themselves. As I have shown, this shattering event is the harbinger of evil in existence, because both the vessels and their contents become separated from their source.

But even at this maturational moment, however, there exist certain primitive reparative capacities. These are physical and cognitive skills which help to overcome fragmentation and promote psychic and emotional integration. One of the most important of these has to do with language, because a baby creates reality through sounds and words. And if he can create reality, then he can change it and make it better. This explains the Kabbalistic maxim, "Redemption comes with the birth of the word." Why? Because words nourish "meaning." They contain projective outbursts and allow fragments of self which have been embedded in others "to come home."

The containing child or adult enters the world of relationships. Then he can become a giver as well as a taker. So the containing/contained function becomes more flexible and stronger. Feelings do not have to well up until bursting point, or be explosively discharged. They can be held, processed, digested, modulated, and otherwise transformed from bad to good.

There is a striking resemblance between the Lurianic account of creation, *tikkun ha-olam*, which can be roughly translated as "repairs to the tears in the universe," and the Kleinian concept of reparation, which can also be seen as making good the "tears" of separation.[7] For it conveys the possibility of overcoming the shock of separateness, aloneness, loss, and jealousy, but especially guilt for the damage one has inflicted on beloved relatives and friends, as well as oneself.

A damaged self denotes not just a part of the body, but a whole range of ruptured thoughts and feelings. It describes an inner world which lies bleeding, shattered and in ruins. Hassidism, in particular, has tried to address this problem through prayer, meditation, and introspection.

In his book on traditional Jewish healing, *The Wings of the Sun* (1995), the Breslov (hassid) lecturer and writer Avraham Greenbaum goes into great detail about how to overcome a broken body and mind. Ultimately (p. 24) he quotes Rabbi Nachman of Breslov (1772–1810) in his *Likutey Moharan* II: "The basic cause of illness is unhappiness, and the great healer is joy" (pp. 5, 113, 123). It is noteworthy that in English "Freud" means "joy."

Similarly, the late Lubavitcher Rebbe, Menachem Mendel Schneerson, emphasized the power of faith and reflection to overcome inner confusion and chaos. He explained, "Everything has its limits, even darkness," and "When the world was made, a limit was set how long it will function in confusion" (2002, p. 286).

Tikkun-actions initially focus on the self, hence, repair of the self (*tikkun ha-nefesh*). They include a variety of internal and external activities: prayer, meditation, introspection, dream processing, symbol formation, speech, artistry, sublimation, gnosis, and the search for meaning. Collectively all of these activities allow the individual to contain previously uncontainable experiences and to heal wounds to the psychic fabric and personal identity.

These wounds or divisions must reach beyond self-structure to the next stage of repair, to healing or reunifying human relationships. This is the action-time for the formation of "whole objects," and whole object relationships. For Kabbalists the comparable occasion is *bohu*, the "World of Repair." It is the occasion for reconciliation and rectification, when the divine characteristics (*sephirot*) "dance" together and when the male and female expressions of the Divine presence on earth establish and reestablish relations with each other.

Bohu (reconciliation) denotes an interplay of reciprocal relationships which leads to the creation of the spiritual and physical universe. It is the point where the devastation caused by the "breaking of the vessels" (*shvirat ha-kelim*), begins to be rectified. The original difficulty occurred because of the lack of reciprocity. The lower *sephirot* (characteristics) were only able to take in divine energies, but not give them out. So the vessels shattered. But once reciprocity was established, then the *sephirot* and their cosmic structure the *Etz Chaim* (the Tree of Life, the *sephirotic tree*) could be constituted and reconstituted.

Rabbi Chaim Vital elaborated the view of the Ari (Isaac Luria) that an exchange, seen as sexual intercourse, has to take place between the male principle as God, and the female principle (the *shekinah*) as humankind. Then humanity can be impregnated by God's qualities or characteristics, so that they permeate "her" existence and allow human-kind to perceive things through "his" eyes, that is, to see and respond to the world as God does.[8]

Therefore, the whole process of rectifying human relationships as well as correcting the cosmos is dependent on a cosmic drama (or should we say dream) about the erotic coupling of the divine personas. Sanford Drob explains:

> These unifications symbolize the dialectical union of such "opposites" as male and female, good and evil, being and nothingness, creation and destruction, self and other, past and present, mind and world, material and spiritual, and so on. (*Symbols of Kabbalah*, 2000b, p. 365)

The Kabbalists realized that the sexual union between a man and a woman was itself the symbolic fulfillment of the relationship between God and the *shekinah* (the female principle, the divine presence in its receptive mode). And since the Old Testament uses the same word (*daat*) to denote both knowledge and sexual relations, knowledge (of all kinds) can be seen as having a deeply erotic nature.[9] As Bakan empha-sizes, Freud's use of the idiom of sexuality is a fundamental instrument for expressing the deepest and most profound problems of mankind. And it is entirely in the spirit of the Kabbalah (op. cit., p. 272).[10] He continues:

> The basic paradigm of knowledge is union or penetration. Sexual union in the *Zohar* is spoken of as "uncovering of nakedness." [The divine quality or *sephirah* of] *binah* [means] understanding and [also means] mother. Thus, when a man sins sexually he "uncovers the nakedness of [his] Mother. Kabbalistically speaking, Freud came to *binah* in his discovery of the unconscious forces in man. He had, in the idea of the Oedipus complex, an image of the "mother lying in her nakedness." (ibid., p. 289)[11]

By grasping the importance of sexuality in human relationships, Freud was not just concerned with the physical act of copulation. Nor did he limit his understanding of the Oedipus complex to a longing for incestuous union with the mother. Rather he saw that it was a complex metaphor that addressed universal mysteries: Who am I? How was I created? Where do I come from? And, Where am I going?

The first questions concern the self. How can I cure a shattered self? How can I become whole? And, in so doing, how can I establish "I-ness" and "Me-ness," that is, a strong personal identity. The second issue has to do with relationships, and the wish of the child to have been present when the parental intercourse took place. Moreover, this wish is not just to have been present, but to have seen that he was created deliberately and lovingly. If this were not the case, then, by his own dream thoughts and actions, he longed to renew their union, so that it was really warm and caring.

The renewal of relationships leads to the third and most important level of reparation—rectification of the world (*tikkun ha-olam*). This is a very big project, so what does it mean in practice? The *Zohar* hints at an answer when it describes divers paths to wisdom:

> Another … way is to know the secrets of souls. What is the soul within me? Where does it come from? Why did it come into this body made of a stinking drop? [How can I …] know and contemplate the world one is in? What is its purpose? And then to seek to know the supernal mysteries of the higher worlds … (Drob, 2000b, p. 373)

Essentially the *Zohar* is calling for self-perfection or self-completion through the process of soul-discovery, not unlike a long and deep psychoanalysis, which as Bruno Bettelheim has pointed out, really means "soul-analysis." This is a path that avoids personal enhancement or narcissistic satisfaction. Rather it has to do with raising the sparks or elements of one's existence, an event which is simultaneously psychological, spiritual, ethical, and political. Each of these goals and actions is dependent on and identical with the other, and not only leads to the redemption of the individual, but to the whole of existence.

Rectification of the world (*tikkun ha-olam*) is a collective task. For "… in everyone there is something of his fellow man" (Elior, 1993, p. 50).[12] We rely on every act of kindness, every bit of self-sacrifice, every prayer to bring this about. Then every time a therapist helps to restore a person to sanity, he thereby becomes a helper to restore another person to sanity, and so on and on, where to reconstruct one person is to redeem the world.

This view is consistent with what Freud said, or is said to have said, when asked what should a normal person be able to do: "To love and to work" (*"Lieben und arbeiten"*).[13] The formulation is deceptively simple, but is quite profound. To love is to treat another individual with respect, mutuality, and kindness. It is the most healing of balms. Concomitantly, to work is to give added value back to the world, to repay it for the blessings that one has received.

Love, work, charity, contemplation, self-sacrifice, and kindred deeds all comprise the active component of repairing the world (*tikkun ha-olam*). But as I explained at the beginning of this chapter, and have been trying to demonstrate through subsequent examples, *tikkun ha-olam* is both a means to an end, and the end itself. The ultimate purpose of the rectification of physical and spiritual realms is peace and wholeness, the total transformation of chaos and fragmentation (*toho*) into reconciliation and integration (*boho*). In human terms the equivalent achievement is a state of self-actualization. Then we should be able to heal, through an act of will, whatever wounds someone has suffered, whether intrapersonally, interpersonally, or transpersonally.

Recent research shows that adults carry within themselves stem or precursor cells that can differentiate and repair damaged tissues when activated.[14] Essentially, people are plastic and restorable. Therefore we can recognize that we are all part of a multidimensional hologram like the Tree of Life (*Etz Chaim*), instead of clinging to the narcissistic idea that we are the center of the universe and everything has to revolve around us.

This is all very well, however, the question remains, what about individuals who abuse this process? What about those who use love and work for self-aggrandizement? Many observers, including Freud, have asserted that ritual practices are obsessive-compulsive neurotic mannerisms or worse, offensive stratagems designed to insulate the self and project superiority over others.

Obviously, actions which appear to be expressions of reparation are often perversions of it. Far from repairing broken hearts and helping others, work and worship, self-sacrifice and charity may simply serve as vehicles of control, contempt, and ways of triumphing over relatives and friends. This very common situation arises when arrogance replaces repentance. Then people refuse to face reality, acknowledge damage, feel regret, make amends, or ask for forgiveness.

Yet, expressly in these situations, the potential for *tikkun* remains present. I am impressed by the way that both psychoanalysis and Kabbalah can utilize the power of language to ameliorate pain, and transform bad into good. We have seen this process in Chapter Nine, "On Opposites," where a small change to a single letter, or vowel, can radically alter the meaning of a thought or word, from bad breast to good breast, from withholder to the source of life. In Hebrew, the words for evil ("rahh," רַע) and friend ("ray," רֵע) demonstrate similar possibilities. They carry the same consonants, *resh* (ר) and *ayin* (ע). The only difference is in the vowels, a tiny line ("ahhh") or two dots ("aye") under the *resh* (ר), which separate pain from pleasure.[15]

A certain breath or intense silence can also bring about profound changes in mood or demeanor. Thus, the Bible's Book of Ezekiel (which is a basic text for the Kabbalah) deploys the word *chashmal* to convey the prophet's vision when he met the Almighty. This word is usually translated as intense energies, or "luminescence." But the Ari (Isaac Luria) asserted that *chashmal* can also be interpreted as the "colour of the speaking silence," or the silence from which transformative insights emerge (Kaplan, 1990, op. cit., pp. 140, 147, 153–154, 165–166).

Chashmal is the "something from nothing." This explains why mystics, like Wilfred Bion, conclude that healing words are connected to the sound of silence. He saw that the greatest light can come from the deepest darkness. Such views are consistent with a successful therapy or analysis. The effort may be long and difficult and painfully silent. As John Thompson's patient declared, the loudest truths may remain unspoken, yet they can yield remarkable repairs of the self and of the soul.

CHAPTER TWELVE

Atonement

This book is dedicated to Dr. David Bakan and Professor Yosef Hayim Yerushalmi, two men who have been instrumental in reintroducing psychoanalysis to its Jewish roots. Bakan (1921–2004) was one of the founders of humanistic psychology.[1] He wrote on a wide variety of topics including psychoanalysis, religion, philosophy, and research methodology. His interest in the Jewish origins of psychoanalysis was aroused by his grandfather who spent hours reading him tales of the hassidim, especially by the Sassover Rebbe, Moishe Leib, who insisted that whoever does not devote one hour a day to himself is not a person and that to help someone out of the mud, one must be willing get into mud oneself.[2]

Bakan's hypothesis is that Freud, consciously or unconsciously, secularized Jewish mysticism and that the origins of psychoanalysis exist within the Kabbalah (ibid., p. xi). He further stated that the discipline that Freud originated is essentially a contemporary version of this outlook, or should we say, "in-look". I have already presented considerable evidence for this conclusion from the works of earlier Kabbalists like Abraham Abulafia, Moses De Leon, Isaac Luria, and Chaim Vital as well as modern thinkers like the Lubavitcher Rebbes, Aryeh Kaplan, Yitzchak Ginsburgh, and Adin Steinsaltz.

Bakan points out these thinkers were strongly influenced by the ideas expounded by the twelfth-century Jewish philosopher Moses Maimonides, in his *The Guide for the Perplexed*.[3] Bakan emphasizes that *The Guide* is essentially a handbook for the interpretation of dreams and visions. In doing so he recalls the Torah (Numbers 12: 6–8) "… if there be a prophet among you, I (God) … make Myself known to him in a vision, I do speak to him in a dream" (op. cit., p. xxv).

Maimonides (aka the Rambam) noted that the "keys" to interpretations of dreams and other phenomena lie in playing close attention to word play and anagrams as well as the operations of the "imaginative faculty" (ibid., p. xxv). According to the Rambam this faculty explains the difference between philosophers and prophets. Only the latter can appreciate the essence of the Divine, which is to create something from nothing. Concomitantly, the human wish to do likewise is very powerful and occurs through the metaphor of sexual intercourse (what the Rambam called *mubashara*). This is a further key to understanding the importance of sexuality and sexual imagery in human relations, a major focus of Freud's conceptions (ibid., p. xxvi).

Bakan was the first scholar to systematically explore the links between psychoanalysis and the Jewish mystical tradition and, by extension, to Judaism itself. But there was one element in his exposition which I found hard to accept. That is the idea that Freud was a secret Sabbatean, or follower of the seventeenth-century mystic, Sabbatai Zevi (1626–1676), a Sephardi rabbi and Kabbalist. Zevi preached during a period of murderous pogroms unleashed by the Cossacks against the Jews of eastern and central Europe. A large percentage of them were killed. Those that survived lived in terror and desperation.[4] Zevi argued that their suffering was a prelude to the coming of the Messiah, when peace and prosperity would reign. To bring this about, he advised his brethren to abolish their sacred rites and rituals. Accordingly, fast days became feast days, morality became amorality, and prior bounds of sexuality were broken (he married a prostitute). Eventually Zevi proclaimed himself the Messiah and prepared his tens of thousands of followers to march to Jerusalem.[5]

On the way he stopped in Istanbul. The sultan, Mehmed IV, got word of Zevi's plans and had him imprisoned. Later he was given the choice of converting to Islam or being impaled. Zevi chose to convert. This act devastated his devotees many of whom refused to believe in his apostasy.[6] They thought it was part of the Messianic scheme. But it was a wrenching moment for the whole of world Jewry and was a major reason why the Hassidic revolution, which the Baal Shem Tov initiated a generation later, was so reviled.[7]

But on rereading Bakan's book, I was struck both by the extent of his sources linking psychoanalysis and Kabbalah (which would have been even stronger if he had had access to the more recent accounts of Emanuel Rice and Marianne Krüll), and the reasons for Bakan associating Sigmund Freud with Sabbatai Zevi. Both men sought to repair the world. With Zevi this was the Jewish world, under threat of physical and spiritual annihilation. With Freud this was damaged souls or selves, Jewish or non-Jewish, and by extension, the world of social relations. Both focused on the freer expression of sexuality, and sought to break the bounds of normality. For Zevi this related to Rabbinic Judaism and with Freud this had to do with the stifling conventions of bourgeois propriety, which forswore the impact of infantile impulses on adult development. And they both saw themselves as Messiahs, Zevi leading Jews to the promised land, and Freud uncovering the unconscious bases of human life, especially the Oedipus complex.

Yet, Zevi was never able to overcome an overgrown ego. He was as much a showman as a Kabbalist. And because he converted to Islam, he became known as the "false Messiah." Freud never converted to Christianity, "the royal road to social acceptance," although numerous disciples did. He remained a proud Jew and keenly aware of the dagger of anti-Semitism.[8]

Professor Yosef Yerushalmi (May 1932–December 2009) is the second person to whom this book is dedicated. He was the most outstanding Jewish historian of the post-Holocaust era and held the Salo Wittimayer Baron Chair of Jewish History, Culture and Society at Columbia University. His most important work (1996) had to do with distinguishing between history and memory. The former is concerned with the collective consciousness of a people and its inspirational power. Thus, in the Passover story, every Jew is enjoined to feel that he or she was personally present at the exodus from Egypt. The story becomes part of their consciousness and gives meaning to their lives.

In contrast, in the modern era, Yerushalmi pointed out that scholars have focused on factual memory, as if the only real and important aspects of retrospection are verifiable facts. Yerushalmi called this preoccupation "the faith of the fallen Jew" (Myers, December 2009). He argued that it caused the Jew (or, for that matter, any member of a particular culture), to be estranged from his essential past or future "hi-story."

As a scientist and archeologist of the mind Freud seemed to have had a foot in both perspectives. His seduction theory aimed to uncover specific events that led to neurotic traits. And in the elaboration of the Oedipus complex he was also concerned with distinct conflicts that might account for specific symptoms. Yet he also held a wider view of the mythological and multigenerational jealousies and desires that surfaced in any given individual. That did, of course, include himself. Indeed, he relied on his own experiences to develop general ideas about human relations.

Then we must consider, if psychoanalysis can be seen as a secular expression of Kabbalah, did Freud have to be a Kabbalist, or a Sabbatean, or, for that matter, a mystic to work out his ideas? The answer is: not necessarily. As a *Galicianer* Jew coming from a Hassidic family steeped in Hassidic and mystical lore, the ideas were "in the air." As Yerushalmi would say, they were part of his "hi-story," whether Freud acknowledged this or not.

Bakan concurred. He emphasized that it did not matter whether Freud was formally conversant with Kabbalistic literature in order to conclude that he was influenced by it. However, Bakan (op. cit., p. xx) also referred to the meeting of the Hassidic savant, Rabbi Chaim Bloch, with Freud. Bloch told Bakan that he saw a copy of the French translation of the *Zohar* in Freud's library as well as other books on Kabbalah in German.[9] Besides, in his discussions with Wilhelm Fliess, Rabbi Safran, and others, Freud showed that he was familiar with Talmudic and Hassidic ideas.[10]

These concepts were part of his heritage. Whether they contributed to his genotype, or genetic inheritance, is a moot point. Freud himself believed in the Lamarkian idea that acquired characteristics can affect and be passed on through the genes, a view that many researchers do not now accept. Certainly it coincided with his phenotype, or cultural inheritance which included his identifications with family and friends as well as everything he heard or saw.[11] This was quite extensive (hence his awareness of Jewish customs and concepts) as Freud had a phenomenal memory, and, as is well known, he lived among and was mostly comfortable with fellow Jews.[12]

Yerushalmi was fascinated by Freud's last major work, *Moses and Monotheism* (1939a, op. cit.), which many people took to be a scandalous attack on Jewish history and culture. Freud began writing it in 1934 and completed the narrative after he moved to London in 1938. A half century later, Yerushalmi responded with a detailed study, *Freud's Moses: Judaism Terminable and Interminable* (1991, op. cit.), in which he queried Freud's facts, but also the criticisms that engulfed the book. Yerushalmi asserts that the "true axis" of the publication is not the sensational idea that Moses was an Egyptian, nor that the Jews killed him, rather it lies in the down-chaining of tradition.

> Moses received the Torah from Sinai and delivered it to Joshua, and Joshua to the Elders, and the Elders to the Prophets, and the prophets delivered it to the Men of The Great Synagogue. (Yerushalmi, 1991, op. cit., p. 29)[13]

The extended tradition (think of the eponymous song from the musical, *Fiddler on the Roof*) is what has given Judaism its "extraordinary hold" on the Jewish people. It is an experience that has gotten under and into their skin. As Yerushalmi underlines, Freud's account is based on a "Lamarckian assumption" that underlies the transmission of Judaism from the individual to the group and back again. He insists that this train of events is related to what Freud called "the return of the repressed," and is the "essential drama" of Freud's work, an astonishing story of "remembering and forgetting."[14]

Yerushalmi began his analysis of *Moses and Monotheism* with a joke, one that Freud told his colleague Theodor Reik, in 1908:

> The boy Itzig is asked in grammar school: "Who was Moses?" and answers, "Moses was the son of an Egyptian princess." "That's not true," says the teacher. "Moses was the son of a Hebrew mother. The Egyptian princess found the baby in a casket." But Itzig answers: "Says she!" (1991, op. cit., p. 1)

Then, to explain the joke, Yerushalmi deploys the delicious phase, the "hermeneutics of suspicion," which echoes Freud's own doubts about Moses's identity. Who was Moses? But, by the same token, who was Freud?

Yerushalmi seems to be sympathetic to Freud's quest. He senses it is part of Freud's struggle with his own origins. Is he really "a godless Jew," as he so often proclaimed? Or, is he a mutant example of *Judaeus Psychologicus*, the Psychological Jew, whose vestigial traits include a fondness for Levy's rye bread? Freud himself said that his book on Moses was akin to a "family romance," an "historical novel," which allowed him to utilize divergent perspectives about his monotheistic roots (ibid., pp. 5, 16–18).

Freud relied on the theses of the German theologian, Ernst Sellin (1867–1946). After studying the Prophet Hosea (who preached five centuries after Moses), Sellin concluded that Moses was an Egyptian, because he had an Egyptian name, and that he had been martyred by his own people who hated his tyrannical leadership (1922, pp. 25, 149). Freud also surmised that Moses had tried to impose on his followers the monotheistic cult of Aton, practiced by pharaoh Amenotep IV (as well as the Egyptian custom of circumcision).

Afterwards, according to Sellin, Moses was "resurrected" by the fusion of his persona with the "Moses" who commanded the cult of the Midianite volcano god, Yahweh. All this led to the creation of mono-theistic Judaism. Meanwhile, Freud insisted on the Lamarckian pre-dilection that the ancient heritage of the Jews "comprises … memory traces of the experience of earlier generations" (ibid., p. 31). Yerushalmi observed that for Freud these lines carry "the oppressive feeling of the longevity and irremediability of being Jewish," a Jewishness which he both loved, and felt was a terrible burden (ibid., p. 32).

What astonishes Yerushalmi about Freud's reconstruction of Jewish history is his recognition of "chosenness." This idea is consistent with Freud's postulating, as an essential fact of Jewish experience, the "return of the repressed." That refers to the intense guilt about the oedi-pal slaying of Moses, the father figure who unveiled monotheism. Be that as it may, I think Freud's guilt had more to do with the return of his Jewish feelings in the last decade of his life and the recognition of his deep attachment to his father. The bond included an intense interest in Egyptian antiquities. It is difficult to appreciate his lifelong passion for collecting statuettes of Egyptian deities without knowing that they were profusely illustrated in the Philippson Bible which Freud studied with his father for many years. The next two pages present a selection of these antiquities as published in this book.[15]

What seems to have happened is that Freud displaced his love for his father onto Egyptian antiquities and his conflicts with his father and grandfather onto the figure of the tyrannical Moses. Yet, Yerushalmi queries whether Jacob Freud is a useful example of an oppressive father. He says that a much better candidate would be Franz Kafka's, father, Herman.[16] Furthermore, he points out that Jacob Freud doted on his son.

> [He] was a loving, devoted, warmhearted father who openly acknowledged his son's precocious brilliance. ("My Sigmund has more intelligence in his little toe than I have in my whole head.") Of course he also expected obedience and respect (we are still in the mid-nineteenth century), but he encouraged his son to surpass him and was proud of his achievements. (1991, op. cit., p. 63)

As for the illustrations in the Philippson Bible, Yerushalmi states that they would not necessarily have been seen by observant Jews at that time as a violation of the prohibition of graven images. Since the German-Hebrew text was completely acceptable for the Orthodox reader, it was clear that in this "modern" edition of the Bible, the pictures were only there to provide background information (ibid., p. 64).

Two further issues need to be clarified. The first is the claim that Moses was an Egyptian because he had an Egyptian name. This does not follow. People commonly take on the name of their adopted country without giving up their original identity. At the age of two, the child was given over by Yocheved, his mother and wet nurse, to Pharoah's daughter who took him into her home as her son. She gave him the name Moses which, in Egyptian, means son. In contemporary terms she named him "Sonny." The name could also convey "drawn from water," for in Egyptian "*mo*" signifies water and "... *uses*" conveys, drawn from.[17]

The Torah establishes that Moses was the great-great-grandson of the patriarch, Jacob. "And Jacob begot Levi, Levi begot Kohath, Kohath begot Amram, and Amram begot Moses." This family tree confirms his Jewish ancestry (Philippson, 1838–54).

Secondly Yerushalmi muses, "Return of the repressed? What was repressed?" In Judaism the murder of a man as important and famous as Moses would have been recorded and remembered throughout the generations, "eagerly and implacably, in the most vivid detail" (1991, op. cit., p. 85).

> The biblical narratives of the sojourn in the wilderness do not hesitate to tell of constant rebellion by a stiff-necked and ungrateful people which, at one point, seems fully prepared to stone both

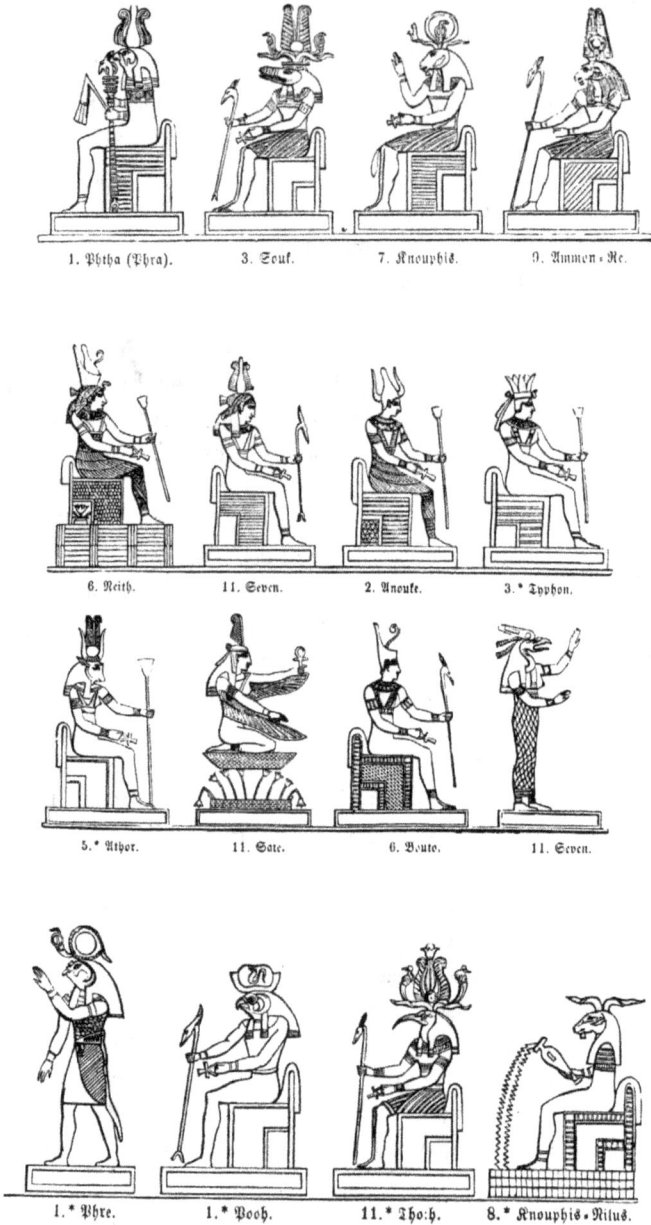

Figure 1. Egyptian gods, woodcuts from Philippson's Bible, 1:869–871 (illustrating Deuteronomy 4: 15–31).

Figure 2. Egyptian temple, woodcut from Philippson's Bible, p. 1164 (illustrating Hezekiah 8: 7–13).

Figure 3. Egyptian funeral ferry, woodcut from Philippson's Bible, 2:459 (illustrating 2 Samuel 19: 17–20).

Moses and Aaron [his brother] to death (Numbers 14:10). The prophets are by the irritating nature of their mission, always at risk. Jeremiah (chapter 26) is almost lynched in the Temple for treason … Zechariah son of Yehoiada the priest is stoned by order of King Joash (ll Chronicles 24:21) … All this is told unabashedly, without any sign of reticence. (ibid., pp. 84–85)

Bahre. Von einem Basrelief in Theben.

Figure 4. Egyptian funeral bier, woodcut from Philippson's Bible, 2:394 (illustrating 2 Samuel 3: 31–35).

Yerushalmi continues that far from lying in the group unconscious, as Freud supposed, he overlooked what "was the most singular aspect of Jewish tradition from the bible onwards, to wit—its almost maddening refusal to conceal the misdeeds of the Jews" (ibid., p. 84). The murder of Moses could not have happened, and certainly not in the way that Sellin and Freud recounted it.

This brings us back to the essential drama of Freud's life, forgetting and remembering, a repetition which occurred when he tried to deny his roots and become a Viennese professional. Nonetheless, the smell of a Jewish delicacy, or the sight of an anti-Semitic act, or the interjection of Yiddishisms and Hebrew into his writings, to cite but a few examples, constantly served to remind him of his origins.[18]

Indeed, Freud's close friend and colleague, Hanns Sachs, noted in his affectionate memoir, *Freud, Master and Friend*, published not long after his death:

> It is as though Freud walked intuitively and unconsciously in the footsteps of his ancestors and followed one of the most ancient Jewish traditions: the belief that all Jews, born or yet to be born,

were present at Mount Sinai, that there they took upon themselves
the "yoke of the Law." (1944, p. 152)[19]

Try as he might, Freud could not escape from his lineage. Max Graf, who
was the father of Freud's famous patient, Little Hans, has described the
formal rituals of the Wednesday Psychological Society, which eventually evolved into the Vienna Psychoanalytical Society:

> First, one of the members would present a paper. Then black cof-
> fee and cakes were served; cigars and cigarettes were on the table
> and consumed in great quantities. After a quarter of an hour, the
> discussion would begin. The last and the decisive word was always
> spoken by Freud himself. There was an atmosphere of the founda-
> tion of a religion in that room. Freud himself was its new prophet
> who made the theretofore prevailing methods of psychological
> investigation appear superficial. Freud's pupils—all inspired and
> convinced—were his apostles … However, after the first dreamy
> period and the unquestioning faith of his first group of apostles, the
> time came when the church was founded. Freud began to organ-
> ize his church with great energy. He was serious and strict in the
> demands he made of his pupils; he permitted no deviations from
> his orthodox teaching. (op. cit., pp. 470–471)[20]

Graf's observations fully accord with the picture I presented of his relationship with Stekel, Adler, and Jung, and later dissidents. Although
a rebel himself from conventional views on infantile and adult development, he treated colleagues who did not agree with him as heretics
and was quite willing to excommunicate them from the psychoanalytic
community. This created a culture of conformity which has carried on
today in analytic institutes where candidates are expected to "toe the
line," whether classical Freudian, Kleinian, Lacanian, or whatever.

Freud himself anticipated such "necessary" outcomes in his epic
attack on organized religion, *The Future of an Illusion* (1927c, op. cit.,
pp. 5–58). He argued:

> If you want to expel religion from our European civilization,
> you can only do it by means of another system of doctrines, and
> such a system would from the outset take over all the psycho-
> logical characteristics of religion—the same sanctity, rigidity and

intolerance, the same prohibitions of thought—for its own defense.
(ibid., p. 51)[21]

One might think that Freud was prophetic in describing the future difficulties of the "psycho-analytical movement." His official biographer,
Ernest Jones, tried to counter the accusation that Freud had created a
new "secular religion." Yet, in his caricature, he seemed to give cre-
dence to the very idea that he was attempting to deny:

> It was this element that gave rise to the general criticism of our
> would-be scientific activities that they partook rather of the nature
> of a religious movement, and amusing parallels were drawn. Freud
> was of course the Pope of the new sect, if not a higher Personage,
> to whom all owed obedience; his writings were the sacred text, cre-
> dence in which was obligatory on the supposed infallibilists who
> had undergone the necessary conversion, and there were not lack-
> ing the heretics who were expelled from the church. (1959, p. 205)

Jones also mentioned that there was a "minute element of truth" in the
"amusing" picture he portrayed. Indeed, if you substitute "Rebbe" for
Pope, "hassidim" for new sect, "God" for high personage and "Bible"
for sacred text, then you can find a fairly accurate description of the
Hassidic milieu from which Freud emerged.

No matter how hard Freud tried to bury, or murder, his *Galicianer*
self, it lay within his soul, if not his genes. For Freud, the "return of
the repressed" was the recreation of a Hassidic "court" replete with
a powerful, charismatic, omniscient Rebbe (akin to Moses, leading
modern man to the promised land of psychological health), a Bible (his
collected works), a multitude of attendants (his inner circle of friends
and colleagues), and a formal structure of meetings and ritual (the
Wednesday Society, later the Vienna Psychoanalytical Society). Thus,
when Karl Abraham first attended one of these occasions, he reported
to his friend, Max Eitingon:

> He [Freud] is all too far ahead of the others. [Isador] Sadger is like
> a Talmud-disciple, he interprets and observes every rule of the
> Master with orthodox Jewish severity. (Gay, op. cit., p. 178)[22]

Although Freud did hope that psychoanalysis would give rise to a
"secular priesthood," he constantly sought to distinguish between religion and mysticism, of which he disapproved, and science, of which he
approved. Freud wanted to be seen and treated as a scientist. In his early

years he was very careful to deny that the discipline of psychoanalysis was a "Jewish science." He thought that any link between his Jewishness and his creation would bring down the hatreds of anti-Semites on his head. This was an important reason for concealing his knowledge of Jewishness, in almost all its forms. Following this lead, his disciples did likewise. However, later in life, he remarked:

> "I don't know whether you're right in thinking that psychoanalysis is a direct product of the Jewish spirit, but if it were I wouldn't feel ashamed." (Clark, op. cit., p. 242)[23]

The Hungarian Jewish neurologist Sándor Ferenczi (1873–1933) was the essential link between Freud, psychoanalysis, science, and Kabbalah. He decided to become a psychoanalyst after reading Freud's *The Interpretation of Dreams*, and quickly became one of Freud's closest disciples and collaborators (ibid., pp. 214–215). In 1909 he accompanied Freud and Jung to Clark University in Worcester, Massachusetts, where Freud delivered five lectures which introduced psychoanalysis to an American audience. Given the importance of this event in the history of the psychoanalytic movement, analysts tend to forget that the really famous speakers were not Freud and Jung, but the scientists Ernest Rutherford and A. A. Michelson, both of whom had recently won Nobel prizes in chemistry and physics respectively. Their work instigated the great discoveries in the twentieth century in relativity, atomic physics, and quantum theory.

No doubt the five men met and discussed psychology and metapsychology, physics and metaphysics. Ferenczi was particularly fascinated by these subjects, even before he read Freud's work. The physicist, Tom Keve, has described Ferenczi's grappling with new paradigms in his paper, "Physics, Metaphysics, and Psychoanalysis." As far back as 1899, Ferenczi announced that the predominant, old, rigid, materialistic, reductionistic model of human relations had to change. Keve points out Ferenczi proposed a holistic, integral world view twenty years before Jung and twenty-five years before quantum theory (ibid., p. 159).

Ferenczi followed up these ideas in the introduction to his 1923 study, *Thalassa* (Greek for sea or ocean), a forerunner of later psychosomatic studies such as Norman Brown's *Life Against Death*. He wrote:

> ... the conviction grew in me, that an interpretation into the psychology of concepts belonging to the field of natural science,

> and into the natural sciences of psychological concepts, was inevitable and might be extremely fruitful. (Szekas-Weisz & Keve, 2012, p. 160)

Ferenczi also had an extensive network of familial and social relations with the most brilliant scientists and mathematicians of his generation. They included John von Neumann, Leo Szilárd, Theodor von Kármán, Eugene Wigner, and Wolfgang Pauli Jnr. Many intermarried within each others' families as well as with prominent psychoanalysts, a connection which Keve demonstrates in his book, *Triad: the Physicists, the Analysts, the Kabbalists* (2000, op. cit.).[24] Von Neumann's brother, Nicholas, recalls that the Ferenczis were neighbors:

> (Sandor) was a close relative and member of the family circle. As a result, discussions about Freud and psychoanalysis were among the subjects frequently encountered around the dinner table. (ibid., p. 164)

Moreover, to an extraordinary extent, their ancestors were rabbis, Kabbalists, and purveyors of sacred texts. The grandfather of Wolfgang Pauli, Jacob Pascheles, was the elder of the Gipsy Synagogue in the old city of Prague, and his father, Wolf (Pauli's great-grandfather), sold and published religious and mystical texts including the legend of *The Golem* (Keve, 2000, op. cit., pp. vi–vii).

Ferenczi's circle included Gershom Scholem who, after leaving Germany to settle in Palestine, founded the modern study of the Kabbalah. Scholem was a close personal friend of Wolfgang Pauli and one can assume that he would often discuss *gematria*, the mystical significance of numbers, with him. One number, 137, is particularly important, for it is "the magic number in physics," the inverse fine structure constant, and represents the strength of electromagnetic interaction (Keve, 2012, op. cit., p. 169).[25]

The Nobel laureate, Richard Feynman, who originated the theory of quantum electrodynamics, has confessed that the number 137 is one of the greatest mysteries in physics:

> ... All good theoretical physicists put the number up on their wall and worry about it ... is it related to pi or perhaps to the base of natural logarithms? Nobody knows. It's one of the greatest damn

mysteries of physics: A magic number that comes to us with no understanding by man. You might say the "hand of God" wrote that number, and "we don't know how He pushed his pencil." (1985, p. 129)

Is it just a coincidence that the *gematria*, the numerical value of the Hebrew word Kabbalah, is 137? In the year 1295 Abraham Abulafia, founder of the school of prophetic Kabbalah wrote that "... the Kabbalistic way consists of an amalgamation in the soul of man of the principles of mathematical and natural science" (Szekas-Weisz & Keve, op. cit., p. 175). The statement echoed Ferenczi's thoughts linking maths and mysticism, psychology and physics, six centuries later. In a paper entitled, "Mathematics," published posthumously, he noted:

> ... armed with the tool of psychoanalysis, we must try to increase our understanding of one special talent—mathematics.
>
> Mathematics is self-observation for the metapsychological processes of thought and action.
>
> The mathematician appears to have a fine self-observation for the metapsychic processes, finds formulas for the operation in the mind ... projects them onto the external world and believes that he has learnt through external experience. (ibid., p. 162)

Keve points out that these views reflect "the deep connections between quantum physics and mathematics on the one side and psyche or psychoanalysis on the other," and lead directly to the idea of an observer created reality. Both the observer and the observed (such as therapist and patient) are one total system. "Hence the observer effects the observed and vice versa, so that—in a sense—one never knows what 'really' happened, or would have happened, if the observation had not been made" (ibid., p. 170).

A further implication is that consciousness and the material world are intrinsically connected. Man is not simply a distinct particle interacting with other particles, but also exists in the form of a wave which can spread out in all directions influencing a multiplicity of other beings. Perhaps a dim awareness of this situation leads to the admonition about being careful with one's actions, as in: "Don't make waves!"

The awareness of quantum reality led Eugene Wigner to propose that consciousness creates actuality, a view very close to a Kabbalistic understanding of the unfolding of the universe. In a reconstructed conversation between Ferenczi and his wife Gizella, Ferenczi exclaimed:

> He [Jung] is right that psychoanalysis has been conceived out of mystical, Jewish tradition. It is the Kabbalah of the twentieth century. It is the *Zohar* transplanted to our age, adapted to our needs, modified by our observations. I said as much to Jung myself, years ago. Of course, Freud will not hear of it. (Keve, 2000, op. cit., p. 84)

The interconnection between the observer and the observed, the analyst and the patient, God and mankind, is a basic Kabbalistic as well as physical concept. Ferenczi utilized the idea in developing his technique of "mutual analysis," whereby both the analyst and the analysand are seen as part of a single system, mutually affecting each other. He felt that the only way of disentangling the personal realities of the participants is to view it as a whole, and to focus on the operation of the system as a whole, not just on the individual involved in it. Freud alluded to this in his elaboration of the transference relationship. Klein and her colleagues greatly expanded systemic analysis by uncovering the role of the countertransference in the analytic relationship and, in particular, the actions of projection and introjection, projective identification and introjective identification.

But Ferenczi's more active role with his patients led to Freud's recriminations and subsequent break with him. A major issue was therapeutic abstinence. Freud emphasized the importance of remaining aloof from his patients while carefully listening to and encouraging their free associations. For Ferenczi this was treating people as particles. He was far more engaged with his patients, a technique of "action analysis" which allowed deeply denied thoughts and feelings to emerge, in the therapist as well as in the patient. This was the opposite of the analytic "blank screen," but also carried with it the danger of over-involvement and making non-therapeutic waves. Nonetheless Ferenczi was a pioneer in working with very disturbed patients and an analyst who anticipated many of the concepts and techniques of modern psychotherapy.[26]

For many reasons, including his split with Freud and his terminal illness from pernicious anemia in the 1930s, Ferenczi died unappreciated and shunned by the psychoanalytic establishment (ibid., pp. 1–8). This began to change with the publication of his *Clinical Diary* (1988) and his correspondence with Freud. His professional resurrection is an overdue atonement for a psychoanalyst who was clearly ahead of his time, especially in the way he tried to integrate psychoanalysis, physics, and Kabbalah.

Once again, this raises the question, is psychoanalysis a Jewish science? The answer depends on how you define Jewish and how you define science. Freud tried to argue that it was not a Jewish science because he did not want it to be the focus of anti-Semitic enmity.

Let us first consider the issue of science. This involves a methodology which can be learned and objectively reviewed, such as when Freud dissected the testicle of an eel. But his far greater accomplishment was to develop a science of subjectivity, a sophisticated way of eliciting the internal life of men and women and children through the analysis of dreams, associations, slips of the tongue, and other inner to outer phenomena.[27] Then we have to consider the founding fathers of psychoanalysis, their Jewish genealogies, and the huge proportion of analysts and therapists who, even today, have Jewish religious or cultural backgrounds. And, as Bakan and Yerushalmi have shown, the concepts and practices of psychoanalysis are deeply rooted in the conceptualizations and customs of Judaism and the Jewish mystical tradition. So yes, it is not difficult to conclude that psychoanalysis is a Jewish science.[28]

Freud's daughter, Anna, made a reparation, a *tikkun*, an atonement, for her father's and her own doubts about the Jewish nature of psychoanalysis in a speech which she wrote and which was delivered on his behalf on the occasion of the creation of the Sigmund Freud Chair of Psychoanalysis at the Hebrew University in Jerusalem in 1977. She said:

> During the era of its existence, psychoanalysis has entered into connexion with various academic institutions, not always with satisfactory results … It has also, repeatedly, experienced rejection by them, been criticized for its methods being imprecise, its findings not open to proof by experiment, for being unscientific, even for being a 'Jewish science.' However the other derogatory comments may be evaluated, it is, I believe the last-mentioned connotation which, under present circumstances, can serve as a title of honor. (Yerushalmi, 1991, op. cit., p. 100)

Indeed, by his last years, Freud had begun to soften his hostility to religious and spiritual phenomena. Thus, in 1930, he wrote to his friend, the

French dramatist and writer, Romain Roland: "I am not an out-and-out skeptic. Of one thing I am absolutely positive, there are certain things we cannot know now" (Clark, 1980, op. cit., p. 496).[29]

In the same year his mother, Amalie, died at the age of ninety-five. Freud meticulously prepared her funeral and burial according to strict Orthodox Jewish standards. He arranged for the entire Freud family to attend, although he did not (Rice, op. cit., pp. 109–110). Just as his teenage friend, Eduard Silberstein, with whom he learned Spanish, noted, Freud never forgot a language, it is highly likely that he never forgot a custom (Clark, op. cit., pp. 21–22).

Likewise, Freud carefully prepared for his own passing. He had been suffering from cancer of the jaw for sixteen years, had endured many operations and, for much of the time, had been in great pain. By the time he moved to London in 1938, his condition had worsened, and by the fall of 1939, he realized that he could not carry on. Freud had an agreement with his personal physician Max Schur, to administer a terminal dose of morphine when requested (Gay, op. cit., pp. 739–740). He chose to exit the world on Saturday, 23 September 1939. This was not just the Sabbath, but it was also the most holy day in the Jewish calendar, *Yom Kippur*, the Day of Atonement, which itself is the culmination of ten days of introspection about one's sinful thoughts and actions (Schneider & Berke, 2011, vol. 13, pp. 1, 9). Yerushalmi suggests that such soul-searching was the impetus for Freud's writing *Moses and Monotheism* during his last decade (1991, op. cit, p. 6).

There are several Jewish primary sources that point to the special merit a person has when dying on the Sabbath and especially, *Yom Kippur*.[30] The Talmudic references are well known to people who have grown up in religious or Hassidic homes as did Freud.

"The death of the righteous affords atonement" (Talmud, Moed Katan 28a).

Here "the righteous" refers to a person who has expressed a willingness to correct his faults. The commentators say that "the atonement" will come both for the deceased and those left behind (Schneider & Berke, 2011, op. cit., p. 12).

> "Dying on Sabbath eve is a good omen … [and] on the termination of the Day of Atonement is a good omen." (Talmud, Ketuboth 103b)

Freud died at 3:00 a.m. on the morning of Yom Kippur. According to the Talmud, dying on the Sabbath, the Day of Rest, is a good sign, for then the soul of the deceased will go immediately into Heaven. Dying on Yom Kippur is a good sign because repentance has begun.[31]

The prominent eighteenth-century Kabbalist Chaim Joseph David Azulai has added: "The Day of Atonement atones for even mental thoughts to change oneself" (2003, p. 271).[32]

Meanwhile, the *Zohar* (Book of Splendor) explicitly states that God is so compassionate that on Yom Kippur ... no sins remain ... that could grant the side of judgment (i.e., severity) dominion (2006, 1:229b, p. 384). In the period of the "Ten Days" (and before) Freud would have been able to make a review of his life history, literally an accounting of his soul (*cheshbon ha-nefesh*). That, in itself, would "qualify" him for a return to the fold, as a "believing Jew," not a Jew who was "godless" or "estranged" (Schneider & Berke, 2011, op. cit., p. 14). As his colleague Karl Abraham wrote:

> "... the Day of Atonement, whose liturgy begins with the somber sound of the Kol Nidre [hymn], speaking of heavy guilt, and ends with the proclamation of the uniqueness of the Lord." (1920)

This soul searching must have been a strenuous mental and emotional effort. Yet, while it was going on, it seemed that Freud remained as recalcitrant as ever regarding ritual, for he directed that he would not be buried, according to the tradition which he well knew, but cremated, and his ashes placed in an 2,300-year-old Greek urn.

Perhaps, unsurprisingly, his wife, Martha, despite her positive feelings about religion and ritual, chose to be cremated and her remains were added to the urn when she died in 1951.

How ironical that sixty-three years later a thief tried to steal the urn where it was on display at the Golders Green Crematorium in north London. But he (or she) slipped while trying to make a getaway and the urn was badly damaged. The police did not mention whether any ashes had escaped (Doherty, 2014, p. 3).

EPILOGUE

In the ensuing generations since Freud passed away many of his descendants have made major contributions to secular knowledge and culture. They include, of course, his daughter, Anna, a founder of child psychoanalysis, particularly through the auspices of the Hampstead Child Therapy Centre (now the Anna Freud Centre) which she helped to establish in London in 1947.

Anna's brother, Martin, was a lawyer who looked after his father's finances, and Ernst, who was a successful architect. Their descendants numbered notable writers, artists and journalists, academics and businesspeople.[1] Many have moved in the highest circles of British aristocracy and government. Freud's grandson Clement (by Ernst) received a knighthood after serving several terms as the Liberal MP for the Isle of Ely.[2] His very rivalrous brother, Lucian, one of the greatest English portrait painters of all time, one-up'd Clement exclaiming:

> Why on earth would I want to speak with him or see him? I was offered a knighthood, but turned it down. My younger brother has one of these. That's all that needs to be said on the matter. (Singh, 2000, p. 3)

185

Their feud lasted over seventy years and was never resolved. Apparently, as teenagers, the two boys were racing in a park. Lucian cried out, "Stop thief," whereupon a passer-by apprehended Clement. This allowed Lucian to rush to the finish line. The prank so enraged Clement that he refused to have anything to with his brother again (Berke, 2012, op. cit., p. 40).

Although he refused a knighthood, Lucian counted many members of the aristocracy as patrons and friends. His second wife was Lady Caroline Hamilton-Temple Blackwood, eldest child of the 4th Marquess of Dufferin and a scion of the Guinness family.[3] Her mother, Maureen Guinness, was so incensed by this liaison with a Bohemian, "Jewish hanger-on," that she tried to hire gangsters to kidnap her daughter or dispose of her lover. What she did not know was that Lucian used to hang out with these same gangsters and they told him what was going on. (He was friends with the notorious Kray brothers and other Paddington hoodlums.) So this put paid to her plot (ibid., pp. 105–115).[4]

Lucian's cousin, Walter Freud (by Martin), was a war hero who parachuted and captured an airfield in Austria single handedly.[5] His son, David, was a controversial banker and Conservative politician. He served as a Parliamentary Under-Secretary of State for Work and Pensions and, under Labour, was put in charge of welfare reform. Eventually he was created a life peer and was known as Baron Freud.[6]

By anyone's standards, Lucian was not just a prolific painter, but a prolific lover. It is said that he fathered forty children, although only fourteen (by six women) are directly known.[7] One of Lucian's daughters, Bella (Freud's great-granddaughter), the sister of the noted novelist Esther, is a well-established fashion designer. On the other hand, Clement's children, while not nearly so numerous, have had a major impact in the media and public relations. Clement's daughter, Emma (Freud's great-granddaughter) has had a thriving career in TV, radio, and films. In 2011 she was appointed Officer of the Order of the British Empire (OBE) for services to Comic Relief.[8] His son Matthew (Freud's great-grandson) is one of the most influential men in England through his enterprise, Freud Communications. It is the eighth largest and possibly the best-connected public relations company in the UK. Matthew's first wife, Caroline Hutton, subsequently married the 9th Earl Spencer, brother of Diana, Princess of Wales. His second wife was Elisabeth Murdoch, daughter of the media magnate, Rupert Murdoch.[9]

Their father, Clement, has successfully reinvented himself time and time again. During the Second World War he acted as an aide to Field Marshal Montgomery. Later he became a "celebrity chef" at the famed Dorchester Hotel. About the same time he developed his career as a sports journalist and TV personality. Clement became a familiar face on TV over a series of dog food advertisements co-starring with a bloodhound called Henry. His trademark was a "hangdog" expression.[10]

In addition to his political career, he became well known as a panelist on the long-running radio show, *Just a Minute*. A fellow participant reminisced, "Clement's way of playing the game was to win: that's what he cared about" (Merton, 2009).[11] As an MP, Clement told the story of leading a trade delegation of British MPs to China in the late 1970s. When they checked into the hotel, he was surprised to discover that a junior member of the delegation had been given the presidential suite, while he had only been offered a poky single room. He went down to the front desk and complained, "I don't mean to make a fuss, but it seems that Mr. Winston Churchill has been given the presidential suite despite the fact that I am the leader of this delegation." The manager explained that this was because Mr. Churchill had such a very famous grandfather. Clement chuckled, "Well this is the first time that I have been out-grandfathered" (Doctorow, 2009, p. 8).

GLOSSARY OF HEBREW AND YIDDISH TERMS

Alter Rebbe: See Shneur Zalman: the first Lubavitcher Rebbe.

Ari: The acronym of Rabbi Isaac Luria, the progenitor of contemporary Kabbalah (1534–1572).

Atzvut: Deep sadness or melancholy. Severe, black depression.

Avodah: Service (as in the service of God).

Ayin Beis: One of the greatest and most profound writings of the Rashab.

Ayn sof: Infinity, the without end.

Baal Shem Tov: "Master of the Good Name," Rabbi Israel ben Eliezer, the founder of Hassidism (1698–1760).

Baal Shem Tov of London: Rabbi Dr. Hayyim Samuel Jacob Falk, noted Kabbalist and alchemist, contemporary of the Besht and sometimes confused with him (1708–1782).

Bahir (The): The Book of Illumination, one of the oldest Kabbalistic texts, generally attributed to Nehuniah ben HaKanna, a first-century Talmudic sage.

Bar mitzvah: Literally "son of the commandment." The ceremony at age thirteen which marks the maturing of a boy and his acceptance of responsibility for fulfilling the rites and rituals of Judaism.

Bechadrei Chareidim: Israeli blog site ("in the rooms of the ultra orthodox").

Be-ha'alotekha: (lit.) When you light … Chapter Eight of Numbers, the fourth book of the Torah.

Be-midbar: Numbers, the fourth book of the Torah.

Berg Yidden: Mountain Jews in the Caucasus.

Besht: The acronym for the Baal Shem Tov.

Binah: A divine attribute or emanation meaning understanding.

Birur: (lit.) Extraction, Kabbalistic concept of extracting or elevating the hidden sparks of holiness within a person and reestablishing their proper place within oneself. Part of the process of personal and cosmic reparation.

Bitul: A state of absolute "egolessness".

Bochur (pl. *bochurim*): Religious student, students.

Bohu: (lit.) "the it is in it." Reconciliation, integration, opposite of *tohu*.

Chabad: The Hebrew acronym for Lubavitch Hassidism representing *Chochmah, Binah,* and *Da'at* (wisdom, understanding, and knowledge).

Chayah: Soul, the fourth and very advanced level of spirituality, known as "the living soul," and to do with volition or divine will.

Chesed: A divine attribute or emanation meaning kindness.

Cheshbon Ha-Nefesh: An accounting of the soul, soul searching.

Chochmah: A divine attribute or emanation meaning wisdom.

Cordovero: Rabbi Moses ben Jacob Cordovero, leading Safed Kabbalist, predecessor of the Ari (1522–1570). Known as the Ramak.

Da'at: A divine attribute or emanation meaning knowledge.

Davin: Pray.

Etz Chaim: The tree of life, basic configuration of the ten sephirot or divine emanations.

Farbrengen: Hassidic gathering, featuring singing of Hassidic melodies, inspiring discussions, often addressed by a rebbe.

Fartrought: To carry or to bear.

Gematria: Jewish numerology, a system of discerning the meaning of a word or phrase by adding the numerical value of the Hebrew letters and relating it to other words or phrases with the same numerical value.

Gevurah: A divine attribute or emanation meaning severity.

Great Maggid: Rabbi Dov Ber of Miedzyrec, the successor to the Baal Shem Tov (–d. 1772).

Gria: The Gaon of Vilna, major Lithuanian Talmudist and religious leader, opponent of hassidim.

Gufe Torah: Bodies (lit.), the main principles of the Torah.

Halacha: The collective body of Jewish law.

Haskalah: "The enlightenment." Jewish movement opposed to strict interpretation of the law.

Hassid (pl. Hassidim): A member of the Hassidic movement, (lit.) pious one.

Hassidic: Pertaining to Hassidism.

Hassidism: A mystical and religious renewal movement rooted in the Kabbalah, which emphasizes the joyful worship of God. The practical application of Kabbalah.

Hassidus: The nature and philosophy of Hassidism.

Hod: A divine attribute or emanation meaning submission.

Kabbalah: The Jewish mystical tradition.

Keter: A divine attribute or emanation meaning crown, referring to will or volition.

Ketoret: Incense.

Klippah (pl. *klippot*): Shells, barriers, as between man and God, responsible for evil.

Lev Nishbar: Contriteness of hearing (lit.), deep remorse, sadness, a heart broken leading to overcoming evil.

Lubavitch: 1. The name of the largest Hassidic movement in the world. 2. The Russian town from which it emanated, and in which it was originally based beginning with the second Rebbe. The word means: "The Town of Love."

Maariv: Evening prayer.

Maharash: The acronym of the fourth Lubavitcher Rebbe, Rabbi Shmuel (1834–1882).

Malchut: A divine attribute or emanation meaning kingship, but referring to the feminine, receptive quality of the Divine.

Mamzer: Bastard.

Maskillim: "Enlightened ones," adherents of the *Haskalah*, reformed Jews opposed to strict rabbinic Judaism and Hassidism.

Mekubal: A person who can directly receive and transmit spiritual experiences.

Merrirut HaNefesh: Bitter depression, bitterness of the soul.

Messiah: (lit.) The anointed one, the redeemer who will bring about *tikkun ha-olam*, the repair of the world.

Mitnagdim: Religious Jewish opponents of Hassidism.

Mittler Rebbe: Rabbi Dov Ber (Schneuri), the second Lubavitcher Rebbe (1773–1827).

Mitzvah: Religious commandment, required deed.

Mizrachi: Religious Zionism movement.

Moses Maimonides: A preeminent medieval Jewish philosopher and physician and one of the greatest and most influential Torah scholars of all time (1135–1204).

Mubashara: Sexual intercourse.

Nachman of Breslov: Hassidic rabbi, great-grandson of the Baal Shem Tov, leader of Breslov Hassidim (1772–1810).

Nefesh: Soul, the lowest level representing the physical dimension of spirituality.

Nefesh B'hamit: (lit.) The animal soul, to do with egotistic and physical desires and cravings.

Nefesh Elokit: (lit.) The Godly soul, the spiritually elevated part of one's being, close to God.

Nemichat Ruach: Lowness of spirit.

Neshamah: Soul, the third level, to do with intellect.

Netzach: A divine attribute or emanation meaning victory or eternity.

Neve Yaakov: "Jacob's oasis," a neighborhood in Jerusalem.

Niggun: Hassidic melody or song.

Nigleh: Revealed, as in Torah *Nigleh*, the revealed Torah.

Nistar: Secret, hidden, as in Torah *Nistar*, the hidden Torah.

Ostjuden: East European Jews, particularly from Galicia, looked down on by other Jews as socially inferior.

Pilpul: Complex Talmudic discussion or reasoning.

Rambam: The acronym for Rabbi Moses Maimonides.

Ramchal: The acronym for Rabbi Moshe Chaim Luzzatto, a great Italian Kabbalist (1707–1746).

Rashab: The acronym of the fifth Lubavitcher Rebbe, Rabbi Shalom Dov Ber Schneersohn (1860–1920).

Rayatz: The acronym of the sixth Lubavitcher Rebbe, Yosef Yitzhak Schneersohn (1880–1950).

Rebbe: Hassidic rabbinic and spiritual leader.

The Rebbe: Rabbi Menachem Mendel Schneerson, the seventh Lubavitcher Rebbe, leader of Lubavitch Hassidism from 1951–1994 (1902–1994).

Rosh Hashanah: The Jewish New Year.

Rosh Yeshivah: Director of a yeshiva.

Ruach: Soul, the second level, to do with emotionality.

Ruach Hakodesh: (lit.) Holy spirit, Godly directed spiritual energy, divine inspiration.

Sabbatean: Follower of the seventeenth-century mystic and "false Messiah," Sabbatai Zevi.

Safed: City in northern Israel, center of Kabbalah.

Sassover Rebbe: Rabbi Moshe Leib Erblich of Sassov, a disciple of the Great Maggid of Miedzyrec, and one of the foremost Hassidic leaders who followed after the Baal Shem Tov.

Shneur Zalman: The first Lubavitcher Rebbe, aka "Der Alter Rebbe" ("The Old Rebbe"). The founder of Lubavitch Hassidism (1745–1813).

Sephirah (pl. *sephirot*): containers or vessels, especially of spiritual energies. The spiritual equivalents of human faculties.

SHaDe: Demon, devil, the bad breast.

SHahD: Breast, the good breast.

Shalem: Whole, wholeness, complete.

Shalom: Peace, peaceful.

Shavuot: Jewish festival of weeks commemorating the giving of the Ten Commandments.

Shekinah: The Divine presence, notably the female, receptive aspect of the Godhead.

Shema Yisroel: Central prayer expressing the oneness of God with everything.

Shevirith ha-kelim: Breaking of the vessels, particularly to do with splintering the *sephirot*.

Shiduch: Arranged marriage.

Shtetl: Small village in central or eastern Europe with a predominant Jewish population.

Sitra achra: (lit.) "the other side," meaning the force of darkness or evil that exists within every person.

Sitting shiva: Ritual mourning.

Tallit: Prayer shawl.

Talmid (pl. *talmidim*): religious student(s).

Talmid Hacham: Torah scholar.

Talmud: Basic compilation of Jewish civil and religious laws.

Tanya: Primary text of Lubavitch Hassidism, meaning "Teachings." Written by Rabbi Shneur Zalman.

Tefillin: Phylacteries.

Teshuvah: Repentance, also signifying a return to whomever one has wronged.

Tiferit: A divine attribute or emanation meaning beauty, splendor.

Tikkun: Reparation, restoration, renewal.

Tikkun Ha-Lev: Repair, restoration of the heart.

Tikkun Ha-Nefesh: Repair, restoration of the self.

Tikkun Ha-Olam: Repair, restoration of the world.

Tohu: Chaos.

Tomchei Temimim: Name of first Lubavitch yeshiva (religious school). Also name of Lubavitch yeshiva network.

Torah: First five books of the Bible (Old Testament).

Tselem: Astral body, disembodied spiritual self.

Tzaddik: Righteous one, particularly a person infused with spiritual powers.

Tzedakah: Charity.

Tzemach Tzedek: Rabbi Menachem Mendel Schneerson (meaning Righteous Offspring), the third Lubavitcher Rebbe (1789–1866).

Tzumtsum: Contraction, withdrawal, concealment, as of the divine radiance.

Valgerinzich: Roaming around.

Yechidah: Soul, the fifth and highest level of spirituality, signifying unification with the Divine.

Yeshiva: Seminary for religious, Talmudic, and Hassidic studies.

Yesod: A divine attribute or emanation meaning foundation or denoting sexuality.

Yetzah harah: The evil impulse.

Yom Kippur: The Day of Atonement.

Zohar: "The Book of Illumination" or "Book of Splendor." The primary text of the Kabbalah. It focuses on the mysteries of the Torah, the nature of God, and the origin and structure of the universe, among many mystical, spiritual, and psychological themes. The traditional view is that the teachings of the Zohar were revealed by God to Abraham and Moses and then passed down orally until it was formalized by Rabbi Shimon Bar Yochai in the second century. Modern academic analysis theorizes that the thirteenth-century Spanish writer Moses de Leon was the actual author and that he ascribed the work to Rabbi Shimon to enhance its acceptability.

NOTES

Introduction

1. Rabbi Lew also related a symposium that had been held in Melbourne, Australia to consider the encounter of Freud with the fifth Lubavitcher Rebbe (the Rashab). The proceedings were eventually published in the *Journal of Judaism and Civilisation: Essays on the Relationship of Judaism with the Arts, Science and Values of General Civilisation*, 1999, Vol. 2, 5759, pp. 1–13, under the leadership of Rabbi Dr. Shimon Cowen, editor of the journal. In the proceedings it was pointed out that it was only in 1998 that specific texts derived from the seventh Lubavitcher Rebbe (Rabbi Menachem Mendel Schneerson) were published that relate to the event and identify Freud as "the famous Professor" (ibid., p. 1).
2. It is important to note that in Judaism it is the mother who is the essential agent in passing on the tradition, especially through familial rites and rituals. Freud did his best to prevent his wife, Martha from engaging in them, an obvious attack displaced from his mother.
3. For infant Sigmund the sudden disappearance of his nursemaid was an emotional catastrophe. Krüll surmises that the event contributed to Freud's heart condition as an adult. He later suffered a further separation from his mother when she contracted TB and had to spend a long convalescence in the Carpathian mountains (ibid., p. 148).

Chapter One

1. *The Jerusalem Post* (2011). His/Her Story: The Mother of Jewish Feminism. 6 June, internet edition.
2. Regarding Freud's famous patients, see Clark, op. cit., pp. 130–132.
3. Schneur Zalman of Liadi (1796). *Likkutei—Amarim—Tanya* [Teachings], bilingual edition. N. Mindel (Trans.). London: Kehot Publishing Society, 1973.
4. Quoted by M. M. Schneerson (1986). *Sihot Kodesh 5712*, "Yud Tet Kislev", pp. 84–89.
5. Shalom Dov Ber Schneersohn (1985+). *Sefer HaMa'amorim* [Collected Writings] (Hebrew and English). New York: Kehot Publishing Society.
6. Rabbi Motti Seligson, personal communication, 26 January 2012. As of 2014, Chabad has facilities in eighty countries and is represented in forty-eight American states (Telushkin, 2014, pp. 444, 515).
7. The words are taken from the singing during the seventh ritual encirclement with the Torah Scrolls, *Hakafot*, on the holiday of Simchat Torah. See *Siddur Tehillat Hashem* (2002, p. 387).
8. Also quoted in Shimon Cowan (1999, pp. 4–5).
9. Translated by Rabbi Shmuel Lew.
10. These "discussions" were not what modern practitioners would consider to be "psychoanalysis." This would only occur decades later with Freud's elaboration of the transference and the development of the "object relations" school of psychoanalysis based on the study of interpsychic processes. Rather the "discussions" can be considered to be more in the nature of supportive psychotherapy or counseling.
11. Personal communication, April 2012.
12. An exception might be Kabbalistic practices which utilize sexual imagery to unite the masculine and feminine aspects of the divine so that humankind can be impregnated with godliness (Berke & Schneider, 2008, p. 232). It is extremely unlikely that Stekel saw sexuality in these terms.

    While many hassids have suffered sexual phantasies, they have been able to overcome them by following the teachings of the Baal Shem Tov (Besht). He explained that oppressive sexual thoughts came from the *sephirah* (divine characteristic) of *hesed* (kindness). And that the way to supersede them is by spiritualizing them, that is, by elevating them to their spiritual roots and Kabbalistic functions.
13. Ayn Beis means 5672, the Hebrew year (1912) in which the Rashab started to write the work.
14. R. Shmuel Lew, R. Mendel Gordon, personal communications, March 2012. Both rabbonim categorically state that the Rashab was not known

to have a stutter or stammer. Rabbi Lew also relates that he knew an elderly hassid, Rabbi Yehudah Chitrik, who was present at many of the Rashab's farbrengens. Chitrik told him that the Rashab spoke in a "strong, baritone voice."

15. R. Shmuel Lew, personal communication, May 2012.
16. As Freud's confidant, Ernest Jones recalls, this "became a standing joke." (ibid., p. 214).
17. Freud also referred to Stekel as an "unbearable human being" (ibid., p. 232) and "a swine," (ibid., p. 214).

Chapter Two

1. This account has been documented from Lubavitch sources as well as newly available accounts provided by direct descendants and relatives of the Bick family: R. N. Kahn (1997, pp. 159–163); Marinowsky (1991, pp. 142–144); Mundshein (1997, pp. 11–13); Y. Y. Neumann (1997, pp. 17–18; also personal communications, 2000, 21 May, 24 July); Oberlander (1997, pp. 1–3; also personal communication, 2000, 12 May); Y. Y. Schneersohn (op. cit.); M. M. Schneerson (1997a, op. cit.).
2. In another version of this story, the Rashab and his son checked into a small inn in a village near Pressburg because they did not want to be recognized. (In a hotel they would have had to hand in their passports.) They wanted to remain anonymous because according to Hassidic teaching, a good deed (mitzvah) done anonymously is a greater mitzvah. In the next morning Yosef Yitzhak started to look for a cab to take them into the city, but his father told him that they would walk. Then they encountered the bochur (student) (Rabbi Yerachmiel Tilles, 2012).
3. Nachama Bick married Zev Wolf Neumann of Pressburg, "a God-fearing Jew, but simple man."
4. When they were in Pressburg the Rashab bought several of Rav Bick's books from his estate. It may be that these are now in the Lubavitch library in Crown Heights, Brooklyn, New York.
5. See also: http://www.jewishencyclopedia.com/articles/14751-wahl-saul.
6. This was recorded by R. Phineas Katzebellenbogen, a descendent of Saul (1734).
7. He was appointed "rex pro tempore" (temporary king). Some accounts say he may have reigned for several days. For generations this story was considered to be more of a legend than a fact, but in the nineteenth century, research by Professor Bershadsky confirmed Saul Wahl's reign (Rosenstein, 1976a).

8. See also http://en.wikipedia.org/wiki/Yitzchak_Yaacov_Reines and http://en.wikipedia.org/wiki/Neve_Yaakov.

9. The Pupa Rav, R. Yaakov Yitzhak Neumann, died in 2007. Prof. Miki Neumann died in 2011. The grandchildren and great-grandchildren of Yaisef and Faiga Lefkowitch live in New York City and remain Orthodox Jews. (See Oberlander, 1997, op. cit., pp. 17–18).

10. Avraham Bick was born in Moholov-Podolyin, about twenty-five miles from Uman, in the Ukraine. He died at the age of sixty-five and was buried in the Jewish cemetery in Pressburg near his father, Yaacov. Miriam Reines lived on until 1926.

11. This paper was presented at a meeting with close colleagues in 1921, but published posthumously.

12. See http://en.wikipedia.org/wiki/Astral_projection. Accessed September 2014.

13. Isaac Newton was born in the same year that Galileo died and straddled the seventeenth and part of the eighteenth century. He passed on in 1727.

Chapter Three

1. This remark was part of a spontaneous exchange about psychoanalysis during the course of a discussion with Michael Eigen in 1978, a year before Bion passed away.

2. See also Sandford Drob (2000a, pp. 246–247).

    Bloch confronted Freud: "Anti-Semites accuse us of killing the founder of Christianity. Now a Jew adds that we also killed the founder of Judaism." Bloch added: "Have you examined the birth records and death records of ancient Egypt and found conclusive evidence that Moses was an Egyptian and the Jews killed him?" (Bakan, op. cit., p. xix).

3. Bloch published part of his interview with Freud in the magazine, *Bitzaron*, November 1950.

    Bloch also noted in Freud's library "a large collection of Judaica, all of which has been expurgated in the official account of his library held in the New York Psychoanalytic Society."

4. The *Zohar*, 5 volumes. H. Sperling, M. Simon, and P. P. Levertoff (Trans.). London: Soncino Press, 1931–1934. A more modern translation by Daniel Matt is the Pritzker Edition. It is being published by the Stanford University Press from 2004 onwards.

5. An alternative translation is: "You (God) enwrap (Yourself) with light as with a garment."

6. Translated from the Hebrew by Dr. Naftali Loewenthal.

Chapter Four

1. The London Gazette: (supplement) no. 30801 p. 8439 (http://www.london-gazette.co.uk/issues30801/supplements/8439.16 July 1940.)
2. Thompson's patient was himself the son of a noted New England psychoanalyst. For a fuller account of Thompson's extraordinary life read the Weindling biography (ibid.).
3. Kingsley Hall was the residential community in the East End of London established by R. D. Laing and his colleagues in 1965 in order to "demystify schizophrenia" (see Barnes & Berke, 1972).
4. I feel very grateful to Thompson for his role in my "catalyzing" this solution. The story was made into a stage play by the playwright, David Edgar, which opened at the Royal Court theatre, London, in 1979, and subsequently has been performed all over the world. As of 2014 it is under option for a feature film.
5. Mary always painted with her fingers somewhat in the very colorful style of German expressionists. She has had and continues to have exhibitions of her work in England and abroad, most recently at the Space Studios, London, in 2011, the Djanogly Art Gallery, Nottingham in 2013, and the Nunnery Gallery, London in 2015. (See www.mary-barnes.co.uk.)
6. See Cordovero, *Pardes Harimonim*, Shaar 4, Chs. 5–6, reprinted 2010 as *Pardes Rimonim* (Orchard of Pomegranates), parts 5–8.

   The sephirotic tree of life (Etz Chaim) is simple, but also very complicated. For a fuller discussion see Berke and Schneider (2008, op. cit., pp. 127–144). See also Eigen, Appendix 1, "Ein Sof and the Sephirot" (2012, op. cit., pp. 79–92).

Chapter Five

1. "The structural model" was first formulated in 1920 in *Beyond the Pleasure Principle*, and was developed and formalized in 1923 in *The Ego and the Id*.

Chapter Six

1. For a further elaboration of this point see Tom Keve (2000).
2. Hassidic thought postulates a further soul, the *nefesh hasichlit* or intellectual soul. It is said to be a tool by which the Godly soul can communicate with the consciousness of a person. Moreover, the *nefesh hasichlit* is said to be the means by which the "upper" spiritual realms can communicate with the "lower" earthy realms, and the Godly soul can communicate with the animal soul. I think it is less complicated to

maintain the picture of an animal soul (*nefesh b'hamit*) and a Godly soul (*nefesh elokit*), whereby each has an intellectual component that allows it to communicate with the other.

3. Mary Edith Barnes, b. 9 February 1923 (Portsmouth), d. 29 June 2001 (Tomintoul, Scotland). See: Barnes & Berke (1972b). Also: www.mary-barnes.co.uk.

Chapter Seven

1. Solomon was Jacob's father's given name. In Hebrew it was Shlomo and in German it was Sigismund. Years later when the name was given by Jacob to his son, the name was shortened to Sigmund, initially by Jacob, and then by Freud himself. See endnote 19 in Yerushalmi (1991, op. cit., p. 132).

2. There are other versions of this account. Rice, for example, quotes from Freud's biographer, Peter Gay. One Friday afternoon after the Freuds had arrived in London, they were visited by "a young Oxford philosopher" (obviously Berlin). Martha Freud exclaimed, "You must know that on Friday evenings good Jewish women light candles for the approach of the Sabbath. But this monster—*Unmensch*—will not allow this, because he says that religion is a superstition" (Rice, op. cit., p. 120).

3. This was written on Freud's seventy-fifth birthday in 1931 (quoted by Rice, op. cit., p. 25).

4. A sheitel is a wig that strictly observant women wear as a sign of modesty. Kosher means according to the Jewish dietary laws (ibid., pp. 11–12).

5. Ernest Simon, b. 1899 (Berlin), d. 1988 (Jerusalem).

6. Karl Ludwig Borne was a Jewish born journalist and political philosopher, b. 1786 (Frankfurt), d. 1837 (Paris). He is credited with numerous aphorisms such as: "Losing an illusion makes you wiser than finding a truth." According to Ernest Jones, he was instrumental in Freud's realising the importance of "free associations" in psychic life. See http://en.wikipedia.org/wiki/Ludwig_Borne.

7. Quoted in Simon, E. (1980). Freud and Moses. In *Entscheidung zun Judentum. Essays und Vortrage*, Frankfurt am Main: Suhrkamp, p. 200f. Passage explained by Dr. Naphtali Loewenthal.

8. The psychoanalyst, Theodore Reik, frequently visited the Freud household and noted that Freud's mother only spoke a Galician Yiddish and had only a minimal knowledge of German (ibid., p. 30).

9. In modern times this hierarchy tends to be reversed. Jews whose ancestors came from Eastern Europe as well as Litvaks and Germans

are at the top, especially if they have assimilated into American and European cultures and have become wealthy businessmen and professionals. The Sephardim are at the bottom because after they were expelled from Arab countries in the 1930s and thereafter, their wealth was confiscated. So they arrived in Israel and other countries relatively impoverished.

10. Rohling's propaganda was part of a pamphlet, *The Talmud Jew*, which went through seventeen editions. Thirty-eight thousand copies of the sixth edition alone were distributed free in Westphalia.

11. See also http//www.guardian.co.uk/world/2012/apr27/vienna-row-legacy-antisemitic-karl-lueger.

12. Freud worked at Brucke's Institute of Physiology from 1876–1882. Then he transferred to a clinical post at the Vienna General Hospital (Clark, op. cit., pp. 41–43).

13. According to Rice (op. cit., pp. 98–100), there is no evidence that the Bernays were Sephardim. This was part of the Freud "family romance." It was also an identity that the Hakkam assumed in order to enhance his prestige (ibid., p. 12).

14. The Bernays did not have the resources to provide a large dowry as would have been required for Martha to marry a man of high social rank. See also Aron (1956–57, p. 292).

15. A painting of Hakkam Bernays used to hang in the hall of Freud's Burgess 19 apartment. Beneath it was a little electric light. It was usually kept off. But when members of the Bernays family came to visit on the Sabbath, Freud always chose this time to turn it on. This was a major religious infraction (Rice, op. cit., p. 13).

16. Tysmenitz was destroyed by the Nazis in 1942. The town is now located in the Ukraine and is called Tysmenytsia. A memorial to the town and its former inhabitants was published in 1974 by Shlomo Blond, titled in translation *Tysmienica: A Memorial to the Ruins of a Destroyed Jewish Community*. The original book can be seen online at the New York Public Library site: Tysmenytsia. See also http//www.jewishgen/Yiizkor/Tysmienica/Tysmienica.html.

   Considerable information about Tysmenitz was also published by Krüll (op. cit., pp. 85–88).

17. In Tysmenitz and the nearby town of Brody the *mitnagdim* (non-hassidim) were in the majority. But they were surrounded by countless famous Hassidic towns.

   Rebbi Naftali Tzvi Horowitz of Robshitz, 22 May 1760–8 May 1827. Known as the Robshitzer Rebbe, he was renowned for his profound wisdom and good humor. He was a master of the Kabbalistic interpretation of the Torah.

Rebbi Yachiel Michel Rabinowitz of Zlotchov, 1721–1786. His seventh generation descendent, Aharon Pinchas Rabinowitz, is the current Zlotchover-Ropshitzer Rebbe of Baltimore, Maryland. So 200 years after R. Naftali the two Hassidic groups seem to have amalgamated.

18. Jocasta discovered the reason for the plague before Oedipus did, and tried to stop her son and husband from finding out with the view that it was better "to let sleeping dogs lie." When this did not work, she hanged herself.

19. This is a three generational model. With the oedipal myth the situation does not become clear without tracing the pattern of parental infanticide back seven generations, from Gaea to Uranus to Chronos to Zeus to Tantalus to Pelops to Laius (ibid., pp. 11–12).

20. In addition to Jacob (18 December 1815–23 October 1896), Shlomo had two further sons, Abae and Josef, and a daughter (Krüll, op. cit., pp. 234–235, Table 3, Jacob Freud Family Tree).

21. In an earlier study, *Totem and Taboo*, (1912–13), Freud called religion an obsessional neurosis. See also Gay (op. cit., p. 526).

    Jones complemented Freud's views in his essay on "The God Complex." He wrote: "... how closely the ideas of God and Father are associated, so much so that, from a purely psychological point of view, the former idea [God] may be regarded as a magnified, idealized, and projected form of the latter [Father] (1964, p. 244).

22. Most scholars assumed that the nursemaid was Monika Zajic, a member of the family in the house in which the Freuds lived. However, recent research indicates that the woman was a Czech Catholic woman named Resi Wittek (ibid., pp. 119–122).

23. All perished in 1942, Rosa in Auschwitz, Mitzi in Treblinka, Dolfi in Theresienstadt, and Paula in Treblinka. See Jacob Freud Family Tree (ibid., p. 234).

24. Klein emphasizes the Jewish sources of psychoanalysis, both as a theory and organization, which he contends have often been overlooked because of an "unusual blend of assimilation and dissimulation."

25. However, like so many Viennese Jews, Freud was also ambivalent about his Zionism. Earlier, in a letter to Albert Einstein (February 1930), he doubted whether the Islamic or Christian world would allow Palestine to become a Jewish state. He preferred a "rational" attitude which would have enabled a Jewish homeland to be founded on "historically unencumbered soil" and railed against the "unrealistic fanaticism" of his fellow Jews (quoted by Gay, op. cit. p. 598).

26. The dedication was signed: "Jacob, son of Reb Sh. Freud. In the capital city of Vienna, 29th of Nissan, 5851, May 6 [1]891." This is a further indication of the religious nature of Jacob. An assimilated Jew would not have signed his name in this manner (Rice, op. cit., p. 370).

Chapter Eight

1. The *shekinah* is the feminine, receptive aspect of the divine. In analytical psychology this became "the anima" or female aspect of the self.
   Numerous books, plays and films have emerged about Spielrein and her relationship with Jung and Freud. See Kerr, 1993, also the 2001 film, *A Most Dangerous Method*, starring, Keira Knightley.

2. Freud refused, probably because of her intense sexual wishes toward Jung, which he feared could have been transferred to him. Previously Jung had confessed to Freud about their sexual relationship. Nonetheless, Spielrein became one of the first female psychoanalysts. Her many contributions to Freudian and Jungian analysis have been overlooked, most likely because she was a focus of friction and embarrassment between Freud and Jung and their followers.

3. Quoted from Freud's letter to Abraham, 23 July 1908, 57.

4. From Freud to Abraham, 23 July 1908, 57 and Freud to Abraham, 20 July 1908, 57.

5. Gutman Locks (1985) has listed all the words of the Torah (first five books of the Old Testament) according to their numerical value. Gematria means counting. There are many different systems of counting, but whichever is used, the whole point is to discover the deeper, sublime meanings of the mysteries of existence.

6. The same quote from the Kabbalah was used for the title of Fromm-Reichman's biography: Hornstein, G. (2000). *To Redeem One Person is to Redeem the World: The Life of Frieda Fromm-Reichman.*

7. This is particularly the case via the Kabbalistic representation of the Tree of Life (*Etz Haim*) describing the ten qualities of the Godhead. See www.corax.com/tarot/tree-of-life.html.

8. My discussion of the Freud–Safran meetings is based on a published paper that my colleague, Professor Stanley Schneider and I co-authored (Schneider & Berke, 2010, pp. 15–23).
   We are indebted to Rabbi Dr. Nathan Lopes Cardozo, dean of the David Cardozo Academy for Jewish Studies in Jerusalem, for bringing these letters to our attention and for providing us with copies of them. Rabbi Dr. Cardozo received copies of these letters from Dr. Eisenstein, during a lecture tour in the United States in the early 1960s.

9. Eisenstein refers to the rabbi's "encounter" with Freud. In fact there were several meetings. In Safran's obituary in *Le Monde*, in July 2006, by Prof. Carol Iancu of Paul Valery University in Montpelier, France, Iancu (2006) refers to "numerous encounters" between Safran and Freud.

    In several phone calls that Prof Schneider made to Rabbi Safran during the period 2004–05, he referred to his "meetings" with Freud.

10. The *Talmud* consists of a body of teachings comprising civil, religious, sociological, and philosophical discussions. The writing and final edition of the Talmud took place between the third and sixth centuries C.E.

    It is complemented by the *Midrash* which consists of Jewish commentaries on the Hebrew scriptures, compiled between 400 and 1300 C.E. The Midrash is based on exegesis, metaphors, and legends.

    On a deeper level both the Talmud and Midrash are connected with the Kabbalah. This has to do with an "inner" or "higher" reality, beyond "external" reality, which mystics attempt to "experience" and "know." This inner reality is associated with the Divine, and therefore is related to the Godhead, which is the source of everything.

11. Jacques Derrida, 15 July 1930–9 October 2004. He is an important twentieth-century thinker associated with poststructuralism and postmodern philosophy. He is famous for developing a form of linguistic analysis known as deconstruction.

12. The Aramaic translation of the Bible was made by Onkelos, a convert to Judaism (35–120 C.E.). His translation is the accepted rendition of how to understand the text. Many later Jewish Bible commentators built their understanding of the text upon the translation of Onkelos.

13. These words were written on his tombstone. He died in Brody in 1717 (Aron, op. cit., p. 291). See also Krüll, op. cit., p. 234.

14. Freud confided to Abraham: "The idea is to put Lamarck entirely on our ground and to show that the 'necessity' that, according to him, creates and transforms organs is nothing but the power of unconscious ideas over one's body … in short the omnipotence of thoughts. This would actually supply a psychoanalytic explanation of adaptation" (quoted by Clark, op. cit., p. 381, from Freud–Abraham, 11 Nov. 1917, *Abraham Letters*, p. 261).

Chapter Nine

1. Psalm 139, Verse 12. An alternative translation is: "Even the darkness obscures nothing from You; and the night shines like the day—the

darkness is as light." The *Bahir* is generally attributed to Nehuniah ben HaKanna, a first-century Talmudic sage.

2. Dressler (1891–1954) was also a noted educator who expounded that branch of Judaism known as *Musar*. Musar is a path of contemplative practices that have developed to help an individual soul to pinpoint and then break through the barriers that surround and obstruct the flow of inner light (truth, understanding, morality, spirituality). Musar, in particular, is concerned with ethical guidance.

3. *Minutes*, ll, pp. 396–398, quoted by Edward Timms (2013, p. 218).

4. Wilhelm Fleiss (1858–1928) was a German Jewish Otorhinolaryngologist who for many years was a close friend and colleague of Freud. He developed three major Kabbalistic ideas: bisexuality, numerology, and predestination. Fliess was the source of Freud's theory of bisexuality (Bakan, op cit., pp. 58–63).

5. The work of Abel which particularly influenced Freud was his essay "On the Antithetical Meaning of Primal Words" (1884). Freud later wrote an essay with the identical title which, in turn, was said by Jacques Derrida to be a precursor to the semantic insights of deconstruction theory.

6. Moscati was professor of Semitic philology at the University of Rome as well as an award-winning archeologist for his excavations in the Middle East as well as Sardinia and North Africa.

7. Kutscher was a prominent Israeli philologist and Hebrew linguist.

8. The "ah" vowel is called a *"pah'tach."* The "ay" vowel is called a *"tzay'reh."*

9. Further words with the same consonants but different vowels yield SHeDaDe and signifies "destroy." Concomitantly SHeDooD signifies "despoiling." (Both SHeDaDe and SHeDooD connote a total reorganization.)

10. A quiescent is a half consonant, a weak letter. In Hebrew quiescents are: aleph, hay, vav and yod (יהוא).

11. The difference between shin and sin is that the shin (שׁ) has a dot on top of the letter on the right side (hence the "sh" sound), while the sin (שׂ) has a dot on the top of the letter on the left side (hence the "s" sound).

12. The final form of the consonant *noon* (נ), that is, when it comes at the end of a word, is (ן).

13. The basic Hebrew vowels are *pah'tach* (ah) and *tzay'reh* (ay). Others include *kah'matz*, pronounced (ah) in sephardi pronunciation or (ohr) in ashkenazi pronunciation; *see'gool* (eh); *khee'reek* (ee) and *koo'bootz* (oo). Vav may be a consonant or a vowel depending whether it comes with a dot at the top or middle of the letter, or not.

14. The primary definition of broadcast is to sow, to scatter seed over a wide area. Clearly, the word relates to feeding and procreation and demonstrates another direct link with SHahD (שד), the breast.

15. The small consonant Yod (י) when added to the end of a word in Hebrew denotes possession. So SHahD (שד), breast plus Yod (י) literally equals my breast or my source. In spiritual terms the word denotes my Source, the Source of all or SHaD'i (שדי), the Almighty.

16. Envy and greed rarely operate separately. "Grenvy" signifies the fusion of greed and envy as well as the simultaneous expression of them. The term was suggested by Dr. Nina Coltart (see Berke, 1988, op. cit., p. 26).

17. Diana of Ephesus is one of many images of "the great many-breasted mother" that have appeared and been worshipped throughout the ages. The typical statue of Diana of Ephesus depicts a large, voluptuous woman with arms outstretched and with a plethora of breasts covering her body (E. Neumann, 1963, plate 35; see also Neumann's discussion, ibid., pp. 126–127).

18. Stan Tenen is the director of the Meru Foundation, which was established in 1983 to study ancient alphabets and texts from a modern mathematical perspective.

19. Personal communication, July 1992. See also Tenen (2011).

20. Much of the material for this chapter comes from the paper which I co-authored with Stanley Schneider (Berke & Schneider, 1994, pp. 491–498).

Chapter Ten

1. According to the Alter Rebbe even the divine soul has a militant aspect to it.

2. Weinberg writes that this is only one side of the coin. The other is a spiritually motivated depression where a person becomes aware that he exists in a state of concealment from his godly soul. This realization can lead to a sudden burst of desire to change his ways and reconnect with the Godhead (spiritual center).

3. In *Tanya* in his section on repentance, the Alter Rebbe states that the quality of brokenness can refer to the breaking of the husks or shells which imprison the heart with bad or evil thoughts and intensions. So a broken heart can also be a liberation from "grossness and arrogance" and conveys the crushing of the evil impulse (*Igeret Hateshuvah*, p. 369).

4. David Annesley, personal communication, January 1981.

5. Freud also noted the opposite, that with sexual delight, and feelings of joy or happiness, "… the whole body blossoms out and shows signs of a renewal of youth" (ibid., p. 287).

6. Quoted from Freud (1950a [1887–1902]) *Aus den Anfängen der Psychoanalyse*, p. 82 (*The Origins of Psycho-Analysis*), with corrections by Schur 1972, p. 43).

7. Letter is available on PEPWeb, correspondence edited by Ernst Freud.

8. Freud tended to feel very low after his books were published, thinking that they were not good enough. Gay comments, for example, "Sunk in his 'familiar depression' after reading the proofs of *The Ego and the Id*, Freud denigrated it as 'unclear, artificially put together, and nasty in its diction'" (op. cit., p. 411). The same was the case after the publication of *The Interpretation of Dreams* (ibid., pp. 133–134). To make matters worse, the book sold just over 300 copies in the first six years after publication.

9. The *Journal* was edited by Ferenczi, Rank, and Jones, all dedicated to following a "strict Freudian line." Stekel's *Zentralblatt* continued to be published before expiring at the outbreak of the First World War (ibid., p. 315).

10. Later when Ernest Freud edited his father's correspondence he left out the word "Jew" in "Jew boy" as too derogatory.

11. Jung suffered from a weak father and a strong, but crazy mother (Ann Shearer, personal communication, January 2014). Freud had a stronger father (but with moments of weakness such as by not responding to an anti-Semitic bully) and an overweening and possessive mother (whom he felt he had to visit every Sunday). Both Freud and Jung sought out idealized father substitutes whom they ultimately rejected, Freud with Fliess, and Jung with Freud (see Shearer, 2011, pp. 121–132).

12. Quoted from Freud–Putnam, 19 June 1914, *Putnam Letters*, p. 176.

13. Freud also wrote to Karl Abraham: "Jung is crazy, but I have no desire for a separation and should like to let him wreck himself first. Perhaps my *Totem* paper will hasten the breach against my will …" (quoted by Clark, op. cit., p. 330, from Freud–Abraham, 1 June 1913, *Abraham Letters*, p. 141).

14. Jung's ideas about the collective unconscious, for example, were close to Freud's interest in Lamarckism, the inheritance of acquired characteristics. And the concept of "the anima" is directly connected to the ideas of Spielrein and the Kabbalistic concept of the *shekinah*, the feminine emanation of the Godhead.

15. Aryan was superior. Jewish was inferior. In private Jung was much less guarded in his remarks (see Aryeh Maidenbaum, 2013).

Once Jung left the psychoanalytic circle, Freud bitterly complained about Jung's "anti-Semitic condescension towards me" (Clark, op. cit., p. 243). Nonetheless, he had many Jewish supporters including Gershom Scholem, the first professor of Jewish mysticism at the Hebrew University in Jerusalem. For an extended discussion of the issue see Yerushalmi, op. cit., pp. 48–50.

16. Quoted from Freud–Abraham, 26 July 1914, *Abraham Letters*, p. 186.
17. See Anna Freud to Jones, 21 January 1955, Jones papers, Archives of the British Psychoanalytical Society.
18. See also www.heretical.com/freudian/coca1884.html.

Chapter Eleven

1. Jacob Freud died on 23 October 1896.
2. Translated from the Hebrew by Rabbi Jules Harlow (Rice, op. cit., pp. 31, 37). This was in the 1839 edition. Freud also possessed a complete eight volume set of the 1858 edition (ibid., p. 38). This is the transcription of the Hebrew script.

בן יקיר לי שלמה

כשבע בימי שני חייך החל רוח ה' לפעמך
ודבר בך: לך, קרא בספרי אשר כתבתי
ויבקעו לך מעינות בינה דעה והשכל
ספר הספרים הנהו בארו חפרו חכמים
ומחוקקים למדו דעת ומשפט
מחזה שדי חזית שמעת ורבות עשית
ותדא על כנפ' הרוח
מן אז היה הספר כמוס בשברי לוחות
בארון עמדי
ליום נמלאו שנותיך לחמשה ושלושים
נתתי עליו מכסה עד חדש
וקראתי לו עלי באר ענו לה
ואקריבנו לפניך לזכרון
ולמזכרת אהבה   מאביך
אוהבך אהבת עולם   יעקב בר"ש פרייד
בעיר הבירה וויען כ"ט ניסן תרנ"א 6 מאי 891

3. Yerushalmi has provided an alternative, what he called a "literal ... abrasively unliterary" translation:

> Son who is dear to me. Shelomoh. In the seventh in the days of the years of your life the Spirit of the Lord began to move you and spoke within you: Go, read in my Book that I have written and there will burst open for you the wellsprings of

understanding, knowledge, and wisdom. Behold, it is the Book of Books, from which Sages have excavated and lawmakers learned knowledge and judgement. A vision of the Almighty did you see; you heard and strove to do, and you soared on the wings of the Spirit.

Since then the book has been stored like the fragments of the tablets in an ark with me. For the day on which your years were filled to five and thirty I have put upon it a cover of new skin and have called it: "Spring up, O well, sing ye unto it." And I have presented it to you as a memorial and as a reminder of love from your father, who loves you with an everlasting love. (op. cit., p. 71)

4. In addition Rice quotes from a modern biblical commentator about Joseph: "He is the all vicissitudes of life. He is the ideal son, the ideal brother, the ideal servant, the ideal administrator" (ibid., p. 69).
5. The Rambam (Moses Maimonides) outlined several stages of *teshuvah* in his seminal work, *Mishneh Torah*. The first step is recognition. A person has to see that he has done wrong. Next is confession, when he openly acknowledges what he has done. Third, is regret. This allows the person to learn from his mistakes. And finally there is resolve, the decision not to repeat the wrongdoing in the future. Collectively these four stages comprise repentance, which is only complete when the impetus to act wrongly or wickedly has ended. In fact, for sins against one's fellow men, the Rambam adds a fifth step, which includes apology, asking forgiveness and restitution.

Maimonides (Moses ben Maimon), 1135–1204, was a physician, rabbinic sage, mystic, and philosopher.
6. Galbanum was obtained from various Asiatic plants (genus ferula) of the umbel family.
7. The Kleinian and Lurianic systems are discussed at length by Harriet Lutsky in "Reparation and Tikkun: A Comparison of the Kleinian and Kabbalistic Concepts" (1989, pp. 449–458).
8. Vital, C. (1587). *Etz Chaim* (The Tree of Life), Hechal 6 Gate 1 *Shaar Tikkun Nukvah* (Gate of the Restoration of the Feminine) (pp. 1146–1156). Jerusalem: Videvsky, 1988.
9. Hence, according to Jewish tradition, to "know" a woman is to have sexual relations with her. *Daat* (knowledge) comes from the union of the two "higher" intellectual faculties of *sephirot* or *chochmah* (wisdom, seen as male) and *binah* (understanding, seen as female). This knowledge, in turn, serves to answer the great mystery of existence, "Where do I come from?"
10. See also his entire chapter on sexuality, pp. 271–301.

11. Bakan points out that Freud's association of the "mother lying in her nakedness" comes directly from his 1928 paper, "A Religious Experience" (pp. 167–172).

12. Rachel Elior is quoting Rabbi Moshe Cordovero, who was one of the great sixteenth-century Kabbalists, in *Elima Rabbai* (fol. 25a). He lived in Safed in northern Israel at the same time as the Ari (Isaac Luria).

13. These words, which are very familiar to all psychoanalysts, may not have been written down, but seem to be part of an oral tradition. They have been quoted in several places including by Erik Erikson in *Childhood and Society* (1950, pp. 264–265).

14. "From bone marrow, the raw material of cures" (*International Herald Tribune*, 22–23 June 2002, pp. 1, 5). This is an example of repair (*tikkun*) from within. "Firing up artificial memory: Scientists develop circuits to mimic neural activity" (*International Herald Tribune*, 22–23 June 2002, p. 14). It is also possible to make repairs from without, as in the development of exoskeletons to help paraplegic persons walk.

15. For further discussion see Mordechai Gafni, "Shattered Vessels, Stained Hands," (2001, p. 16).

Chapter Twelve

1. He taught at the University of Chicago, Ohio State, and Harvard, and was professor emeritus at York University, Department of Psychology, Toronto.

2. Bakan's grandfather was Yitzchak Yosef Rosenstrauch, whom Bakan describes as an "uneducated man" (until his old age, when he taught himself Yiddish), but a devoted Jew (op. cit., p. xv). Rabbi Moishe Leib Erblich of Sassov (1745–1807) was a third generation disciple of the Baal Shem Tov.

3. Moses ben Maimon (Maimonides) was also known as the Rambam (Hebrew acronym for "our rabbi/teacher Moses son of Maimon"). He was born in Cordoba, Spain in 1135 and died in Cairo in 1204. He is generally considered to be one of the greatest Jewish scholars of all time. See *The Guide for the Perplexed*, translations of 1950 and 1963.

4. Bakan points out that the Cossacks were an advance guard in the fight of the Polish nobility against the Turks and Tartars. Their leader was the notorious Bogdan Chmielnicki. They attacked the Jews because many Jews acted as tax collectors for the Poles (often the only work they were allowed). See extended discussion in "The Chmielnicki Period" (in Bakan, op. cit., pp. 85–88).

5. In 1666 practically the whole Jewish community of Avignon, France was ready to follow Zevi to Jerusalem (see en.wikipedia.org/wiki/

Sabbatai_Zevi, p. 5 (accessed 8 December 2013). In the same year Zevi's secretary, Samuel Primo, wrote a circular to all Jews on his behalf:

> The first-begotten Son of God, Shabbethai Tebi, Messiah and Redeemer of the people of Israel, to all the sons of Israel, Peace! Since we have been deemed worthy to behold the great day and the fulfillment of God's word by the Prophets, your lament and sorrow must be changed into joy, and your fasting into merriment; for ye shall weep no more. Rejoice with song and melody, and change the day formerly spent in sadness and sorrow into a day of jubilee, because I have appeared. (ibid., p. 5)

The circular aroused tremendous controversy. There were Jews who considered it to be blasphemous. Many rabbis condemned it and some went as far as to formally excommunicate him.

6. Many followers also converted to Islam, but secretly practiced Judaism, like the *Marranos* in Spain. They became known as *Dönmeh*, and often rose to prominent positions in Turkey. Recently some of their descendants have applied to be accepted as Jews in Israel (ibid., pp. 7–8). See also http://www.shavei.org/category/communities/other_communities/asia/donmeh-turkey/?lang=en.

7. The founder of Hassidism, the Baal Shem Tov (Besht), was himself considered by many non-Hassidic Jews to be a secret Sabbatean, that is, a person who did not abide by the Jewish code of law, and thereby brought disaster onto his brethren.

8. "The essential fact remains that unlike so many of his Viennese Jewish contemporaries, Freud never acted upon whatever negative impulses he may have harbored in the one way that really counted—to disavow his Jewish identity. Quite the opposite" (Yerushalmi, 1991, op. cit., p. 11).

9. These books, his edition of the Talmud, and other books on Judaica are not listed among the books held in the Freud Library at the New York Psychiatric Library (ibid., p. xx). Interestingly, the Freud Museum in London holds a complete twelve volume German translation of the Babylonian Talmud from Freud's library, as well as a complete four volume set of the Babylonian Talmud in the original Aramaic. Freud took both editions with him when he left Vienna for London (Rice, op. cit., pp. 94–95).

10. Emanuel Rice has documented that Freud did have a lengthy and rigorous religious education (op. cit., pp. 48–54).

11. When challenged about the biological inheritance of acquired characteristics, Freud replied: "But we can't bother with the biologists. We

have our own science ... we must go our own way" (quoted by Bakan, op. cit., p. 156).

12. All the original members of Freud's Wednesday Society (discussion group launched in 1902) were Jews (Yerushalmi, 1991, op. cit., p. 41). The Wednesday Society then became the Wednesday Psychological Society and finally in 1908, the Vienna Psychoanalytic Society (Gay, op. cit., pp. 173–179). Clark says it was 1906 (op. cit., p. 213).

Freud felt particularly at home at the Vienna lodge of B'nai B'rith (Sons of the Covenant), which he joined in September 1897, and he remained a member until he left Vienna in 1938. From 1897 until 1917 he delivered twenty-seven lectures there. He used to regularly attend meetings at this Jewish society where, as Clark put it, he "found refuge from an unappreciative outer world." Freud commented:

> I felt as though I were despised and universally shunned. In my loneliness I was seized with a longing to find a circle of picked men of high character who would receive me in a friendly spirit in spite of my temerity. Your society was pointed out to me as the place where such men were to be found. (1941e, op. cit., p. 273, quoted by Clark, op. cit., p. 196)

13. Quoted by Yerushalmi from the Mishnaic tractate *Avot* (Sayings of the Fathers), known as "Chain of Tradition," (*shalshelet ha-qabbalah*).

14. For a further of discussion of Freud's "Lamarckian assumptions" see Yerushalmi, ibid., pp. 29–33.

15. Marianne Krüll reproduced these illustrations in her book, *Freud and His Father* (op. cit., pp. 158–159).

16. Herman Kafka (1852–1931) was the Czech son of a ritual slaughterer. Physically robust, he disparaged his writer son, Franz (1883–1924), at almost every opportunity.

17. In Egyptian, *Moshe* may also used as a suffix, as in *Ah-mose*, son of the moon. Aryeh Kaplan says that *moshe* may be Semitic in origin, introduced by the Semitic Canaanite rulers of the fifteenth dynasty of Egypt (1981, op. cit., p. 263). See also "As for Moses being an Egyptian, what's in a name?" (Yerushalmi, 1991, op. cit., pp. 85–86).

18. Yerushalmi has documented Freud's use of Yiddishisms and Hebrew words (1991, op. cit., pp. 68–70).

19. Sachs (1881–1947) was one of the earliest psychoanalysts and became a member of Freud's Secret Committee of six in 1912.

20. Graf is quoted by Clark (op. cit., p. 217); see also Gay (op. cit., p. 174).

21. Also quoted by Dinah Mendes (2011).
22. Both Sadger and Eitingon became prominent psychoanalysts.
23. Freud to Enrico Morselli (professor of psychiatry, University of Genoa), 1926, quoted in Jonathan Miller (1972, p. 15), as well as by Clark, who points out that six decades after Freud feared that psychoanalysis would be attacked for being predominantly Jewish, researchers found out that analysts were generally "… upwardly mobile, politically liberal (urban) Jewish men" (ibid., p. 243).
24. John von Neumann, father of modern computers; Leo Szilárd, inventor of the nuclear chain reaction; Theodor von Kármán, father of aerodynamics; Wolfgang Pauli, quantum physicist and Nobel laureate, friend and collaborator of Carl Jung; Eugene Wigner, quantum physicist and Nobel laureate. Keve discusses them in his paper and also in his book, *Triad*.
25. Another way of understanding the fine structure constant is that it represents the probability that an electron will absorb or emit a photon (a particle of light). (The actual number is one over 137.) It is defined as the charge of an electron (q) squared over Planck's constant (h) times the speed of light (c). Essentially the equation links electromagnetism (q), relativity (c) and Planck's constant (h).
26. These include the elaboration of such constructs as "identification with the aggressor," "splitting," "projective identification," and the "corrective emotional experience" S. Kahn (1996). See also: http://pandc.ca/?cat=sigmund_freud&page=ferenczi_mutual_analysis, p. 1.

    His technical advances include empathic reciprocity, self-disclosure, and mutual encounter.
27. To an increasing extent even these subjective phenomena are available for third party or objective observation through the use of sophisticated MRI and EEG technology (Kaku, 2014, pp. 65–75).
28. That psychoanalysis remains so controversial and open to attack from so many quarters tends to confirm Freud's fears of it being a discipline that attracts anti-Semitic hostility.
29. Romain Roland (1866–1944) was also a distinguished essayist, art historian and mystic, who won the Nobel Prize for Literature in 1915.
30. Significantly, three generations of Freud's family, notably, Freud himself, his father, Jacob, and his grandfather, Shlomo, all died on the Jewish Sabbath (Schneider & Berke, 2011, op. cit., p. 1).
31. Since Yom Kippur is the culmination of the Ten Days of Repentance, one can assume that Freud had long begun his self-introspection and questioning of his life (ibid., p. 13).

32. Azulai (1724–1806) was known by the acronym, Hida (see Schneider & Berke, 2011, op. cit., p. 13). His sayings are very familiar to those well versed in Kabbalah.

Epilogue

1. The writers include Sophie (Martin's wife), and her daughter, Andrea Freud Loewenstein (Freud's great-granddaughter) and Clement (Freud's grandson), and Esther, Jane (McAdam), and Susie (Boyt) (all great-granddaughters via Freud's grandson, Lucian). No doubt they will themselves produce future generations of notable writers.

    The academics include George Freud Loewenstein (Freud's great-grandson), the son of Sophie, the Herbert Simon Professor of Economics and Psychology at Carnegie Mellon University. He is a leader in the fields of behavioral economics and neuroeconomics.

2. After being elected an MP, Clement was hailed by the London *Jewish Chronicle* as the first Jewish Liberal MP for decades. Whereupon Clement called up the paper and vehemently complained that he was not Jewish and did not want to be called Jewish. He had converted to Anglicanism (Church of England) many years before (Matthew Rosen-Marsh, personal communication, April 2014). (He was told this by his father, Peter, who was a journalist on the *Jewish Chronicle* at the time.)

3. Lucian and Caroline married impulsively at the Chelsea Register Office on 9 December 1953 (Greig, 2013, p. 112).

4. Anti-Semitism pervaded aristocratic circles at the time. Caroline's mother despised Jews. When asked about his mother-in-law's anti-Semitism, Lucian replied: "Perhaps that came into it. But I had never really seen myself as a Jew in any absolute identifying way, although of course I was and I am" (ibid., p. 116).

    It will be interesting to see if Freud's "Jewish genes" assert themselves in succeeding generations.

5. http://en.wikipedia.org/wiki/Walter_Freud (p. 1). Walter was also a major figure in investigating German war crimes.

6. http://en.wikipedia.org/wiki/David_Freud,_Baron_Freud (pp. 1–3). It was said that David Freud will be remembered in the city as one of the key players in several of the most embarrassing and badly managed deals in investment banking history (ibid., p. 2).

7. The children include two by his first wife, Kathleen Garman, four by Susie Boyd, four by Katherine McAdam, two by Bernadine Coverley, one by Jacquetta Eliot, the Countess of St. Germans, and one by Celia Paul (http://en.wikipedia.org/wiki/Freud_family, p. 4). Many of these children did not know their father until they were

grown up (Parr, 2011). See also: http://www.dailymail.co.ukfemail/ article-2018102/Lucian-Freud-told-...r-deathbed-I-want-know-Im-selfish-extraordinary-reconciliation.html (pp. 1–9).

8. http://en.wikipedia/wiki/Emma_Freud (pp. 1–2).
9. http://en.wikipedia/wiki/Matthew_Freud (pp. 1–2).
10. http://en.wikipedia/wiki/Clement_Freud (pp. 1–7).
11. Quoted in http://en.wikipedia/wiki/Clement_Freud (p. 3).

REFERENCES

Abel, K. (1884). On the antithetical meaning of primal words (Über den Gegensim der Urworte). Leipzig, Germany: Wilhelm Friedrich, 1884 (digitalized).

Aberbach, D. (1980). "Freud's Jewish Problem". *Commentary, 69.*

Abraham, K. (1920). The Day of Atonement. In: K. Abraham (Ed.), *Clinical Papers and Essays on Psycho-Analysis.* London: Karnac, 1979.

Abraham, Hilda and Freud, Ernest, eds., *A Psycho-Analytic Dialogue: The Letters of Sigmund Freud and Karl Abraham, 1907–1926,* Trans. by Bernard Marsh & Hilda Abraham, London: Hogarth Press and the Institute of Psycho-Analysis, 1965.

Annesley, D. (1981). Personal communication, 10 January.

A Psychiatric Glossary (1980). Washington, DC: American Psychiatric Association.

Aron, W. (1956–57). Notes on Sigmund Freud's Ancestry and Jewish Contacts. *Yivo Annual of Jewish Social Science, Vol. XI.* New York: Yivo Institute for Jewish Research.

Azulai, H. J. D. (2003). *Sefer Orot HaHida* (The Light of the Hida). (S. Vaanunu, compiler). Jerusalem.

Bacon, F. (1890). Of envy. In: S. H. Reynolds (Ed.), *The Essays or Counsels, Civil and Moral.* Oxford: Clarendon.

Bakan, D. (1965). *Sigmund Freud and the Jewish Mystical Tradition*. London: Free Association (revised edition, 1990).

Barnes, M., & Berke, J. H. (1972a). *Mary Barnes: Two Accounts of a Journey Through Madness*. New York: Harcourt Brace.

Barnes, M., & Berke, J. H. (1972b). *Mary Barnes: Two Accounts of a Journey Through Madness (3rd edition)*. New York: Other Press, 2002.

Bentall, R. (2003). *Madness Explained: Psychosis & Human Nature*. London: Allen Lane.

Berke, J. H. (1988). *The Tyranny of Malice: Exploring the Dark Side of Character and Culture*. New York: Summit.

Berke, J. H. (1996). Psychoanalysis and Kabbalah. *Psychoanalytic Review, 83*.

Berke, J. H. (2012). *Why I Hate You and You Hate Me: The Interplay of Envy, Greed, Jealousy and Narcissism in Everyday Life*. London: Karnac.

Berke, J. H., & Schneider, S. (1994). Antithetical meaning of "the breast." *International Journal of Psychoanalysis, 75*(3).

Berke, J. H., & Schneider, S. (2008). Faces, guises and roles. In: *Centers of Power: The Convergence of Psychoanalysis and Kabbalah*, Plymouth, UK: Jason Aronson.

Bettelheim, B. (1955). *Symbolic Wounds*. London: Thames and Hudson.

Bettelheim, B. (1983). *Freud and Man's Soul*. London: Chatto & Windus.

Bion, W. R. (1962). *Learning from Experience*. London: Karnac, 1977.

Bloch, C. (1950). Pgishati im Freud vehitvakhuti ito Moshe Rabenu. *Bitzaron, XXIII*(2): 104.

Bloch, J. S. (1923). *My Reminiscences*. Vienna: R. Lowit.

Blond, S. (1974). *Tysmienica: A Memorial to the Ruins of a Destroyed Jewish Community* (translation of *Tismentis: a matseyve oyf de. khurves fun a farnikheter yidisher kehile*). Tel Aviv: Hamenora (Hebrew and Yiddish).

Brown, N. O. (1959). *Life Against Death: The Psychoanalytical Meaning of History*. Middletown, CT: Wesleyan University Press.

Carotenuto, A. (1982). *A Secret Symmetry: Sabina Spielrein between Jung and Freud*. A. Pomerans, J. Sherby, & K. Winston (Trans.). New York: Pantheon.

Castaneda, C. (1968). *The Teachings of Don Juan: A Yaqui Way of Knowledge*. New York: Pocket Books.

Cirlot, J. E. (1962). *A Dictionary of Symbols*. London: Routledge & Kegan Paul.

Clark, R. W. (1980). *Freud: The Man and the Cause*. London: Jonathan Cape and Weidenfeld & Nicolson.

Cordovero, M. *Pardes Harimonim*, Shaar 4, Chs. 5–6. Reprinted as *Pardes Rimonim* (Orchard of Pomegranates) parts 5–8. Providence, RI: Providence University Press, 2010.

Cowan, S. (1999). The encounter of Freud and the fifth Lubavitcher Rebbe: A Symposium. *Journal of Judaism and Civilization, 2*.

Dennett, D. C. (1991). *Consciousness Explained*. Boston: Little, Brown.

Doctorow, C. (2009). Boing boing. http://boingboing.net/2009/04/19/clement-freuds-funni.html.

Doherty, R. (17 January 2014). Callous thief tries to steal Freud's ashes. *Jewish Chronicle*, London.

Donleavy, P., & Shearer, A. (2008). *From Ancient Myth to Modern Healing: Themis: Goddess of Heart-Soul, Justice and Reconciliation*. London: Routledge.

Dov Ber of Lubavitch (1963). *On Ecstasy*. L. Jacobs (Ed. & Trans.). Chappaqua, NY: Rossel.

Dressler, E. (1943). *Michtav Eliyahu* (A letter from Eliyahu) (in Hebrew). Jerusalem: *Sifriyat, 5*, 1997.

Drob, S. (2000a). *Kabbalistic Metaphors: Jewish Mystical Themes in Ancient and Modern Thought*. New York: Jason Aronson.

Drob, S. (2000b). *Symbols of the Kabbalah: Philosophical and Psychological Perspectives*. Northvale, NJ: Jason Aronson.

Eigen, M. (2012). *Kabbalah and Psychoanalysis*. London: Karnac.

Eigen, M. (2014). *A Felt Sense: More Explorations of Psychoanalysis and Kabbalah*. London: Karnac.

Elior, R. (1993). *The Paradoxical Ascent to God*. Albany, NY: State University of New York Press.

Encyclopaedia Judaica (1972). Vol. 7. Jerusalem: Keter.

Erikson, E. H. (1950). *Childhood and Society*. New York: W. W. Norton, 1963.

Fenwick, P. (2000). Personal communication, 3 July.

Fenwick, P., & Fenwick, E. (1995). *The Truth in the Light: An Investigation of over 300 Near-Death Experiences*. London: Headline.

Ferenczi, S. (1923). *Thalassa: A Theory of Genitality*. London: Karnac, 1989.

Ferenczi. S. (1988). *The Clinical Diary of Sándor Ferenczi*. J. Dupont (Ed.), M. Balint & N. Z. Jackson (Trans.). Cambridge, MA: Harvard University Press.

Feynman, R. (1985). *QED: The Strange Theory of Light and Matter*. Princeton, NJ: Princeton University Press.

Fichtner, G. (2010). Freud and the Hammerschlag family: A formative relationship. *International Journal of Psychoanalysis, 91*.

Frankel, E. (1994). Yom Kippur, Teshuvah and Psychotherapy. *Tikkun, 9*.

Frankl, V. (1984). *Man's Search for Meaning*. New York: Washington Square/Pocket.

Freud, E., Freud, L., & Grubrich-Simitis, I. (1978). *Sigmund Freud: His Life iin Pictures and Words*. C. Trollope (Trans.). London: Andre Deutsch.

Freud, M. (1957). *Glory Reflected: Sigmund Freud—Man and Father*. London: Angus & Robertson.

Freud, M. (1983). *Sigmund Freud: Man and Father*. New York: Jason Aronson.

Freud, S. (1884e). Über Coca. *Zentralblatt für die gesamte Therapie, 2*. See also: www.heretical.com/freudian/coca1884.html.

Freud, S. (1890a). Psychical (or mental) treatment. *S. E., 7.* London: Hogarth.

Freud, S. (1891b). *On Aphasia* (A Critical Study). E. Stengel (Trans.). New York: International Universities Press, 1953.

Freud, S. (1900a). *The Interpretation of Dreams. S. E., 4–5.* London: Hogarth.

Freud, S. (1905a). On psychotherapy. *S. E., 7.* London: Hogarth.

Freud, S. (1910e). The antithetical meaning of primal words. *S. E., 11.* London: Hogarth.

Freud, S. (1912–13). *Totem and Taboo. S. E., 13.* London: Hogarth.

Freud, S. (1914d). On the history of the psycho-analytic movement. *S. E., 14.* London: Hogarth.

Freud, S. (1915c). Instincts and their vicissitudes. *S. E., 14.* London: Hogarth.

Freud, S. (1916–17). *Introductory Lectures on Psycho-Analysis. S. E., 15–16.* London: Hogarth.

Freud, S. (1917e). Mourning and melancholia. *S. E., 14.* London: Hogarth.

Freud, S. (1919e). A child is being beaten. *S. E., 17.* London: Hogarth.

Freud, S. (1920b). A note on the prehistory of the technique of analysis. *S. E., 18.* London: Hogarth.

Freud, S. (1920g). *Beyond the Pleasure Principle. S. E., 18.* London: Hogarth.

Freud, S. (1922a). Dreams and telepathy. *S. E., 18.* London: Hogarth.

Freud, S. (1923b). *The Ego and the Id. S. E., 19.* London: Hogarth.

Freud, S. (1927c). *The Future of an Illusion. S. E., 21.* London: Hogarth.

Freud, S. (1928a). A religious experience. *S. E., 21.* London: Hogarth.

Freud, S. (1933a). New introductory lectures on psycho-analysis. Lecture XXX, "Dreams and Occultism." *S. E., 22.* London: Hogarth.

Freud, S. (1934b). Preface to the Hebrew translation of *Totem and Taboo. S. E., 13.* London: Hogarth.

Freud, S. (1935a). Postscript to *An Autobiographical Study. S. E., 20.* London: Hogarth.

Freud, S. (1939a). *Moses and Monotheism.* K. Jones (Trans.). *S. E., 23.* London: Hogarth.

Freud, S. (1941d). Psycho-analysis and telepathy. *S. E., 18.* London: Hogarth.

Freud, S. (1941e). Address to the Members of the *B'nai B'rith. S. E., 20.* London: Hogarth.

Freud, S. (1950a). A project for a scientific psychology. *S. E., 1.* London: Hogarth.

Freud, S. (1950a [1887–1902]). *Aus den Anfängen der Psychoanalyse,* p. 82 (*The Origins of Psycho-Analysis*). Wein: Springer-Verlag, 2004.

Freud, S. (1954). *The Origins of Psychoanalysis: Letters to Wilhelm Fliess, Drafts and Notes 1887–1902.* M. Bonaparte, A. Freud, & E. Kris (Eds.), E. Mosbacher & J. Strachey (Trans.). New York: Basic Books.

Freud, S. (1960). *Letters of Sigmund Freud*. E. Freud (Ed.), T. Stern & J. Stern (Trans.). New York: Basic Books.

Freud, S., & Breuer, J. (1895d). *Studies on Hysteria. S. E., 2*. London: Hogarth.

Gafni, M. (2001). Shattered vessels, stained hands. *Wellsprings, 48, Spring/Summer*.

Gay, P. (1988). *Freud: A Life for Our Time*. London: J. M. Dent & Sons.

Geller, J. (1970). *On Freud's Jewish Body: Mitigating Circumcisions*. New York: Fordham University Press.

Ginsburgh, Y. (1990). *The Hebrew Letters: Channels of Creative Consciousness*. Jerusalem: Gal Einai.

Glazer, A., & Kallus, M. (2011). *Pillar of Prayer: Sacred Study and the Spiritual Life from the Baal Shem and His Circle*. Louisville, KY: Fons Vitae.

Glitzenstein, C. (1972). *Sefer HaToldos* [Biography]. New York: Kehot Publishing Society (Hebrew and Yiddish).

Gottlieb, F. (1989). *The Lamp of God*. New York: Jason Aronson.

Graf, M. (1942). Reminiscences of Professor Sigmund Freud. *Psychoanalytic Quarterly, 11*.

Greenbaum, A. (1995). *The Wings of the Sun: Traditional Jewish Healing in Theory and Practice*. Jerusalem: Breslov Research Institute.

Greig, G. (2013). *Breakfast with Lucian: A Portrait of the Artist*. London: Jonathan Cape.

Grosskurth, P. (1987). *Melanie Klein: Her World and Her Work*. London: Hodder & Stoughton.

Hinshelwood, R. D. (1991). *A Dictionary of Kleinian Thought*. London: Free Association.

Hornstein, G. (2000). *To Redeem One Person is to Redeem the World: The Life of Frieda Fromm-Reichman*. New York: Free Press.

Iancu, C. (2006). Le sauveur d'un peuple: Le grand rabbin Alexandre Safran. *Le Monde*, 31 July.

Idel, M. (1995). *Hasidism: Between Ecstasy and Magic*. Albany, NY: State University of New York Press.

James, W. (1890). *The Principles of Psychology*. New York: Holt.

James, W. (1901). *The Varieties of Religious Experience*. New York: Mentor, 1958.

Jobey, L. (2013). Interview with Michael Clark. *Financial Times Weekend Magazine*, 16 November.

Jones, E. (1953, 1955, 1957). *Sigmund Freud: Life and Work, Vols. 1, 2, 3*. London: Hogarth.

Jones, E. (1959). *Memories of a Psycho-Analyst*. London: Free Association.

Jones, E. (1964). *Essays in Applied Psycho-Analysis, Vol. ll*. London: Hogarth.

Jung, C. G. (1963). *Memories, Dreams, Reflections*. R. & C. Winston (Trans.). London: Collins and Routledge & Kegan Paul.

Kahn, R. N. (1997). *Extraordinary Chassidic Tales*. B. Majerczyk (Trans.). New York: Ostar, Sifrei Lubavitch.

Kahn, S. (1996). Ferenczi's mutual analysis: A case where the messenger was killed and his treasure buried. (Paper presented at annual meeting of the Eastern Psychological Association, Philadelphia, PA.)

Kaku, M. (2014). *The Future of the Mind*. London: Allen Lane.

Kaplan, A. (1989). *Meditation and Kabbalah*. York Beach, ME: Samuel Weiser.

Kaplan, A. (1990). *Inner Space*. New York: Maznaim.

Katz, M. (2010). An occupational neurosis: A psychoanalytic case history of a rabbi. *AJS Review, 34*(1), April: 1–31.

Kerr, J. (1993). *A Most Dangerous Method: The Story of Jung, Freud, and Sabina Spielrein*. New York: Alfred A. Knopf.

Keve, T. (2000). *Triad: the Physicists, the Analysts, the Kabbalists*. London: Rosenberger & Krausz.

Keve, T. (2012). Physics, metaphysics, and psychoanalysis. In: J. Szekacs-Weisz & T. Keve (Eds.), *Ferenczi and His World* (pp. 157–178). London: Karnac.

Klein, D. B. (1981). *Jewish Origins of the Psychoanalytic Movement*. Chicago: University of Chicago Press.

Klein, G. (1959). Consciousness in psychoanalytic theory: Some implications for current research in perception. *Journal of the American Psychiatric Association, 7*: 5–34.

Klein, M. (1935). A contribution to the psychogenesis of manic-depressive states. In: *Love, Guilt, Reparation and Other Works 1921–1945*. London: Hogarth, 1975.

Klein, M. (1940). Mourning and its relation to manic-depressive states. In: *Love, Guilt, Reparation and Other Works 1921–1945*. London: Hogarth, 1975.

Klein, M. (1946). Notes on some schizoid mechanisms. In: *Envy and Gratitude and Other Works 1946–1963*. London: Hogarth, 1975.

Kohut, H. (1977). *The Restoration of the Self*. New York: International Universities Press.

Krüll, M. (1986). *Freud and His Father*. A. Pomerans (Trans.). New York: W. W. Norton.

Kutscher, E. Y. (1966). *Words and their History*. Jerusalem: Kiryat Sepher (Hebrew).

Kutscher, E. Y. (1982). *A History of the Hebrew Language*. Jerusalem: Magnes.

Laplanche, J., & Pontalis, J.-B. (1973). *The Language of Psycho-Analysis*. London: Hogarth and the Institute of Psychoanalysis.

Leet, L. (2003). *The Kabbalah of the Soul: The Transformative Psychology and Practices of Jewish Mysticism.* Rochester, VT: Inner Traditions.

Living Torah: The Five Books of Moses and the Haftarot (1981). A. Kaplan (Trans.). New York: Maznaim.

Locks, G. (1985). *The Spice of Torah-Gematria.* New York: Judaica.

Loewenthal, N. (1990). *Communicating the Infinite: The Emergence of the Habad School.* Chicago: University of Chicago Press.

Lutsky, H. (1989). Reparation and Tikkun: A comparison of the Kleinian and Kabbalistic concepts. *International Review of Psycho-Analysis, 16.*

Maidenbaum, A. (2013). Carl Jung and the question of anti-Semitism. www.jewishcurrents.org/Carl Jung-and-the-question-of-anti-semitism/ 15187.

Maimonides, M. (1950). *The Guide for the Perplexed.* M. Freidlander (Trans.). New York: Dover.

Maimonides, M. (1963). *The Guide for the Perplexed.* S. Pines (Trans.). Chicago: University of Chicago Press.

Maimonides, M. (2006). *Moreh Nevuchim* (Guide for the Perplexed). Y. Kapach (Ed.). Jerusalem: Mossad HaRav Kook (Hebrew).

Maimonides, M. (Ed.) (2010). *Mishneh Torah: Sefer Hamadah—Book of Knowledge.* E. Touger (Trans.). New York: Maznaim.

Marinowsky, H. O. (1991). *Al Avortaynu v'al Yichus* (On Our Forefathers and Their Backgrounds). Kfar Chabad, Israel (Hebrew).

Markel, H. (2011). *An Anatomy of Addiction: Sigmund Freud, William Halsted and the Miracle Drug Cocaine.* New York: Pantheon.

Maslow, A. (1970). *Religions, Values, and Peak-Experiences.* New York: Viking Penguin.

May, R., Angel, E., & Ellenberger, H. (Eds.) (1958). *Existence: A New Dimension in Psychiatry and Psychology.* New York: Basic Books.

McGuire, W. (Ed.) (1974). *The Freud/Jung Letters: The Correspondence between Sigmund Freud and C. G. Jung.* R. Manheim & R. F. C. Hull (Trans.). London: Hogarth and Routledge & Kegan Paul.

Mendes, D. (2011). Totem and Tefillin. A review of *The Jewish World of Sigmund Freud: Essays on Cultural Roots and the Prohibition of Religious Identity.* A. Richards (Ed.). Jefferson, NC: McFarland.

Merton, P. (2009). Clement Freud on *Just a Minute*: A celebration. *BBC Radio 4,* 21 May.

Miller, J. (Ed.) (1972). *Freud: The Man, His World, His Influence.* Boston: Littlehampton.

Moscati, S. (1960). *Ancient Semitic Civilizations.* New York: Capricorn (Putnam).

Mundshein, Y. (1997). *Ha'Orot U'Beorim* (Explanations and Comments) *Vol. 732.* Brooklyn, NY: Oholei Torah (Hebrew).

Mundshein, Y. (2000). *Aynayne Mayseeach Daas Mayahnyanahv* (I Do Not Stop Thinking of Your Situation). *Kfar Chabad, 911*, 11 Tammuz 5760 (13 July) (Hebrew).

Myers, D. N. (December 2009). Yosef Yerushalmi, 77, polymath historian. *The Forward*. See also http://forward/com/articles/121176/yosef-yerushalmi-polymath-historian/.

Neumann, E. (1954). *The Origins and History of Consciousness*. New York: Bollingen Series.

Neumann, E. (1963). *The Great Mother: An Analysis of the Archetype*. New York: Bollingen Series.

Neumann, Y. Y. (1997). *Ha'Orot U'Beorim* (Explanations and Comments), *Vol. 736*. Brooklyn, NY: Oholei Torah (Hebrew).

Neumann, Y. Y. (2000). Personal communications, 21 May, 24 July.

Oberlander, B. (1997). *Ha'Orot U'Beorim* (Explanations and Comments), *Vol. 731*. Brooklyn, NY: Oholei Torah (Hebrew).

Oberlander, B. (2000). Personal communication, 12 May.

Osis, K., & Haraldsson, E. (1997). *At the Hour of Death*. New York: Hastings House.

Parr, A. (24 July 2011). Lucian Freud told daughter on deathbed "I want you to know I'm very selfish" in extraordinary reconciliation. *The Daily Mail*.

Philippson, L. (Ed.) (1838–54). *Die Israelitische Bibel. Enthaltend: Den heiligen Urtext, die deutsche Übertragung, die allgemeine ausführliche Erläuterung mit mehr als 500 englischen Holzschnitten. 2nd corrected ed., 3 vols*. Leipzig, Germany, 1858–59.

Phillips, A. (1994). *On Flirtation: Psychoanalytic Essays on the Uncommitted Life*. London: Harvard University Press.

Reich, W. (1980). *Character Analysis, 3rd ed*. New York: Farrar, Straus & Giroux.

Rice, E. (1990). *Freud and Moses: The Long Journey Home*. Albany, NY: State University of New York Press.

Roazen, P. (1963). *Meeting Freud's Family*. Amherst, MA: University of Massachusetts Press.

Rosen-Marsh, M. (2014). Personal communication, 25 April.

Rosenstein, N. (1976a). *The Unbroken Chain: Biographical Sketches and Genealogy of Illustrious Jewish Families from the 15th–20th Century*. New York: Shengold.

Rosenstein, N. (1976b). *The Unbroken Chain: Biographical Sketches and Genealogy of Illustrious Jewish Families from the 15th–20th Century, 2 volumes, revised edition*. Lakewood, NJ: C.I.S., 1990.

Rycroft, C. (1972). *Critical Dictionary of Psychoanalysis*. London: Penguin.

Sabbadini, A. (1997). Sounds, children, identity and a "quite unmusical" man. *British Journal of Psychotherapy, 14*(2).

Sachs, H. (1944). *Freud, Master and Friend*. Cambridge, MA: Harvard University Press.

Safran, A. (1977). *The Kabbalah: Law and Mysticism in the Jewish Tradition*. New York: Feldheim.

Safran, A. (1987). *Israel in Time and Space: Essays on Basic Themes in Jewish Spiritual Thought*. New York: Feldheim.

Safran, A. (1991). *Wisdom of the Kabbalah*. New York: Feldheim.

Samuels, A. (1986). *A Critical Dictionary of Jungian Analysis*. London: Routledge & Kegan Paul.

Schneersohn, Shalom Dov Ber (1977+). *Ayin Beis, Beshoo Shemi Kdimu, 3 Volumes*. New YorK: Kehot (Hebrew).

Schneersohn, Shalom Dov Ber (1985+). Sefer HaMa'amorim (Collected Writings). New York: Kehot (Hebrew and English).

Schneersohn, Y. Y. (1992). *Sefer HaSichot: 1920–1927* (Book of Essays). New York: Kehot (Hebrew and Yiddish).

Schneerson, M. M. (1986). Yud Tet Kislev. New York: *Sihot Kodesh 5712*.

Schneerson, M. M. (1997a). *R'Shimos* (Diaries) *vol. 94*. New York: Kehot (Hebrew and Yiddish).

Schneerson, M. M. (1997b). Addendum to the *R'Shimos*.

Schneerson, M. M. (2002). *Bringing Heaven Down to Earth: 365 Meditations*. Tzvi Freeman (Comp.). New York: Class One.

Schneider, S., & Berke, J. H. (2000). Sigmund Freud and the Lubavitcher Rebbe. *Psychoanalytic Review, 87*(1).

Schneider, S., & Berke, J. H. (2010). Freud's meeting with Rabbi Alexandre Safran. *Psychoanalysis and History, 12*(1).

Schneider, S., & Berke, J. H. (2011). Freud's atonement. *Mental Health, Religion and Culture, 13*.

Schneur, Zalman of Liadi (1796). *Likkutei—Amarim—Tanya* (Teachings), *bilingual ed*. N. Mindel (Trans.). New York: Kehot, 1973.

Scholem, G. G. (1941). *Major Trends in Jewish Mysticism (3rd edition)*. New York: Schocken, 1955.

Scholem, G. G. (1991). *On the Mystical Shape of the Godhead*. New York: Schocken.

Schur, M. (1972). *Freud, Living and Dying*. New York: International Universities Press.

Segal, H. (1986). A psychoanalytic approach to the treatment of psychoses. In: *The Work of Hanna Segal*. New York: Jason Aronson.

Seligson, M. (2012). Personal communication, 26 January.

Sellin, E. (1922). *Mose und Seine Bedeutung für die israelitisch-jüdische Religionsgeschichte* (Moses and His Significance for the History of the Israelite-Jewish Religion). Berlin.

Shearer, A. (2011). Psyche's Babel: archetypal patterns in psychological organisations. *International Journal of Jungian Studies, 4*(2).

Siddur Tehillat Hashem (2002). New York: Merkos L'Inyonei Chinoch.

Simon, E. (1980). Freud and Moses. In: *Entscheidung zum Judentum. Essays und Vorträge*. Frankfurt, Germany: Suhrkamp.

Singh, A. (2000). The Freud family feud that lasted a lifetime. *The Daily Telegraph*, 17 April.

Steinsaltz, A. (Even Yisroel) (1988). Garments of the soul. In: *The Long Shorter Way*. Northvale, NJ: Jason Aronson.

Steinsaltz, A. (2002). *Teshuvah*. London: British Friends of Rabbi Steinsaltz.

Steinsaltz, A. (2003). *Opening the Tanya*. New York: Jossey-Bass.

Stekel, W. (1908). A vocational neurosis. In: R. Gabler (Trans.), *Conditions of Nervous Anxiety and their Treatment* (pp. 211–220). London: Kegan Paul, Trench, Trubner, 1923. (From *Nervöse Angstzustände und ihre Behandlung*. Berlin: Urban und Schwartzenberg.)

Stekel, W. (19 January 1910). The psychology of doubt. *Protokolle, ll.*

Szekacs-Weisz, J., & Keve, T. (Eds.) (2012). *Ferenczi and His World*. London: Karnac.

Tanach (The Bible). New York: Art Scroll, 1970.

Tarnas, R. (1991). *Passion of the Western Mind*. New York: Ballantine.

Tart, C. (1972). *Altered States of Consciousness*. New York: John Wiley & Sons.

Tehillim (Psalms). *Ohel Yosef Yitzchak*. New York: Kehot, 2001.

Telushkin, J. (2014). Rebbe. New York: HarperCollins.

Tenen, S. (2011). *The Alphabet that Changed the World: How Genesis Preserves a Science of Consciousness in Geometry and Gesture*, Berkeley, California: North Atlantic Books.

Tilles, Y. (20 May 2012). A Rebbe goes shopping. http://www.chabad.org/library/article_cdo/aid/2030/jewish/A-Rebbe-Goes-Shopping.

Timms, E. (2013). Wilhelm Stekel's dialogue with Sigmund Freud: The case for brief therapy and the symbolism of dreams. *Psychoanalysis and History*, 15(2).

Underhill, E. (1912). *Mysticism*. London: Methuen.

Vanggaard, T. (1972). *Phallos: A Symbol and its History in the Male World*. New York: International Universities Press.

Viereck, G. S. (1930). *Glimpses of the Great*. London: Duckworth.

Vital, C. (1587). *Etz Chaim* (The Tree of Life), Hechal 6 Gate 1 *Shaar Tikkun Nukvah* (Gate of the Restoration of the Feminine) (pp. 1146–1156). Jerusalem: Videvsky, 1988.

Walter, B. (1947). *Theme and Variations*. London: Hamish Hamilton.

Ward, I. (Ed.) (1993). *Is Psychoanalysis Another Religion? Contemporary Essays on Spirit, Faith and Morality in Psychoanalysis*. London: Freud Museum.

Weinberg, L. (1987). *Lessons in Tanya*. New York: Kehot.

Weindling, P. J. (2010). *John W. Thompson: Psychiatrist in the Shadow of the Holocaust*. Rochester, NY: University of Rochester Press.

Winnicott, D. W. (1960). Ego distortion in terms of true and false self. In: *The Maturational Processes and the Facilitating Environment* (1972). London: Hogarth.

Wittels, F. (1924). *Sigmund Freud*. E. & C. Paul (Trans.). New York: Dodd, Mead.

Yerushalmi, Y. H. (1991). *Freud's Moses: Judaism Terminable and Interminable*. New Haven, CT: Yale University Press.

Yerushalmi, Y. H. (1996). *Zakhor: Jewish History and Jewish Memory*. New York: Schocken, 1982.

The Zohar (The Book of Illumination) (edition of 1931–1934, Vols. 1–5). H. Sperling & M. Simon (Trans.). London: Soncino.

The Zohar (2004+) (Vols. 1–8). D. L. Matt (Trans. and Commentary). Stanford, CA: Stanford University Press: Pritzker Edition.

INDEX

Abel, K. 124
Aberbach, D. 97
Abraham, K. 102
AJS Review 16
Albert Einstein College of Medicine
    (AECM) 50
"alpha-elements," 52
analytical psychology 146
Angel, E. 61
Annesley, D. 208
Aron, W. 203
Aryan psychology 147
astral projection 32
Austro-Hungarian Empire 79
Autobiographical Study, An 96
Ayin Beis 17
Azulai, H. J. D. 183, 216

Bacon, F. 142
Bahir, The 120
Bakan, D. xiv, 165

Bakan's hypothesis 165
Barnes, M. 201–201
Belz Hassidic community 27
Bentall, R. 58, 60
Berke, J. H. 12–13, 19, 46–47, 70, 90,
    183, 186, 201–202, 205
"beta-elements" 52
"beta-waves" 53
Bettelheim, B. 60, 64–65
Beyond the Pleasure Principle 109
"binary opposites" 106, 119
Bion, W. R. 38, 48–49, 163
"Bionesque" 49
bipolar 121
black depression 137
Bloch, C. 39, 85, 168
Bloch, J. S. 85
Blond, S. 89, 203
Book of Lamentations 34
British Psychoanalytical
    Society 48

For Product Safety Concerns and Information please contact our EU
representative GPSR@taylorandfrancis.com
Taylor & Francis Verlag GmbH, Kaufingerstraße 24, 80331 München, Germany

* 9 7 8 1 7 8 0 4 9 0 3 1 1 *